# Seventeen Contradictions and the End of Capitalism

T0058739

*The Limits to Capital* (1982)
*The Condition of Postmodernity* (1989)
*The New Imperialism* (2003)
*A Brief History of Neoliberalism* (2005)
*Spaces of Global Capitalism* (2006)
*The Communist Manifesto: New Introduction* (2009)
*Cosmopolitanism and the Geographies of Freedom* (2009)
*Social Justice and the City: Revised Edition* (2009)
*A Companion to Marx's* Capital (2010)
*The Enigma of Capital* (2010)
*Rebel Cities: From the Right to the City to the Urban Revolution* (2012)
*A Companion to Marx's* Capital, *Volume Two* (2013)

# Seventeen Contradictions and the End of Capitalism

DAVID HARVEY

OXFORD
UNIVERSITY PRESS

# OXFORD
UNIVERSITY PRESS

Oxford University Press is a department of the University of Oxford.
It furthers the University's objective of excellence in research, scholarship,
and education by publishing worldwide.

Oxford   New York
Auckland   Cape Town   Dar es Salaam   Hong Kong   Karachi
Kuala Lumpur   Madrid   Melbourne   Mexico City   Nairobi
New Delhi   Shanghai   Taipei   Toronto

With offices in
Argentina   Austria   Brazil   Chile   Czech Republic   France   Greece
Guatemala   Hungary   Italy   Japan   Poland   Portugal   Singapore
South Korea   Switzerland   Thailand   Turkey   Ukraine   Vietnam

Oxford is a registered trade mark of Oxford University Press
in the UK and certain other countries.

Published in the United States of America by
Oxford University Press
198 Madison Avenue, New York, NY 10016

Library of Congress Cataloging-in-Publication Data
Harvey, David (1935–)
Seventeen contradictions and the end of capitalism / David Harvey.
    p. cm.
Includes bibliographical references and index.
ISBN: 978-0-19-936026-0 (hardcover); 978-0-19-023085-2 (paperback)
1. Capitalism.  2. Financial crises.  3. Business & Economics—Economics
—Macroeconomics.  4. Political Science —Public Policy—Economic Policy.
5. Business & Economics—Economic History  I. Title.
HB501.H35977  2014
330.12'2—dc23     201401076

To John Davey
In recognition of his wise counsel and support for
almost everything I have ever published

# Contents

# Prologue

# The Crisis of Capitalism This Time Around

Crises are essential to the reproduction of capitalism. It is in the course of crises that the instabilities of capitalism are confronted, reshaped and re-engineered to create a new version of what capitalism is about. Much gets torn down and laid waste to make way for the new. Once-productive landscapes are turned into industrial wastelands, old factories are torn down or converted to new uses, working-class neighbourhoods get gentrified. Elsewhere, small farms and peasant holdings are displaced by large-scale industrialised agriculture or by sleek new factories. Business parks, R&D and wholesale warehousing and distribution centres sprawl across the land in the midst of suburban tract housing, linked together with clover-leafed highways. Central cities compete with how tall and glamorous their office towers and iconic cultural buildings might be, mega-shopping malls galore proliferate in city and suburb alike, some even doubling as airports through which hordes of tourists and business executives ceaselessly pass in a world gone cosmopolitan by default. Golf courses and gated communities pioneered in the USA can now be seen in China, Chile and India, contrasting with sprawling squatter and self-built settlements officially designated as slums, favelas or *barrios pobres*.

But what is so striking about crises is not so much the wholesale reconfiguration of physical landscapes, but dramatic changes in ways of thought and understanding, of institutions and dominant ideologies, of political allegiances and processes, of political subjectivities, of technologies and organisational forms, of social relations, of the cultural customs and tastes that inform daily life. Crises shake our mental conceptions of the world and of our place in it to the very core. And we, as restless participants and inhabitants of this new emerging world, have to adapt, through coercion or consent, to the new state of things, even as we, by virtue of what we do and how we think and behave, add our two cents' worth to the messy qualities of this world.

In the midst of a crisis it is hard to see where the exit might be. Crises are not singular events. While they have their obvious triggers, the tectonic shifts they represent take many years to work out. The long-drawn-out crisis that began with the stock market crash of 1929 was not finally resolved until the 1950s, after the world had passed through the Depression of the 1930s and the global war of the 1940s. Likewise, the crisis whose existence was signalled by turbulence in international currency markets in the late 1960s and the events of 1968 on the streets of many cities (from Paris and Chicago to Mexico City and Bangkok) was not resolved until the mid-1980s, having passed through the early 1970s collapse of the Bretton Woods international monetary system set up in 1944, a turbulent decade of labour struggles in the 1970s and the rise and consolidation of the politics of neoliberalisation under Reagan, Thatcher, Kohl, Pinochet and, ultimately, Deng in China.

With the benefit of hindsight it is not hard to spot abundant signs of problems to come well before a crisis explodes into full view. The surging inequalities in monetary wealth and incomes of the 1920s and the property market asset bubble that popped in 1928 in the USA presaged the collapse of 1929, for example. Indeed, the manner of exit from one crisis contains within itself the seeds of crises to come. The debt-saturated and increasingly deregulated global financialisation that began in the 1980s as a way to solve conflicts with labour by facilitating geographical mobility and dispersal produced its denouement in the fall of the investment bank of Lehman Brothers on 15 September 2008.

It is, at the time of writing, more than five years since that event, which triggered the cascading financial collapses that followed. If the past is any guide, it would be churlish to expect at this point any clear indications of what a revivified capitalism – if such is possible – might look like. But there should by now be competing diagnoses of what is wrong and a proliferation of proposals for putting things right. What is astonishing is the paucity of new thinking or policies. The world is broadly polarised between a continuation (as in Europe and the United States) if not a deepening of neoliberal, supply-side and monetarist remedies that emphasise austerity as the proper medicine to cure our ills; and the revival of some version, usually watered down, of a Keynesian demand-side and debt-financed expansion (as in China) that ignores Keynes's emphasis upon the redistribution of income to the lower classes as one of its key components. No matter which policy is being followed, the result is to favour the billion-aires club that now constitutes an increasingly powerful plutocracy both within countries and (like Rupert Murdoch) upon the world stage. Everywhere, the rich are getting richer by the minute. The top 100 billionaires in the world (from China, Russia, India, Mexico and Indonesia as well as from the traditional centres of wealth in North America and Europe) added $240 billion to their coffers in 2012 alone (enough, calculates Oxfam, to end world poverty overnight). By contrast, the well-being of the masses at best stagnates or more likely undergoes an accelerating if not catastrophic (as in Greece and Spain) degradation.

The one big institutional difference this time around seems to be the role of the central banks, with the Federal Reserve of the United States playing a leading if not domineering role on the world stage. But ever since the inception of central banks (back in 1694 in the British case), their role has been to protect and bail out the bankers and not to take care of the well-being of the people. The fact that the United States could statistically exit the crisis in the summer of 2009 and that stock markets almost everywhere could recover their losses has had everything to do with the policies of the Federal Reserve. Does this portend a global capitalism managed under the dicta-torship of the world's central bankers whose foremost charge is to protect the power of the banks and the plutocrats? If so, then that seems to offer very little prospect for a solution to current problems of stagnant economies and falling living standards for the mass of the world's population.

There is also much chatter about the prospects for a technological fix to the current economic malaise. While the bundling of new technologies and organisational forms has always played an important role in facilitating an exit from crises, it has never played a determinate one. The hopeful focus these days is on a 'knowledge-based' capitalism (with biomedical and genetic engineering and artificial intelligence at the forefront). But innovation is always a double-edged sword. The 1980s, after all, gave us deindustrialisation through automation such that the likes of General Motors (which employed well-paid unionised labour in the 1960s) have now been supplanted by the likes of Walmart (with its vast non-unionised low-wage labour force) as the largest private employers in the United States. If the current burst of innovation points in any direction at all, it is towards decreasing employment opportunities for labour and the increasing significance of rents extracted from intellectual property rights for capital. But if everyone tries to live off rents and nobody invests in making anything, then plainly capitalism is headed towards a crisis of an entirely different sort.

It is not only the capitalist elites and their intellectual and academic acolytes who seem incapable of making any radical break with their past or defining a viable exit from the grumbling crisis of low growth, stagnation, high unemployment and the loss of state sovereignty to the power of bondholders. The forces of the traditional left (political parties and trade unions) are plainly incapable of mounting any solid opposition to the power of capital. They have been beaten down by thirty years of ideological and political assault from the right, while democratic socialism has been discredited. The stigmatised collapse of actually existing communism and the 'death of Marxism' after 1989 made matters worse. What remains of the radical left now operates largely outside of any institutional or organised oppositional channels, in the hope that small-scale actions and local activism can ultimately add up to some kind of satisfactory macro alternative. This left, which strangely echoes a libertarian and even neoliberal ethic of anti-statism, is nurtured intellectually by thinkers such as Michel Foucault and all those who have reassembled postmodern fragmentations under the banner of a largely incomprehensible post-structuralism that favours identity politics and eschews class analysis. Autonomist, anarchist and localist perspectives and actions are everywhere in evidence. But to the degree that this left seeks to change the world without taking power, so an increasingly consolidated plutocratic capitalist class remains unchallenged in its ability to dominate the world without constraint. This new ruling class is aided by a security and surveillance state that is by no means loath to use its police powers to quell all forms of dissent in the name of anti-terrorism.

It is in this context that I have written this book. The mode of approach I have adopted is somewhat unconventional in that it follows Marx's method but not necessarily his prescriptions and it is to be feared that readers will be deterred by this from assiduously taking up the arguments here laid out. But something different in the way of investigative methods and mental conceptions is plainly needed in these barren intellectual times if we are to escape the current hiatus in economic thinking, policies and politics. After all, the economic engine of capitalism is plainly in much difficulty. It lurches between just sputtering along and threatening to grind to a halt or exploding episodically hither and thither without warning. Signs of danger abound at every turn in the midst of prospects of a plentiful life for everyone somewhere down the road. Nobody seems to have a coherent understanding of how, let alone why, capitalism is so troubled. But it has always been so. World crises have always been, as Marx once put it, 'the real concentration and forcible adjustment of all the contradictions of bourgeois economy'.[1] Unravelling those contradictions should reveal a great deal about the economic problems that so ail us. Surely that is worth a serious try.

It also seemed right to sketch in the likely outcomes and possible political consequences that flow from the application of this distinctive mode of thought to an understanding of capitalism's political economy. These consequences may not seem, at first blush, to be likely, let alone practicable or politically palatable. But it is vital that alternatives be broached, however foreign they may seem, and, if necessary, seized upon if conditions so dictate. In this way a window can be opened on to a whole field of untapped and unconsidered possibilities. We need an open forum – a global assembly, as it were – to consider where capital is, where it might be going and what should be done about it. I hope that this brief book will contribute something to the debate.

New York City,
January 2014

# Introduction
## On Contradiction

'There must be a way of scanning or X-raying the present which shows up a certain future as a potential within it. Otherwise, you will simply succeed in making people desire fruitlessly ...'

Terry Eagleton, *Why Marx Was Right*, p. 69

'In the crises of the world market, the contradictions and antagonisms of bourgeois production are strikingly revealed. Instead of investigating the nature of the conflicting elements which erupt in the catastrophe, the apologists content themselves with denying the catastrophe itself and insisting, in the face of their regular and periodic recurrence, that if production were carried on according to the textbooks, crises would never occur.'

Karl Marx, *Theories of Surplus Value*, Part 2, p. 500

There are two basic ways in which the concept of contradiction is used in the English language. The commonest and most obvious derives from Aristotle's logic, in which two statements are held to be so totally at odds that both cannot possibly be true. The statement 'All blackbirds are black' contradicts the statement that 'All blackbirds are white.' If one statement is true, then the other is not.

The other mode of usage arises when two seemingly opposed forces are simultaneously present within a particular situation, an entity, a process or an event. Many of us experience, for example, a tension between the demands of working at a job and constructing a satisfying personal life at home. Women in particular are perpetually being advised on how they might better balance career objectives

1

with family obligations. We are surrounded with such tensions at every turn. For the most part we manage them on a daily basis so that we don't get too stressed out and frazzled by them. We may even dream of eliminating them by internalising them. In the case of living and working, for example, we may locate these two competing activities in the same space and not segregate them in time. But this does not necessarily help, as someone glued to their computer screen struggling to meet a deadline while the kids are playing with matches in the kitchen soon enough has to recognise (for this reason it often turns out to be easier to clearly separate living and working spaces and times).

Tensions between the competing demands of organised production and the need to reproduce daily life have always existed. But they are often latent rather than overt and as such remain unnoticed as people go about their daily business. Furthermore, the oppositions are not always starkly defined. They can be porous and bleed into each other. The distinction between working and living, for example, often gets blurred (I have this problem a lot). In much the same way that the distinction between inside and outside rests on clear borders and boundaries when there may be none, so there are many situations where clear oppositions are hard to identify.

Situations arise, however, in which the contradictions become more obvious. They sharpen and then get to the point where the stress between opposing desires feels unbearable. In the case of career objectives and a satisfying family life, external circumstances can change and turn what was once a manageable tension into a crisis: the demands of the job may shift (change of hours or location). Circumstances on the home front may be disrupted (a sudden illness, the mother-in-law who took care of the kids after school retires to Florida). People's feelings on the inside can change also: someone experiences an epiphany, concludes 'this is no way to live a life' and throws up their job in disgust. Newly acquired ethical or religious principles may demand a different mode of being in the world. Different groups in a population (for example, men and women) or different individuals may feel and react to similar contradictions in very different ways. There is a powerful subjective element in defining and feeling the power of contradictions. What is unmanageable for one may mean nothing special for another. While the reasons may vary and conditions may differ, latent contradictions may suddenly intensify to create violent crises. Once resolved, then the contradictions can just as suddenly subside (though rarely without leaving marks and sometimes scars from their passage). The genie is, as it were, temporarily stuffed back into the bottle, usually by way of some radical readjustment between the opposing forces that lie at the root of the contradiction.

Contradictions are by no means all bad and I certainly don't mean to imply any automatic negative connotation. They can be a fecund source of both personal and social change from which people emerge far better off than before. We do not always succumb to and get lost in them. We can use them creatively. One of the ways out of a contradiction is innovation. We can adapt our ideas and practices to new circumstances and learn to be a far better and more tolerant person from the experience. Partners who had drifted apart may rediscover each other's virtues as they get together to manage a crisis between work and family. Or they may find a solution through forming new and enduring bonds of mutual support and caring with others in the neighbourhood where they live. This kind of adaptation can happen at a macroeconomic scale as well as to individuals. Britain, for example, found itself in a contradictory situation in the early eighteenth century. The land was needed for biofuels (charcoal in particular) and for food production, and, at a time when the capacity for international trade in energy and foodstuffs was limited, the development of capitalism in Britain threatened to grind to a halt because of intensifying competition on the land between the two uses. The answer lay in going underground to mine coal as a source of energy so the land could be used to grow food alone. Later on, the invention of the steam engine helped revolutionise what capitalism was about as fossil fuel sources became general. A contradiction can often be the 'mother of invention'. But notice something important here: resort to fossil fuels relieved one contradiction but now, centuries later, it anchors another contradiction between fossil fuel use and climate change. Contradictions have the nasty habit of not being resolved but merely moved around. Mark this principle well, for we will come back to it many times in what follows.

The contradictions of capital have often spawned innovations, many of which have improved the qualities of daily life. Contradictions when they erupt into a crisis of capital generate moments of 'creative destruction'. Rarely is it the case that what is created and what is destroyed is predetermined and rarely is it the case that everything that is created is bad and everything that was good was destroyed. And rarely are the contradictions totally resolved. Crises are moments of transformation in which capital typically reinvents itself and morphs into something else. And the 'something else' may be better or worse for the people even as it stabilises the reproduction of capital. But crises are also moments of danger when the reproduction of capital is threatened by the underlying contradictions.

In this study I rely on the dialectical rather than the logical Aristotelian conception of contradiction.[1] I do not mean to imply by this that the Aristotelian definition is wrong. The two definitions – seemingly in contradiction – are autonomous and compatible. It is just that they refer to very different circumstances. I find that the dialectical conception is rich in possibilities and not at all difficult to work with.

At the outset, however, I must first open up what is perhaps the most important contradiction of all: that between reality and appearance in the world in which we live.

Marx famously advised that our task should be to change the world rather than to understand it. But when I look at the corpus of his writings I have to say that he spent an inordinate amount of time seated in the library of the British Museum seeking to understand the world. This was so, I think, for one very simple reason. That reason is best captured by the term 'fetishism'. By fetishism, Marx was referring to the various masks, disguises and distortions of what is really going on around us. 'If everything were as it appeared on the surface', he wrote, 'there would be no need for science.' We need to get behind the surface appearances if we are to act coherently in the world. Otherwise, acting in response to misleading surface signals typically produces disastrous outcomes. Scientists long ago taught us, for example, that the sun does not actually go around the earth, as it appears to do (though in a recent survey in the USA it seems 20 per cent of the population still believe it does!). Medical practitioners likewise recognise that there is a big difference between symptoms and underlying causes. At their best, they have transformed their understanding of the differences between appearances and realities into a fine art of medical diagnosis. I had a sharp pain in my chest and was convinced it was a heart problem, but it turned out to be referred pain from a pinched nerve in my neck and a few physical exercises put it right. Marx wanted to generate the same sorts of insights when it came to understanding the circulation and accumulation of capital. There are, he argued, surface appearances that disguise underlying realities. Whether or not we agree with his specific diagnoses does not matter at this point (though it would be foolish not to take note of his findings). What matters is that we recognise the general possibility that we are often encountering symptoms rather than underlying causes and that we need to unmask what is truly happening underneath a welter of often mystifying surface appearances.

Let me give some examples. I put $100 in a savings account at a 3 per cent annual compound rate of interest and after twenty years it has grown to $180.61. Money seems to have the magical power to increase itself at a compounding rate. I do nothing but my savings account grows. Money seems to have the magical capacity to lay its own golden eggs. But where does the increase of money (the interest) really come from?

This is not the only kind of fetish around. The supermarket is riddled with fetishistic signs and disguises. The lettuce costs half as much as half a pound of tomatoes. But where did the lettuce and the tomatoes come from and who was it that worked to produce them and who brought them to the supermarket? And why does one item cost so much more than another? Moreover, who has the right to attach some kabbalistic sign like $ or € or £ over the items for sale and who puts a number on them, like $1 a pound or €2 a kilo? Commodities magically appear in the supermarkets with a price tag attached such that customers with money can satisfy their wants and needs depending upon how much money they have in their pockets. We get used to all this, but we don't notice that we have no idea where most of the items come from, how they were produced, by whom and under what conditions, or why, exactly, they exchange in the ratios they do and what the money we use is really all about (particularly when we read that the Federal Reserve has just created another $1 trillion of it at the drop of a hat!).

The contradiction between reality and appearance which all this produces is by far the most general and pervasive contradiction that we have to confront in trying to unravel the more specific contradictions of capital. The fetish understood in this way is not a crazy belief, a mere illusion or a hall of mirrors (though it will sometimes seem that way). It really is the case that money can be used to buy commodities and that we can live out our lives without much concern about anything other than how much money we have and how much that money will buy in the supermarket. And the money in my savings account really does grow. But ask the question 'What is money?' and the answer is usually a baffled silence. Mystifications and masks surround us at every turn, though occasionally, of course, we get shocked when we read that the thousand or so workers who died when a factory building collapsed in Bangladesh were making the shirts we are wearing. For the most part we know nothing about the people who produce the goods that support our daily life.

We can live perfectly well within a fetish world of surface signals, signs and appearances without needing to know all that much about how it works (in much the same way that we can turn on a switch and have light without knowing anything about electricity generation). It is only when something dramatic happens – the supermarket shelves are bare, the prices in the supermarket go haywire, the money in our pocket suddenly becomes worthless (or the light does not go on) – that we typically ask the bigger and broader questions as to why and how things are happening 'out there', beyond the doors and unloading bays of the supermarket, that can so dramatically affect daily life and sustenance.

In this book I will try to get behind the fetishism and identify the contradictory forces that beset the economic engine that powers capitalism. I do so because I believe that most of the accounts of what is happening currently available to us are profoundly misleading: they replicate the fetishism and do nothing to disperse the fog of misunderstanding.

I here make, however, a clear distinction between *capitalism* and *capital*. This investigation focuses on capital and not on capitalism. So what does this distinction entail? By capitalism I mean any social formation in which processes of capital circulation and accumulation are hegemonic and dominant in providing and shaping the material, social and intellectual bases for social life. Capitalism is rife with innumerable contradictions, many of which, though, have nothing in particular to do directly with capital accumulation. These contradictions transcend the specificities of capitalist social formations. For example, gender relations such as patriarchy underpin contradictions to be found in ancient Greece and Rome, in ancient China, in Inner Mongolia or in Ruanda. The same applies to racial distinctions, understood as any claim to biological superiority on the part of some subgroup in the population vis-à-vis the rest (race is not, therefore, defined in terms of phenotype: the working and peasant classes in France in the mid-nineteenth century were openly and widely regarded as biologically inferior beings – a view that was perpetuated in many of Zola's novels). Racialisation and gender discriminations have been around for a very long time and there is no question that the history of capitalism is an intensely racialised and gendered history. The question then arises: why do I not include the contradictions of race and gender (along with many others, such as nationalism, ethnicity and religion) as foundational in this study of the contradictions of capital?

The short answer is that I exclude them because although they are omnipresent within capitalism they are not specific to the form of circulation and accumulation that constitutes the economic engine of capitalism. This in no way implies that they have no impact on capital accumulation or that capital accumulation does not equally affect ('infect' might be a better word) or make active use of them. Capitalism clearly has in various times and places pushed racialisation, for example, to extremes (including the horrors of genocide and holocausts). Contemporary capitalism plainly feeds off gender discriminations and violence as well as upon the frequent dehumanisation of people of colour. The intersections and interactions between racialisation and capital accumulation are both highly visible and powerfully present. But an examination of these tells me nothing particular about how the economic engine of capital works, even as it identifies one source from where it plainly draws its energy.

The longer answer requires a better understanding of my purpose and of the method I have chosen to pursue. In the same way that a biologist might isolate a distinctive ecosystem whose dynamics (and contradictions!) need to be analysed as if it is isolated from the rest of the world, so I seek to isolate capital circulation and accumulation from everything else that is going on. I treat it as a 'closed system' in order to identify its major internal contradictions. I use, in short, the power of abstraction to build a model of how the economic engine of capitalism works. I use this model to explore why and how periodic crises occur and whether, in the long run, there are certain contradictions that may prove fatal to the perpetuation of capitalism as we now know it.

In the same way that the biologist will readily admit that external forces and disruptions (hurricanes, global warming and sea-level rise, noxious pollutants in the air or contamination of the water) will often overwhelm the 'normal' dynamics of ecological reproduction in the area she has isolated for study, so the same is true in my case: wars, nationalism, geopolitical struggles, disasters of various kinds all enter into the dynamics of capitalism, along with hefty doses of racism and gender, sexual, religious and ethnic hatreds and discriminations. It would take only one nuclear holocaust to end it all well before any potentially fatal internal contradictions of capital have done their work.

I am not saying, therefore, that everything that happens under capitalism is driven by the contradictions of capital. But I do want to identify those internal contradictions of capital that have produced the recent crises and made it seem as if there is no clear exit without destroying the lives and livelihoods of millions of people around the world.

Let me use a different metaphor to explain my method. A vast cruise ship sailing the ocean is a particular and complicated physical site for divergent activities, social relations and interactions. Different classes, genders, ethnicities and races will interact in sometimes friendly and at other times violently oppositional ways as the cruise progresses. The employees, from the captain on down, will be hierarchically organised and some strata (for example, the cabin stewards) may be at loggerheads with their overseers as well as with the demanding people they are required to serve. We could aspire to describe in detail what happens on the decks and in the cabins of this cruise ship and why. Revolutions may break out between decks. The ultra rich may isolate themselves on the upper decks, playing an infinite game of poker which redistributes wealth among them, while paying no mind whatsoever to what transpires below. But it is not my interest here to get into all of this. In the bowels of this ship there is an economic engine that pounds away day and night supplying energy to it and powering it across the ocean. Everything that happens on this ship is contingent on this engine continuing to function. If it breaks down or blows up, then the ship is dysfunctional.

Plainly, the engine we have has been stuttering and grumbling of late. It appears peculiarly vulnerable. In this inquiry I shall try to establish why. If it does break down and the ship lies listless and powerless in the water, then we will all be in deep trouble. The engine will have to be either repaired or replaced with an engine of a different design. If the latter, then this poses the question of how to redesign the economic engine and to what specifications. In so doing it is helpful to know what did or did not work well in the old engine so we can emulate its qualities without replicating its faults.

There are, however, a number of key points where the contradictions of capitalism affect the economic engine of capital with potentially disruptive force. If the engine gets flooded because of external events (such as a nuclear war, a global infectious disease pandemic that halts all trade, a revolutionary movement from above that attacks the engineers below or a negligent captain who steers the boat on to the rocks), then plainly the engine of capital stops for reasons other than its own internal contradictions. I will, in what follows, duly note the primary points where the engine of capital accumulation might be particularly vulnerable to such external influences. But I shall not pursue their consequences in any detail, for, as I began by insisting, my aim here is to isolate and analyse the *internal* contradictions of capital rather than the contradictions of capitalism taken as a whole.

In certain circles it is fashionable to derogatorily dismiss studies such as this as 'capitalo-centric'. Not only do I see nothing wrong with such studies, provided, of course, that the interpretive claims that arise from them are not pressed too far and in the wrong direction, but I also think it imperative that we have much more sophisticated and profound capitalo-centric studies to hand to facilitate a better understanding of the recent problems that capital accumulation has encountered. How else can we interpret the persistent contemporary problems of mass unemployment, the downward spiral of economic development in Europe and Japan, the unstable lurches forward of China, India and the other so-called BRIC countries? Without a ready guide to the contradictions underpinning such phenomena we will be lost. It is surely myopic, if not dangerous and ridiculous, to dismiss as 'capitalo-centric' interpretations and theories of how the economic engine of capital accumulation works in relation to the present conjuncture. Without such studies we will likely misread and misinterpret the events that are occurring around us. Erroneous interpretations will almost certainly lead to erroneous politics whose likely outcome will be to deepen rather than to alleviate crises of accumulation and the social misery that derives from them. This is, I believe, a serious problem throughout much of the contemporary capitalist world: erroneous policies based in erroneous theorising are compounding the economic difficulties and exacerbating the social disruption and misery that result. For the putative 'anti-capitalist' movement now in formation it is even more crucial not only to better understand what exactly it is that it might be opposed to, but also to articulate a clear argument as to why an anti-capitalist movement makes sense in our times and why such a movement is so imperative if the mass of humanity is to live a decent life in the difficult years to come.

So what I am seeking here is a better understanding of the contradictions of *capital*, not of *capitalism*. I want to know how the economic engine of *capitalism* works the way it does, and why it might stutter and stall and sometimes appear to be on the verge of collapse. I also want to show why this economic engine should be replaced and with what.

Part One

# The Foundational Contradictions

*The first seven contradictions are foundational because capital simply could not function without them. Furthermore, they all hang together in such a way as to make it impossible to substantially modify, let alone abolish, any one of them without seriously modifying or abolishing the others. Challenging the dominant role of exchange value in the provision of a use value like housing, for example, implies changes in the form and role of money and modifying, if not abolishing, the private property rights regime with which we are all too familiar. The search for an anti-capitalist alternative consequently appears a rather tall order. Simultaneous transformations would have to occur on many fronts. Difficulties on one front have also often been contained by strong resistances elsewhere such that general crises are avoided. But the interlinkages between the contradictions on occasion turn toxic. An intensification of a contradiction of one sort can become contagious. When contagions multiply and magnify (as clearly happened in 2007–9), then a general crisis ensues. This is dangerous for capital and creates opportunities for systemic anti-capitalist struggle. This is why an analysis of the contradictions that produce such general crises is so important. If oppositional and anti-capitalist movements in particular know what broadly to expect as the contradictions unfold, then they will be better positioned to take advantage of, rather than being surprised and stymied by, the way the contradictions move around and deepen (both geographically and sectorally) in the course of crisis formation and resolution. If crises are transitional and disruptive phases in which capital is reconstituted in a new form, then they are also phases in which deep questions can be posed and acted upon by those social movements seeking to remake the world in a different image.*

# Contradiction I
# Use Value and Exchange Value

Nothing could be simpler. I walk into a supermarket with money in my pocket and exchange it for some food items. I cannot eat the money but I can eat the food. So the food is useful to me in ways that the money is not. The food is shortly thereafter used up and consumed away, while the bits of paper and coins that are accepted as money continue to circulate. Some of the money taken in by the supermarket is paid out in the form of wages to a cashier who uses the money to buy more food. Some of the earnings go to owners in the form of profit and they spend it on all sorts of things. Some of it goes to the middlemen and eventually to the direct producers of the food, who all also spend it. And so it goes on and on. In a capitalist society millions of transactions of this sort take place every day. Commodities like food, clothing and cellphones come and go, while the money just keeps on circulating through people's (or institutions') pockets. This is how daily life is currently lived by much of the world's population.

All the commodities we buy in a capitalist society have a use value and an exchange value. The difference between the two forms of value is significant. To the degree they are often at odds with each other they constitute a contradiction, which can, on occasion, give rise to a crisis. The use values are infinitely varied (even for the same item), while the exchange value (under normal conditions) is uniform and qualitatively identical (a dollar is a dollar is a dollar, and even when it is a euro it has a known exchange rate with the dollar).

Consider, as an example, the use value and the exchange value of a house. As a use value, the house provides shelter; it is a place where people can build a home and an affective life; it is a site of daily and biological reproduction (where we cook, make love, have arguments and raise children); it offers privacy and security in an unstable world. It can also function as a symbol of status or social belonging to some subgroup, as a sign of wealth and power, as a mnemonic of historical memory (both personal and social), as a thing of architectural significance; or it simply stands to be admired and visited by tourists as a creation of elegance and beauty (like Frank Lloyd Wright's Falling Water). It can become a workshop for an aspiring innovator (like the famous garage that was the epicentre of what became Silicon Valley). I can hide a sweatshop in the basement or use it as a safe house for persecuted immigrants or as a base for trafficking sex slaves. We could go on to list a whole raft of different uses to which the house can be put. Its potential uses are, in short, myriad, seemingly infinite and very often purely idiosyncratic.

But what of its exchange value? In much of the contemporary world we have to buy the house, lease it or rent it in order to have the privilege of using it. We have to lay out money for it. The question is: how much exchange value is required to procure its uses and how does this 'how much?' affect our ability to command the particular uses we want and need? It sounds a simple question but actually its answer is rather complicated.

Once upon a time, frontier pioneers built their own houses for almost no monetary cost: the land was free, they used their own labour (or procured the collective help of neighbours on a reciprocal basis – you help me now with my roof and I will help you next week with your foundations) and acquired many of the raw materials (timber, adobe etc.) from all around them. The only monetary transactions would have been those concerned with the acquisition of axes, saws, nails, hammers, knives, harnesses for the horses and suchlike. Systems of housing production of this sort can still be found in the informal settlements constituting the so-called slums of many cities in developing countries. This is how the favelas of Brazil get built. The promotion of 'self-help housing' by the World Bank from the 1970s onwards formally identified this system of housing provision as appropriate for low-income populations in many parts of the world. The exchange values involved are relatively limited.

Houses can also be 'built to order'. Someone has land and pays architects, contractors and builders to construct a house according to a given design. The exchange value is fixed by the cost of raw materials, the wages of labour and payment for the services required to build the house. The exchange value does not dominate. But it can limit the possibilities of creating use values (there is not enough money to build a garage or a whole wing of the aristocratic mansion does not get built because the funding runs out). In advanced capitalist societies many people add to the existing use values of a house in this way (building an extension or a deck, for example).

In much of the advanced capitalist world, however, housing is built speculatively as a commodity to be sold on the market to whoever can afford it and whoever needs it. Housing provision of this sort has long been evident in capitalist societies. This is the way in which the famous Georgian terraces of Bath, Bristol, London and the like were built at the end of the eighteenth century. Later on, such speculative building practices were harnessed to erect the tenement blocks of New York City, the terraced housing for the working classes in industrial cities such as Philadelphia, Lille and Leeds, and the tract housing of the typical American suburb. The exchange value is fixed by the basic costs of the house's production (labour and raw materials), but in this case there are two other costs added in: first, the profit mark-up of the speculative builder, who lays out the initial necessary capital and pays the interest on any loans involved, and, second, the cost of acquiring, renting or leasing the land from property owners. The exchange value is set by the actual costs of production plus profit, interest on loans and capitalised rent (land price). The aim of the producers is to procure exchange values not use values. The creation of use values for others is a means to that end. The speculative quality of the activity means, however, that it is *potential* exchange value that matters. The builders of the housing actually stand to lose as well as to gain. Obviously, they try to orchestrate things, particularly housing purchases, to ensure that this does not happen. But there is always a risk. Exchange value moves into the driver's seat of housing provision.

Seeing the need for adequate use values going unmet, a variety of social forces, ranging from employers anxious to keep their labour force domesticated and to hand (like Cadbury) to radical and utopian believers (like Robert Owen, the Fourierists and George Peabody) and the local and national state, have from time to time launched a variety of housing programmes with public, philanthropic or paternalistic funding to provide for the needs of the lower classes at a minimum cost. If it is widely accepted that everyone has a right to 'a decent home and a suitable living environment' (as stated in the preamble to the US Housing Act of 1949), then, obviously, use value considerations are brought back to the forefront of struggles over housing provision. This political stance very much affected housing policies in the social democratic era in Europe and had spillover effects in North America and in selected parts of the developing world. The involvement of the state in housing provision has, obviously, waxed and waned over the years, as has the interest in social housing. But exchange value considerations often creep back in as the fiscal capacities of the state are put to the test by the need to subsidise affordable housing out of shrinking public coffers.

There have been, then, a variety of ways in which the tension between use values and exchange values in housing production has been managed. But there have also been phases when the system has broken down to produce a crisis of the sort that occurred in the housing markets of the United States, Ireland and Spain in 2007–9. This crisis was not unprecedented. The Savings and Loan Crisis in the USA from 1986 on, the collapse of the Scandinavian property market in 1992 and the end of the Japanese economic boom of the 1980s in the land market crash of 1990 are other examples.[1]

In the private market system that now dominates in much of the capitalist world, there are additional issues that need to be addressed. To begin with, the house is a 'big ticket item' that will be consumed over many years and not, like food, be instantaneously used up. Private individuals may not have the money up front to buy the house outright. If I cannot buy it with cash, I have two basic choices. Either I can rent or lease from an intermediary – a landlord – who specialises in buying speculatively built housing in order to live off the rents. Or I can borrow to buy, either getting loans from friends and relatives or taking out a mortgage with a financial institution. In the case of a mortgage, I have to pay the full exchange value of the house plus the monthly interest over the lifetime of the mortgage. I end up owning the house outright after, say, thirty years. Consequently, the house becomes a form of saving, an asset whose value (or at least that part of the value that I have acquired through my monthly payments) I can cash in at any time. Some of that asset value will have been sucked up by the costs of maintenance (for example, painting) and the need to renew deteriorated items (for example, a roof). But I can still hope to increase the net value I command as time goes on by paying off my mortgage.

The mortgage finance of a housing purchase is, however, a very peculiar transaction. The total paid out on a $100,000 mortgage over thirty years at 5 per cent is around $195,000, so the mortgagee in effect pays a premium of $95,000 extra in order to acquire an asset valued at $100,000. The transaction hardly makes sense. Why would I do this? The answer, of course, is that I need the use value of the house as somewhere to live and I pay $95,000 to live in the house until I take full ownership. It is the same as paying $95,000 rent to a landlord over thirty years except in this case I ultimately secure the exchange value of the whole house. The house becomes, in effect, a form of saving, a repository of exchange value for me.

The exchange value of housing is not, however, fixed. It fluctuates over time according to a variety of social conditions and forces. To begin with, it is not independent of the exchange values of surrounding houses. If all the houses around me are deteriorating or people of 'the wrong sort' are moving in, then my house value is very likely to fall even though I keep it in tip-top shape. Conversely, 'improvements' in the neighbourhood (for example, gentrification) will increase the value of my house even though I myself have invested nothing. The housing market is characterised by what economists call 'externality' effects. Homeowners often take action, both individual and collective, to control such externalities. Propose building a halfway house for released criminals in a 'respectable' neighbour-hood of homeowners and see what happens! The result is a lot of 'not in my back yard' politics, exclusions of unwanted populations and activities, and neighbourhood organisations whose missions are almost exclusively oriented to the maintenance and improvement of neighbourhood housing values (good neighbourhood schools have a big effect, for example). People act to protect the value of their savings. But people can also lose their savings when the state or investors take over housing in a neighbourhood destined for redevel-opment and let that housing deteriorate, thus destroying the market value of the housing that remains.

If I do invest in improvements, then I might want to be careful to do only those that clearly add to the house's exchange value. There are lots of 'advice books' for homeowners on this topic (building a new state-of-the-art kitchen adds value but mirrors on all the ceilings or an aviary in the back yard does not).

Home ownership has become important for larger and larger segments of the population in many parts of the world. The main-tenance and improvement of housing asset values have become important political objectives for larger and larger segments of the population and a major political issue because the exchange value for consumers is as important as the exchange value earned by producers.

But over the last thirty years or so, housing has become an object of speculation. I buy a house for $300,000 and three years later its value has appreciated to $400,000. I can then capitalise upon the extra value by refinancing for $400,000 and walk away with the extra $100,000, which I can use as I wish. The enhanced exchange value of housing becomes a hot item. The house becomes a convenient cash cow, a personal ATM machine, thus boosting aggregate demand, including, of course, the further demand for housing. Michael Lewis in *The Big Short* explains the sort of thing that happened during the run-up to the crash of 2008. The childminder of one of his lead informants ended up owning, with her sister, six houses in Queens in New York City. 'After they bought the first one, and its value rose, the lenders came and suggested they refinance and take out $250,000 – which they used to buy another.' Then the price of that one rose too and they repeated the experiment. 'By the time they were done they owned five of them and the market was falling and they couldn't make any of the payments.'[2]

Speculation in housing market asset values became rife. But speculation of this sort always has a 'Ponzi' element attached. I buy a house on borrowed money and the prices go up. More people are then attracted to the idea of buying into housing because of rising property values. They borrow even more money (easy to do when lenders are flush with money) to buy into a good thing. Housing prices go up even more, so even more people and institutions get into the game. The result is a 'property bubble' which eventually pops. How and why such bubbles in asset values like housing form, how big or small they are and what happens when they pop depends on the configurations of different conditions and forces. For the moment all we have to accept, on the evidence of the historical record (from the property market crashes of 1928, 1973, 1987 and 2008 in the United States, for example), is that such manias and bubbles are part and parcel of what capitalist history is about. As China has moved closer to adopting the ways of capital, so it has also become increasingly subject to speculative booms and bubbles in its housing markets. We will revisit the question why in what follows.

In the recent property market crash in the United States, about 4 million people lost their homes through foreclosure. For them, the pursuit of exchange value destroyed access to housing as a use value. An untold number of people are still 'under water' in their mortgage finance. This refers to a situation in which someone who purchased a house at the height of the boom now owes a financial institution more money than the house is worth on the market. Owners cannot get out of ownership and move without taking a substantial loss. At the height of the boom, housing prices were so high that many could not get access to use values without assuming a debt that would ultimately prove unpayable. After the crash, the financial drain of being stuck with a certain bundle of use values has had remarkably dire effects. The reckless pursuit of exchange value destroyed, in short, the capacity for many to acquire and afterwards sustain their access to housing use values.

Similar problems have occurred in rental markets. In New York City, where some 60 per cent of the population are renters, many large rental complexes were bought out at the height of the boom by private equity funds looking to make a killing by raising rents (even in the face of strong regulatory laws). The funds deliberately ran down the current use values to justify their plans for reinvestment, but then themselves went bankrupt in the financial crash, leaving tenants with deteriorated use values and higher rents living in fore-closed properties whose ownership obligations were often unclear (who you call to fix a non-functioning furnace in a housing complex in foreclosure is not at all obvious). Nearly 10 per cent of the rental housing stock has suffered from these sorts of problems. The ruthless pursuit of maximising exchange values has diminished access to housing use values for a large segment of the population. And to top it all, of course, the housing market crash triggered a global crisis from which it has proved very difficult to recover.

Housing provision under capitalism has moved, we can conclude, from a situation in which the pursuit of use values dominated to one where exchange values moved to the fore. In a weird reversal, the use value of housing increasingly became, first, a means of saving and, second, an instrument of speculation for consumers as well as producers, financiers and all the others (real estate brokers, loan officers, lawyers, insurance agents etc.) who stood to gain from boom conditions in housing markets. The provision of adequate housing use values (in the conventional consumption sense) for the mass of the population has increasingly been held hostage to these ever-deepening exchange value considerations. The consequences for the provision of adequate and affordable housing for an increasing segment of the population have been disastrous.

In the background to all this has been the shifting terrain of public opinion and public policy on the proper role of the state in the provision of adequate use values and basic needs to populations. Since the 1970s, a 'neoliberal consensus' has emerged (or been imposed) in which the state withdraws from obligations for public provision in fields as diverse as housing, health care, education, transportation and public utilities (water, energy, even infrastructures). It does so in the interests of opening up these arenas to private capital accumulation and exchange value considerations. Everything that happened in the housing field has been affected by these shifts. Why this shift to privatisation occurred is a particular question we are not at this point concerned to answer. All that I think it is important to record at this point is that shifts of this sort have occurred such that state involvement in housing provision (with its particular implication for how the use value–exchange value contradiction has been managed) has been radically transformed throughout much (though not all) of the capitalist world over the last forty years.

Obviously, I have chosen this case of the use value and exchange value of housing because it is a perfect example of how a simple difference, between the use value and the exchange value of a commodity in the market, can evolve into an opposition and an antagonism before becoming so heightened into an absolute contradiction as to produce a crisis not only in housing but throughout the whole financial and economic system. It did not, presumably, have to evolve that way (or did it? – this is a crucial question we must ultimately answer). But that it did evolve that way in the United States and in Ireland, Spain and to some degree Britain, as well as in various other parts of the world, after 2000 or so to produce the macroeconomic crisis of 2008 (a crisis not yet resolved) is unquestionable. And that it was a crisis in the exchange value side that denied more and more people adequate use values in housing in addition to a decent standard of life is also undeniable.

The same thing happens to health care and education (higher education in particular) as exchange value considerations increasingly dominate the use value aspects of social life. The story we hear everywhere repeated, from our classrooms to throughout virtually all the media, is that the cheapest, best and most efficient way to procure use values is through unleashing the animal spirits of the entrepreneur hungry for profit to participate in the market system. For this reason, many categories of use values that were hitherto supplied free of charge by the state have been privatised and commodified – housing, education, health care and public utilities have all gone in this direction in many parts of the world. The World Bank insists that this should be the global norm. But it is a system that works for the entrepreneurs, who by and large make hefty profits, and for the affluent, but it penalises almost everyone else to the point of somewhere between 4 and 6 million foreclosures in the case of housing in the USA (and countless more in Spain and many other countries). The political choice is between a commodified system that serves the rich well enough and a system that focuses on the production and democratic provision of use values for all without any mediations of the market.

So let us reflect, then, in a more abstract theoretical way on the nature of this contradiction. Exchange of use values between individuals, organisations (such as businesses and corporations) and social groups is plainly important in any complex social order characterised by intricate divisions of labour and extensive trade networks. Barter in such situations has limited utility because of the problem of the 'double coincidence of wants and needs'. You have to have a commodity I want and I have to have a commodity you want in order for simple barter to take place. Barter chains can be constructed but they are limited and cumbersome. Therefore some independent measure of the value of all commodities on the market – a single metric of value – becomes not only advantageous but necessary. I can then sell my commodity for some general equivalent of value and use that general equivalent to buy whatever I want or need from elsewhere. The general equivalent is, of course, money. But this takes us on to the field of the second contradiction of capital. What is money?

# Contradiction 2

# The Social Value of Labour and Its Representation by Money

Exchange value requires a measure of 'how much' commodities are worth relative to each other. This measure is called money. So what is this 'money' that we so unthinkingly use and reuse on a daily basis? We worry when we do not have enough of it, plot ways (sometimes devious or illegal) to get more of it, even as we find ourselves often struggling to organise our lives to live within the parameters defined by how much of it we possess. It sometimes seems as if money is the supreme God of the commodity world and that we must all bow down before it, submit to its dictates and worship before the altar of its power.

We know very well what the basic technical functions of the capitalist form of money are. It is a means or medium of circulation (facilitating exchanges in a way that solves the problem of the 'non-coincidence of interests' that so limits direct barter). It provides a single measuring rod for the economic values of all commodities in the market. And it provides a way to store value. But what does money represent and how does it proliferate in its social and political functions and meanings to make it seem as if it is the lust for money that makes the social and economic world go round?

Money, in the first instance, is a means whereby I can make a claim on the social labour of others: that is, a claim on that labour which is expended on the production of goods and services for others in the marketplace (this is what differentiates a 'commodity' from a 'product' like the tomatoes I grow in my back yard for my own consumption). It is a claim that does not have to be exercised instantaneously (because money stores value), but at some point it has to be exercised, otherwise money is not fulfilling its destiny and function.

In a complex society, such as that which capital has constructed, we depend heavily upon the labour of others to provide us with all the use values we need to live. We take the availability of many of these use values for granted. We turn on a switch and the electricity comes on, the gas stove lights up at the press of a button, the windows can be opened and closed, our shoes and shirts fit, the coffee and tea of a morning are always there, the bread and the buses, the cars and the pencils and pens, the notepaper and the books, all are available to us, and there are dentists and doctors and chiropractors and hairdressers, teachers, researchers, lawyers and bureaucrats producing knowledge and rules – all to be had at a price! But these things and services absorb human labour both directly and indirectly through the labour that accumulates in the steel that goes into the nail that builds the house. Most of us participate to some degree or other, directly or indirectly, in the activity of providing goods and services to others.

It is the social value of all that activity, of all that labouring, that underpins what it is that money represents. 'Value' is a social relation established between the labouring activities of millions of people around the world. As a social relation, it is immaterial and invisible (like the relation between me, the writer, and you, the reader of this text). But, like moral and ethical values more generally, this immaterial value has objective consequences for social practices. In the case of social labour, 'value' speaks to why shoes cost more than shirts, houses cost more than cars and wine costs more than water. These differences in value between commodities have nothing to do with their character as use values (apart from the simple fact that they must all be useful to someone somewhere) and everything to do with the social labour involved in their production.

Being immaterial and invisible, value requires some material representation. This material representation is money. Money is a tangible form of appearance as well as a symbol and representation of the immateriality of social value. But, like all forms of representation (maps come to mind), there is a gap between the representation and the social reality it is seeking to represent. The representation does a good job of capturing the relative value of social labour in some respects, but it misses out and even falsifies in others (much as maps are accurate representations of some features of the world around us but misleading about others). This gap between money and the value it represents constitutes the second foundational contradiction of capital.

Money, we can say at the outset, is inseparable but also distinct from the social labour that constitutes value. Money hides the immateriality of social labour (value) behind its material form. It is all too easy to mistake the representation for the reality it seeks to represent, and to the degree that the representation falsifies (as to some degree it always does) we end up believing in and acting upon something that is false. In the same way we cannot see the social labour in any commodity, so we are particularly blinded to the nature of social labour by the money that represents it. We will look at examples shortly. The inseparability of value from its representation is important. It derives from the simple fact that without money and the commodity transactions it facilitates, value could not exist as an immaterial social relation. In other words, value could not form without the aid of the material representation (money) and the social practices of exchange. The relation between money and value is dialectical and co-evolutionary – they both emerge together – rather than causal.

But the relation can also be misleading because the 'gap' between social value and its representation is riddled with potential contradictions, depending upon the form the money takes. Commodity moneys (like gold and silver) are rooted in tangible commodities with definite physical qualities. On the other hand, coins, paper and fiat moneys (the former issued by private entities and the latter by the state) and the more recent forms of electronic moneys are symbols merely. 'Money of account' dispenses with actual money payments at the moment of sale or purchase in favour of the payment of net balances at the end of a certain period. For firms that buy and sell, the net balances of multiple money transactions are usually far less than the total transactions because purchases and sales offset each other. Only the residual net balance claims are actually paid. Banks, for example, clear cheques from each other (this is now done electronically but it used to be done manually at clearing houses – five times a day in New York – with each bank sending runners to deposit cheques at the window of the bank the cheque was drawn upon). At the end of the day or clearing period, the net transfers between the banks may be close to zero even though a vast number of transactions have taken place. This can be so because the cheques drawn on one bank are offset by the cheques deposited by many others. Money of account therefore greatly reduces the actual amount of 'real' money needed. This kind of money also underpins a vast array of credit instruments and loans used to promote both production and consumption (in housing markets, for example, developers borrow to build speculative housing and consumers use mortgage finance to buy that housing). Credit moneys in themselves constitute a hugely complicated world (that some theorists regard as radically different from other moneys).

From all of this arises a peculiar and seemingly tautological use for money. Money, which supposedly measures value, itself becomes a kind of commodity – *money capital*. Its use value is that it can be used to produce more value (profit or surplus value). Its exchange value is the interest payment, which in effect puts a value on that which measures value (a highly tautological proposition!). This is what makes money as a measure so special and so odd. Whereas other standard measures, like inches and kilos, cannot be bought and sold in themselves (I can only buy kilos of potatoes, not kilos full stop), money can be bought and sold in itself as money capital (I can buy the use of $100 for a certain period of time).

The simplest way to conjure up a material representation for value is to select one commodity as the value representative for all the rest. For a variety of reasons, the precious metals, gold and silver in particular, emerged historically as best suited to fulfil this role. The reasons they were selected are important. To begin with these metals were relatively scarce and there is a fairly constant accumulated supply. I cannot go into my back yard and dig up some gold or silver whenever I want. The supply of the precious metals is relatively inelastic, so they maintain their relative value against all other commodities over time (though bursts of production activity, like the California gold rush, did create some problems). Most of the world's gold is already mined and above ground. Second, these metals do not oxidise and deteriorate (as would happen if we chose raspberries or potatoes as our money commodity): this means that they maintain their physical characteristics over the time of a market transaction and, even more importantly, they can function relatively safely as a long-term store of value. Third, the physical properties of these metals are known and their qualities can be assayed accurately so their measure is easily calibrated, unlike, say, the bottles of vodka (where consumer taste could be erratic) that emerged as a form of commodity money in Russia when the monetary system collapsed in the 1990s and trading collapsed into a multilateral bartering system.[1] The physical and material properties of these elements of the so-called natural world are used to anchor and represent the immateriality of value as social labour.

But commodity moneys are awkward to use on a daily basis for the exchange of low-value commodities. So coins, tokens and eventually bits of paper and then electronic moneys became much more practicable in the marketplaces of the world. Imagine what it would be like if we had to pay for a cup of coffee on the street with the exact weight of gold or silver! So while the commodity moneys may have provided a solid physical material basis to represent social labour (the British currency notes still promise 'to pay the bearer' even though these notes have long ago ceased to be freely convertible into gold and silver), they were quickly displaced by far more flexible and manageable money forms. But this creates another oddity. Moneys which were originally required to give physical form to the immateriality of social labour get represented by symbols, by representations and, ultimately, by numbers in computerised accounts.

When money commodities are represented by numbers, this introduces a serious and potentially misleading paradox into the monetary system. Whereas gold and silver are relatively scarce and of constant supply, the representation of money as numbers allows the quantity of money available to expand without any technical limit. We thus see the Federal Reserve in our time adding trillions of dollars to the economy at the drop of a hat through tactics like quantitative easing. There seems no limit to such possibilities except that imposed by state policies and regulation. When the metallic basis of global moneys was totally abandoned in the 1970s, we indeed found ourselves in a potentially limitless world of money creation and accumulation. Furthermore, the rise of moneys of account and even more importantly of credit moneys (beginning with the simple use of IOUs) places a great deal of money creation in the hands of individuals and the banks rather than in the hands of state institutions. This calls forth regulatory impositions and interventions on the part of the state apparatus in what is often a desperate attempt to manage the monetary system. Astonishing and legendary episodes of inflation, such as that which occurred in the Weimar Republic in 1920s Germany, have emphasised the key role of the state in relation to maintaining confidence in the qualities and meaning of the paper money it issues. We will return to this when we look at the third foundational contradiction.

All these oddities in part arise because the three basic functions of money have quite different requirements if they are to be effectively performed. Commodity moneys are good at storing value but dysfunctional when it comes to circulating commodities in the market. Coins and paper moneys are great as a means or medium of payment but are less secure as a long-term store of value. Fiat currencies issued by the state with compulsory circulation (compulsory because taxes have to be paid in this currency) are subject to the policy whims of the issuing authorities (for example, debts can be inflated away by just printing money). These different functions are not entirely consistent with each other. But nor are they independent. If money cannot store value at all for more than an ephemeral moment, then it would be useless as a medium of circulation. On the other hand, if we are looking for money only as a means of circulation, then fake moneys can do the job just as well as the 'real' money of a silver coin. This is why gold and silver, which are great as measurers and storers of value, in turn need representing in the form of notes and paper/credit moneys if commodity circulation is to remain fluid. So we end up with representations of representations of social labour as the basis of the money form! There is, as it were, a double fetish (a double set of masks behind which the sociality of human labour for others is hidden).

With the aid of money, commodities can be labelled in the market with an asking price. That price may or may not be realised depending on conditions of supply and demand. But this labelling carries with it another set of contradictions. The price actually realised in an individual sale depends on particular conditions of supply and demand in a particular place and time. There is no immediate correspondence between this singular price and the generality of value. It is only in competitive and perfectly functioning markets that we can anticipate the convergence of all these singular realised market prices around some average price that represents the generality of value. But notice it is only because prices can diverge from value that the prices can move around so as to give a firmer representation of what the value might be. However, the market process offers many opportunities and temptations to disrupt this convergence. Every capitalist longs to be able to sell at a monopoly price and to avoid competition. Hence the name branding and the logo-laden sales practices that allow Nike to charge a monopoly price that permanently ensures departure from unified standards of value in sneaker production. This quantitative divergence between prices and values poses a problem. Capitalists necessarily respond to prices and not to values because in the marketplace they see only prices and can have no direct means of identifying values. To the degree that there is a quantitative departure of prices from values, so capitalists find themselves having to respond to the misleading representations rather than to the underlying values.

Furthermore, there is nothing to stop me putting this label called price on anything, no matter whether it is the product of social labour or not. I can hang the label on a plot of land and extract a rent for its use. I can, like all those lobbyists on K Street in Washington, legally buy influence in Congress or cross the line to sell conscience, honour and reputation to some highest bidder. There is not only a quantitative but a qualitative divergence between market prices and social values. I can make a fortune out of trafficking women, peddling drugs or clandestinely selling arms (three of the most lucrative businesses in contemporary capitalism). Even worse (if that is possible!), I can use money to make more money, as if it is capital when it is not. The monetary signals diverge from what the logic of social labour should be all about. I can create vast pools of fictitious capital – money capital loaned out to activities that create no value at all even as they are highly profitable in money terms and return interest to me. State debt to fight wars has always been funded by the circulation of fictitious capital – people lend to the state and get repaid with interest out of state tax revenues even though the state is destroying and not creating any value at all.

So here is yet another paradox. Money that is supposed to represent the social value of creative labour takes on a form – fictitious capital – that circulates to eventually line the pockets of the financiers and bondholders through the extraction of wealth from all sorts of non-productive (non-value-producing) activities. If you do not believe this, then you have to look no further than the recent history of the housing market to see exactly what I mean. Speculation on housing values is not a productive activity, yet vast amounts of fictitious capital flowed into the housing market up until 2007–8 because the rate of return on investments was high. Easy credit meant rising housing prices and high rates of turnover meant a plethora of opportunities to earn exorbitant fees and commissions on housing transactions. The bundling together of the mortgages (a form of fictitious capital) into collateralised debt obligations created a debt instrument (an even more fictitious form of capital) that could be marketed worldwide. These instruments of fictitious capital, many of which turned out to be worthless, were marketed to unsuspecting investors around the world as if they were investments certified by the rating agencies to be 'as safe as houses'. This was fictitious capital run wild. We are still paying the price for its excesses.

The contradictions that arise around the money form are, therefore, multiple. Representations, as we have already noted, falsify even as they represent. In the case of gold and silver as representations of social value, we see that we are taking the particular circumstances for the production of those precious metals as a general measure of the value congealed in all commodities. We in effect take a particular use value (the metal gold) and use it to represent exchange value in general. Above all, we take something that is inherently social and represent it in such a way that it can be appropriated as a form of social power by private persons. This last contradiction has deep and in some ways devastating consequences for the contradictions of capital.

To begin with, the fact that money permits social power to be appropriated and exclusively utilised by private persons places money at the centre of a wide range of noxious human behaviours – lust and greed for money power inevitably become central features in the body politic of capitalism. All sorts of fetishistic behaviours and beliefs centre on this. The desire for money as a form of social power becomes an end in itself which distorts the neat demand–supply relation of the money that would be required simply to facilitate exchange. This throws a monkey wrench into the supposed rationality of capitalist markets.

Whether greed is an innate human behaviour or not can doubtless be debated (Marx, for example, did not believe so). But what is certain is that the rise of the money form and the capacity for its private appropriation has created a space for the proliferation of human behaviours that are anything but virtuous and noble. Accumulations of wealth and power (accumulations that were ritually disposed of in the famous potlatch system of pre-capitalist societies) have not only been tolerated but welcomed and treated as something to be admired. This led the British economist John Maynard Keynes, writing on 'Economic Possibilities for our Grandchildren' in 1930, to hope that:

> When the accumulation of wealth is no longer of high social importance, there will be great changes in the code of morals. We shall be able to rid ourselves of many of the pseudo-moral principles which have hag-ridden us for two hundred years, by which we have exalted some of the most distasteful of human qualities into the position of the highest virtues. We shall be able to afford to dare to assess the money motive at its true value. The love of money as a possession – as distinguished from the love of money as a means to the enjoyments and realities of life – will be recognized for what it is, a somewhat disgusting morbidity, one of those semi-criminal, semi-pathological propensities which one hands over with a shudder to the specialists on mental disease. All kinds of social customs and economic practices, affecting the distribution of wealth and of economic rewards and penalties, which we now maintain at all costs, however distasteful and unjust they may be in themselves, because they are tremendously useful in promoting accumulation of capital, we shall then be free, at last, to discard.[2]

So what should the critical response be to all this? To the degree that the circulation of speculative fictitious capital inevitably leads to crashes which exact a huge toll from capitalist society in general (and even more tragically from the most vulnerable populations therein), so an outright assault on the speculative excesses and the (largely fictitious) monetary forms that have evolved to promote them necessarily become the focus of political struggle. To the degree that these speculative forms have underpinned the immense increases in social inequality and the distribution of wealth and power such that an emergent oligarchy – the infamous 1 per cent (which is really the even more infamous 0.1 per cent) – now effectively controls the levers of all global wealth and power, so this also defines obvious lines of class struggle crucial to the future well-being of the mass of humanity.

But this is only the more obvious tip of the iceberg. Money is, it bears repeating, as inseparable from value as exchange value is inseparable from money. The bonds between the three are tightly woven. If exchange value weakens and ultimately disappears as the guiding means by which use values are both produced and distributed in society, so the need for money and all of the lustful pathologies associated with its use (as capital) and possession (as a consummate source of social power) will also disappear. While the utopian aim of a social order without exchange value and therefore moneyless needs to be articulated, the intermediate step of designing quasi-money forms that facilitate exchange but inhibit the private accumulation of social wealth and power becomes imperative. This can be done in principle. Keynes, in his influential *General Theory of Employment, Interest, and Money*, for example, cites 'the strange, unduly neglected prophet Silvio Gesell', who long ago proposed the creation of quasi-money forms that oxidise if not used. The fundamental inequality between commodities (use values) that decay and a money form (exchange value) that does not has to be rectified. 'Only money that goes out of date like a newspaper, rots like potatoes, evaporates like ether, is capable of standing the test as an instrument of exchange of potatoes, newspapers, iron and ether,' wrote Gesell.[3] With electronic moneys, this is now practicable, in ways that were not possible before. An oxidisation schedule can easily be written into monetary accounts such that unused moneys (like unused airline miles) dissolve after a certain period of time. This cuts the bond between money as a means of circulation and money as a measure and even more significantly as a store of value (and hence a primary means for the accumulation of private wealth and power).

Obviously, moves of this sort would require wide-ranging adjustments of other facets of the economy. If money oxidises it would be impossible to use that money to save for future needs. Investment pension funds, for example, would disappear. This is not so appalling a prospect as it might appear. To begin with, investment pension funds are vulnerable to becoming worthless anyway (because of underfunding, mismanagement, collapses in stock market values or inflation). The value of monetarily based pension funds is contingent and not secure, as many pensioners are now finding out. Social Security, on the other hand, is a form of pension right that does not in principle depend upon using money to save for the future. Today's workers provide for those who preceded them. Far better to organise future incomes by this means than by saving and hoping investments will pay off. A guaranteed minimum income (or minimal access to a collectively managed pool of use values) for all would obviate entirely the need for a money form that would allow private savings to guarantee future economic security.

The focus would then have to be on what really matters, which is the continuous creation of use values through social labour and the eradication of exchange value as the principal means by which the production of use values is organised. Marx, for one, believed that reforms within the monetary system would not in themselves guarantee the dissolution of the power of capital and that it was illusory to believe that tinkering with monetary forms could be the cutting edge of revolutionary change. He was, I believe, correct in this supposition. But what I think his analysis also makes clear is that the evolution of an alternative to capital would require as a necessary but not sufficient condition a radical reconfiguration of how exchange is organised and the ultimate dissolution of the power of money not only over social life but, as Keynes indicates, over our mental and moral conceptions of the world. Envisaging a moneyless economy is one way to get a measure of what an alternative to capitalism might look like. The possibility of this, given the potentialities of electronic moneys or even substitutes for money, may not be so far off. The rise of new forms of cybercurrency, such as Bitcoin, suggest that capital itself is now on the way to invent new monetary forms. It is opportune and wise, therefore, for the left to frame political ambitions and political thought around this ultimate objective.

An alternative monetary politics of this sort becomes more imperative when we consider a particularly dangerous immediate problem. The contemporary form that money assumes has achieved the status of a double fetish – an abstracted representation (pure numbers stored on a computer screen) of a concrete representation (like gold and silver) of the immateriality of social labour. When money takes the form of mere numbers, then its potential quantity is limitless. This permits the illusion to flourish that limitless and unending growth of capital in its money form is not only possible but desirable. Against this, even a casual examination of the conditions pertaining to the development of social labour and the augmentation of value shows that compounding growth for ever is impossible. This opposition, as we will see later, lies at the root of one of the three most dangerous contradictions of capital, that of compounding growth.

When money was constrained by being anchored, however weakly, in the material availability and relative scarcity of the physical money commodities, then there was a material restraint upon the infinite creation of money. The abandonment of the metallic base of the world's money supply in the early 1970s created a whole new world of possible contradictions. Money could be printed ad infinitum by whoever was authorised to do so. The money supply lay in the hands of fallible human institutions such as the central banks. The danger was accelerating inflation. It is no accident that after a brief period of rising inflation towards the end of the 1970s in the United States in particular, the world's central bankers (led by Paul Volcker at the US Federal Reserve) all converged on the sole policy of containing inflation at all costs, thereby abandoning responsibility for employment and unemployment. When the European Central Bank was formed to deal with the euro, its sole mandate was to control inflation and nothing else. That this played out disastrously when the sovereign debt crises hit several European countries after 2012 testifies to a chronic inability within the institutions that capital sets up to regulate its own excesses, to understand the contradictory logic embedded in the monetary form that capital now necessarily assumes. It is therefore no surprise that the crisis that broke out in 2007–8 was a crisis that took in the first instance a financial form.

# Contradiction 3

# Private Property and the Capitalist State

Commodities do not take themselves to market. Individual agents – buyers and sellers – come together in the market to trade commodities for money and vice versa. For this to occur, both buyers and sellers must have exclusive rights of disposal and appropriation over the commodities and the moneys that they hold. Exchange value and money jointly presume the existence of individual private property rights over both commodities and money.

To clear the air, let me first make a distinction between individual appropriation and private property. We all of us, as living persons, appropriate things in the course of actively making use of them. I appropriate food when I eat it, I appropriate a bicycle when I ride it, I appropriate this computer while writing this. My use of many of the processes and things available to me precludes anyone else from using them when I am using them. There are, however, some items whose use is not exclusionary. If I watch a TV programme this does not prevent others from so doing. And there are other goods ('public goods') that are often held and used in common, though usually with limitations. I use the street, as do many others, but there is a limit to how many people a street can hold and there are certain activities that either by custom or by law are prohibited upon the street (for example, defecation on the streets of New York). For many processes and things, however, an exclusive relationship exists between the user(s) and that which is being used. This is not the same thing as private property.

Private property establishes an exclusive ownership right to a thing or a process whether it is being actively used or not. At the root of commodity exchange there lies the presupposition that I do not myself actively want or need the commodity I offer for trade. Indeed, the very definition of a commodity is something that is produced for someone else to use. Private property rights confer the right to trade away (alienate) that which is owned. A difference then emerges between what are called usufructuary rights (rights that pertain to active use) and exclusionary permanent ownership rights. This difference has often been the source of confusion, particularly throughout the history of colonialism. Indigenous populations frequently operate on the basis of usufructuary rights to land, for example (this is the case with shifting agriculture). Colonial powers typically imposed exclusionary ownership rights and this was the source of a great deal of conflict. Populations that moved around from one site to another, following their herds or moving from exhausted land to fresh and more fertile land, suddenly found themselves barred from moving by the existence of fences and barbed wire. They often found themselves prevented from using land that they had traditionally regarded as open for use because someone now owned it in perpetuity even if it was not used. The indigenous population in North America suffered greatly from this. In contemporary Africa people's customary and collective resource rights are currently being pell-mell converted to an exclusionary private property rights regime by what many regard as fraudulent agreements between, for example, village chiefs (who have customarily held the land in trust for their people) and foreign interests. This constitutes what is generally referred to as a huge 'land grab' by capital and foreign states for control over Africa's land and resources.

Private property rights presuppose a social bond between that which is owned and a person, defined as a juridical individual, who is the owner and who has the rights of disposition over that which is owned. By a marvellous sleight of juridical reasoning, it has transpired that ownership is vested not only in individuals like you and me but also in corporations and other institutions which, under the law, are defined as legal persons (even though, as many like to point out, corporations cannot be jailed when they do wrong in the same way that living persons can). The existence of this social bond is recognised in almost all bourgeois constitutions and connects ideals of individual private property with notions of individual human rights, the 'rights of man' and doctrines and legal protections of those individual rights. The social bond between individual human rights and private property lies at the centre of almost all contractual theories of government.

Private property rights are in principle held in perpetuity. They do not expire or dissipate through lack of use. They can pass from one generation to another through inheritance. As a result, there is an inner connection between private property rights and non-oxidisable forms of money. Only the latter can last in perpetuity. But the evolution of forms of paper and fiat money whose relative value is subject to degradation (through, for example, inflation) undermines the initially secure connection between the perpetuity and stability of money forms and that of private property. Furthermore, under the doctrine of *res nullius*, most famously embraced by John Locke, only that private property in land which is productive of value (that is, which involves the application of productive social labour for commodity production) is deemed legitimate. Failure to produce value (and surplus value) not only justified the wholesale dispossession of the land rights of the Irish by the British, it also justified the wiping out and dispossession of 'unproductive' indigenous populations to make way for the 'productive' colonisers particularly throughout the Americas and now across much of Africa. The contemporary version of this doctrine in advanced capitalist societies is that of eminent domain, through which the appropriation of private property in land to bring it into a condition of higher and better usage is legally justified. Private property in both land and money is only, therefore, contingently perpetual.

The imposition of private property rights depends upon the existence of state powers and legal systems (usually coupled with monetary taxation arrangements) that codify, define and enforce the contractual obligations that attach to both private property rights and the rights of juridical individuals. There is a good deal of evidence that the coercive power of the state played an important role in opening spaces within which capital could flourish well before private property regimes became dominant. This was as true in the transition from feudalism to capitalism in Europe as it later became when the Chinese set up special economic zones for capitalist activity in southern China after 1980. But in between usufructuary and private property rights lies a plethora of common property or customary rights, which are often confined to a given polity (like a village community or more broadly across a whole cultural regime). These rights are not necessarily open to all, but they do presuppose sharing and cooperative forms of governance between the members of the polity. The eradication of usufructuary rights and the infamous process of enclosure of the commons have led to the dominance of a system of individualised private property rights backed by state power as *the* basis for exchange relations and trade. This is the form consistent with capital circulation and accumulation.

To be private property, however, a thing or process has to be clearly bounded, nameable and identifiable (in the case of land, this rests on cadastral mapping and the construction of a land registry). Not everything is susceptible to that condition. It is almost impossible to imagine the air and the atmosphere being divisible into private property entities that can be bought and sold. What is remarkable, however, is the lengths to which capital has gone to extend the reach of an individualised private property rights regime deep into the heart of biological processes and other aspects of both the social and the natural world in order to establish proprietary rights. There is a fierce ongoing struggle over the proprietary rights to knowledge of natural processes, for example. The field of intellectual property rights in particular is currently riddled with controversy and conflict. Should knowledge be universally available to all or privately owned?

An individualised private property rights regime lies at the basis of what capital is about. It is a necessary condition and construction in the sense that neither exchange value nor money could operate in the way it does without this legal infrastructure. But this rights regime is beset by contradictions. As in the case of money, the contradictions are multiple rather than singular. This is so in part because of the way in which the contradictions between use value and exchange value and between money and the social labour which it represents spill over into the individualised private property rights regime.

The first and most obvious line of contradiction is between the supposedly 'free' exercise of individual private property rights and the collective exercise of coercive regulatory state power to define, codify and give legal form to those rights and the social bond that knits them so closely together. Legal definitions of the individual and, hence, a culture of individualism arose with the proliferation of exchange relations, the rise of monetary forms and the evolution of the capitalist state. All but the most rabid of libertarians and the most extreme of anarchists will agree, however, that some semblance of state power has to exist in order to sustain the individualised property rights and structures of law that, according to theoreticians like Friedrich Hayek, guarantee the maximum of non-coercive individual liberty. But these rights have to be enforced and it is at this point that the state, with its monopoly over the legitimate use of force and violence, is called upon to repress and police any transgressions against the private property rights regime. The capitalist state must use its acquired monopoly over the means of violence to protect and preserve the individualised private property rights regime as articulated through freely functioning markets. The centralised power of the state is used to protect a decentralised private property system. However, the extension of the status of personhood and juridical individual to powerful corporations and institutions obviously corrupts the bourgeois utopian dream of a perfected world of individual personal liberty for all on the basis of democratically dispersed ownership.

There are many problems within the realm of market exchange that prompt the state to go far beyond a simple 'nightwatchman' role as guardian of private property and of individual rights. To begin with, there are problems of the provision of collective and public goods (such as highways, ports and harbours, water and waste disposal, education and public health). The field of physical and social infra-structures is vast and of necessity the state must be involved either in directly producing or in mandating and regulating the provision of these goods. In addition, the state apparatus itself must be built not only to administer but to secure the institutions it has to protect (hence the creation of military and police capacities and powers and the funding of these activities through taxation).

Above all, the state has to find a way to govern and administer diverse, often restive and fractious populations. That many capitalist states have ended up doing so through the institution of democratic procedures and mechanisms of governmentality to elicit consent rather than by resorting to coercion and force has led some to suggest, erroneously in my view, an inherent bond between democratisation and capital accumulation. That some form of bourgeois democracy has proved to be generally more effective and efficient as a form of governance within capitalism in general is, however, undeniable. But this outcome has not necessarily been a consequence of capital's rise to dominance as the economic engine of a social formation: it owes its dynamic to broader political forces and to long-standing attempts to find collective forms of governance that effectively bridge the tension between the potential arbitrariness of state autocratic power and the popular desire for individual liberty and freedom.

Then there is the pervasive problem of what to do about market failures. These arise because of so-called externality effects, defined as real costs which are not (for some reason) registered in the market. The most obvious field of externalities is pollution, where firms and individuals do not pay for deleterious effects on air, water and land qualities through their actions. There are other forms of both positive and negative externality effects that typically lead to calls for collective rather than individual action – the exchange value of housing, for example, is captive to externality effects since investment or disinvestment in one house in a neighbourhood has an effect (either positive or negative) on the value of houses in the immediate vicinity. One form of state intervention designed to cope with problems of this sort is land-use zoning.

Most people concede the legitimacy of state or other forms of collective action to control and regulate those activities that generate strong negative externality effects. In all of these instances the state necessarily has to encroach upon the exercise of individual liberties and private property rights. The contradiction between use and exchange values spills over to have profound effects upon the relation between centralised state power and the free exercise of decentralised individual private property rights. The only interesting question is how far does the state go and to what degree that encroachment might be based on coercion rather than the building of consent (a process that unfortunately entails the cultivation of nationalism). In any case, the state has to have a monopoly over the legalised use of violence to exercise such functions.

That monopoly also becomes explicit in the way the state in both its pre-capitalist and its capitalist incarnations has been pre-eminently a war-making machine embroiled in geopolitical rivalries and geo-economic strategising on the world stage. Within the framework of an emergent and perpetually evolving interstate global system, the capitalist state is involved in the pursuit of diplomatic, trading and economic advantages and alliances to secure its own wealth and power (or, more accurately, the wealth, status and power of its leaders and at least some segments of the population) by enhancing the capacity of property-rights holders to amass more and more wealth in the territory in which they reside. In so doing, war – classically defined as diplomacy by other means – becomes a crucial tool of geopolitical and geo-economic positioning in which the amassing of wealth, competitive power and influence within the territorial confines of the state becomes a distinctive aim.

But to fight wars and engage in such manoeuvrings the state requires adequate economic resources. The monetisation of its war-making activities lay at the root of the construction of what economic historians refer to as the fiscal-military state from the fifteenth century onwards. At the heart of this state lay the construction of what I call the 'state–finance nexus'. In the British case this was most clearly symbolised by the alliance between the state apparatus on the one hand and the London merchant capitalists on the other. The latter effectively funded the state's war-making powers by securing the national debt in return for an exclusive charter to monopolise and manage the monetary system through the formation of the Bank of England in 1694. This was the world's first central bank. It subsequently became a model for the rest of the capitalist world to follow.

This highlights a key relationship between the state and money. Silvio Gesell, I think, has it right:

> Money requires the State, without a State money is not possible; indeed the foundation of the State may be said to date from the introduction of money. Money is the most natural and the most powerful cement of nations ... The fact that money is indispensable, and that State control of money is also indispensable, gives the State unlimited power over money. Exposed to this unlimited power the metal covering of money is as chaff before the wind. Money is as little protected by the money-material from abuse of State power as the constitution of the State is protected from arbitrary usurpation of power by the parchment upon which it is written. Only the State itself, the will of those in power (autocrats or representatives), can protect money from bunglers, swindlers and speculators – on condition that those in power are capable of purposeful use of their power. Up to the present they have never, unfortunately, possessed this capability.[1]

Yet, Gesell surprisingly suggests, 'the security of paper-money is greater than that of metal money'. This is so precisely because 'paper-money is secured by all the interests and ideals which weld people into a State. The paper-money of a State can only go down with the State itself.' The state, which is usually defined by its monopoly over the legitimate use of violence, acquires another key function: it must have monopoly power over money and the currency.

There are two caveats to this argument. First, this monopoly power is generic to the state and not particular. The global monetary system is hierarchical in character. The US dollar has functioned as the reserve currency for the global monetary system since 1945 and the USA has exclusive rights of seignorage (creation) of that money. The monetary powers of other states are circumscribed because international debts are typically denominated in US dollars and have to be paid in dollars. An individual state cannot monetise its debts by printing its own currency because the immediate effect will be to devalue the local currency against the US dollar. There are other currencies which might be used for global trade – pounds sterling (which used to be the global reserve currency), the euro and the yen and maybe in the future the Chinese yuan. But these have so far not threatened the position of the US dollar and occasional proposals to replace the dollar with a market-basket of currencies (of the sort that Keynes originally proposed at Bretton Woods in 1944) have so far been rebuffed by the USA. Considerable benefits accrue to the USA, after all, from its control over the global reserve currency. US imperial power has been exercised either directly or indirectly by dollar diplomacy. The hegemony of the US state in the world system is largely sustained by its control over the world currency and its ability to print money to pay, for example, for its excessive military expenditures. In the face of this, individual states may give up their role over their own currency. Ecuador, for example, uses US dollars. When the euro came into being, the individual states surrendered their monopoly power over their currencies to a set of supra-national institutions (the European Central Bank) dominated by Germany and to a lesser degree by France.

The second caveat is that this monopoly right of the state over the currency can be subcontracted, as it were, to merchant and banking capitalists through the chartering of central banks that are nominally independent of direct democratic or state political control. This is the case with the Bank of England, the US Federal Reserve and the European Central Bank. These powerful institutions exist in a liminal space between the state and the private banks. They are institutions which, along with the Treasury Departments of the state government, form the state–finance nexus that has long functioned as the 'central nervous system' for regulating and promoting capital. The state–finance nexus has all the characteristics of a feudal institution, because its operations are usually hidden from view and shrouded in mystery. It operates more like the Vatican or the Kremlin than like an open and transparent institution. It assumes a human face only at times of difficulty, when, for example, Hank Paulson (Secretary of the Treasury) and Ben Bernanke (Chair of the Federal Reserve) jointly took to the airwaves to dictate national policy in the wake of the collapse of Lehman Brothers in September 2008, when both the Executive Branch and Congress appeared paralysed and fearful. 'When the financial system and the state–finance nexus fails, as it did in 1929 and 2008, then everyone recognises there is a threat to the survival of capital and of capitalism and no stone is left unturned and no compromise left unexamined in the endeavours to resuscitate it.'[2]

But all is not always harmonious in the relation between the capitalist state and private property. To the degree that the state embraces some form of democracy in order to counteract the absolutist and autocratic state forms that can be arbitrarily hostile or unreceptive to certain of the requirements of capital, regarding, for example, freedom of movement, so it is opened up to populist influences of various sorts. If, as sometimes happens, it is captured by organised labour and left political parties, so its powers may be deployed to curb the powers of capital as private property. Capital can then no longer operate freely in many domains of the economy (labour markets, labour processes, income distributions and the like). It finds itself forced to operate in the framework of a veritable regulatory forest that circumscribes its freedoms. From time to time, therefore, the contradiction between state and private property gets heightened into an absolute contradiction that pits public against private, state against market. Fierce ideological and political battles can erupt around this contradiction.

But let me be clear: I am not here trying to write out a general theory of what the capitalist state is all about. I am simply drawing attention to those aspects and specific functions of the state that have to operate in a certain way to support the reproduction of capital. Given its powers of taxation and the state's susceptibility to political influences and interests, state powers can sometimes be redirected politically to economic ends in ways that trump private entrepreneurial activity and interests. During phases of social democratic political control (of the sort that was set up in Britain after the Second World War as well as in some European countries) and under various forms of *dirigiste* governmentality (of the sort characteristic of France under de Gaulle, Singapore under Lee Kuan-Yew and many other East Asian states, including China), state institutions can be created and organised as economic agents that either assume control of the commanding heights of the economy or guide investment decisions. Government planning at a variety of scales (macroeconomic, urban, regional and local) takes centre stage sometimes in competition with but more often in partnership with private and corporate activities. A large segment of capital accumulation then passes through the state in ways that are not necessarily directed to profit-maximising but to social or geopolitical ends. Even in states most devoted to the principles of privatisation and neoliberalisation, the military-industrial complex is set apart from the rest of the economy as a lucrative trough at which private subcontracted interests freely feed.

From the other end of the political spectrum, the manner of organising state finances is something libertarians clearly see as profoundly contradictory to individual liberties and freedoms. It passes monopoly control over money and credit to a non-elected and undemocratic set of institutions, headed by the central bankers. A critic like Thomas Greco therefore argues:

> The politicization of money, banking, and finance (which prevails throughout the world today) has enabled the concentration of power and wealth in few hands – a situation that has been extremely damaging to societies, cultures, economies, democratic government, and the environment. National governments have arrogated to themselves virtually unlimited spending power, which enables them to channel wealth to favored clients, to conduct wars on a massive scale, and to subvert democratic institutions and the popular will. The privileged private banking establishment has managed to monopolize everyone's credit,

enabling the few to exploit the many through their partiality in allocating credit, by charging usury (disguised as 'interest') and increasingly exorbitant fees, and by rewarding politicians for their service in promoting their interests.[3]

The libertarian argument, which is by no means implausible, is that this was what subverted the possibility of a genuine bourgeois democracy characterised by the maximum of individual liberty from the seventeenth century onwards. This is the system that in addition forces compounding growth, invites 'environmental destruction and rends the social fabric while increasing the concentration of power and wealth. It creates economic and political instabilities that manifest in recurrent cycles of depression and inflation, domestic and international conflict, and social dislocation.'[4] For this reason both left and right wings of the political spectrum in the United States tend to be antagonistic to institutions like the Federal Reserve and the International Monetary Fund.

The balance of the contradiction between private interests and individual liberties on the one hand and state power on the other has shifted most decisively in recent years towards the undemocratic, autocratic and despotic centres of the state apparatus, where they are backed by the increasing centralisation and militarisation of social control. This does not mean that the decentred powers of individual property owners are dissolved or even at risk. Indeed, those powers are enhanced as capital is increasingly protected against any and all forms of social opposition: for example, from labour or from environmentalists. Decentralisation is in any case often an optimal strategy for maintaining centralised control. The Chinese have in recent times consciously deployed this principle very effectively. It is nowhere more evident than in the state organisation of money power in commodity markets.

Since I have in preceding sections frequently referred to the housing market and the crisis in the property market as an example, let me briefly explain how it all works in this context. Private property rights underpin home ownership and capitalist states have systematically supported by various means (from active subsidies to advertising and rhetoric of the dreams of home ownership) the extension of home ownership to more and more segments of the population. This has in part been to ensure a continuous growth of the property market as a field of active and lucrative capital accumulation, but it has also performed a crucial ideological function, consolidating popular and populist support for the strategy of providing use values through exchange value mechanisms: in other words, support for the capitalist way. The active governmental support for home ownership in the United States, for political as well as economic reasons, consequently played its part in fostering the sub-prime mortgage crisis that brought down some of the major private investment institutions but also brought the quasi-public institutions of Fannie Mae and Freddie Mac into the ranks of bankruptcy, from which they had to be rescued by temporary nationalisation.

So what, then, must the political strategy in relation to this contradiction between state and private property be? A simple argument to try to restore the balance and enhance individual liberties (as many on both the left and the right of the political spectrum seem to favour these days) cannot suffice, in part because the balance has shifted so dramatically towards arbitrary state power and also because faith in the state as a potentially benevolent agent has largely faded. The return of the state to a pure 'nightwatchman' role will only further unleash the powers of what is already a largely unregulated capital to do as it will without any social or long-term constraints.

The only viable alternative political strategy is one that dissolves the existing contradiction between private and individual interests on the one hand and state power and interests on the other and replaces it with something else. It is in this context that much of the current left concern with the re-establishment and reclamation of 'the commons' makes so much sense. The absorption of private property rights into a comprehensive project for the collective management of the commons and the dissolution of autocratic and despotic state powers into democratic collective management structures become the only worthy long-term objectives.

These objectives make sense when applied to money and credit. The reclamation of money and credit as a form of the democratically regulated commons is imperative if the trend towards autocracy and monetary despotism is to be reversed. Severing the activities of money creation from the state apparatus becomes imperative in the name of strengthening and democratising collective liberties and freedoms. Since the power of the capitalist state rests in part on the twin pillars of a monopoly over the legitimate use of violence and monopoly power over monetary affairs and the currency, the breaking of the latter monopoly would ultimately entail a dissolution (rather than the 'smashing') of capitalist state power. Once deprived of power over its monetary resources, the capacity of the state to resort to militarised violence against its own restive populations would be nullified also. While this might seem far-fetched as an idea, something like it is already partially realised by the fact that the power of the bondholders is being used in countries like Greece, Italy and Spain to dictate state policies towards their own populations. Replace the power of the bondholders by the power of the people and this all too visible trend could just as easily be reversed.

State power is, as already noted, generic rather than particular. Hence this politics would have to dissolve all those international monetary institutions (like the IMF) that have emerged to support the dollar imperialism of the USA and which serve to maintain its financial hegemony within the world system. The disciplinary apparatus that is currently destroying the daily life of the Greek people, as well as the lives of many others who have suffered from the interventions of the IMF (usually in combination with other multilateral state powers, such as, in the Greek case, the European Central Bank and the European Commission), would likewise need to be dissolved to make way for practices and institutions of collective management of the common wealth of populations. Such a solution may appear abstracted and utopian in relation to current practices. But it is vital for alternative politics to have this sort of vision and long-term ambition in mind. Radical agendas, either revolutionary or reformist, must be formulated if civilisation is to be saved from being drowned in the contradiction between callous and unregulated private property and increasingly autocratic and militarised police state powers dedicated to the support of capital rather than to the well-being of the people.

# Contradiction 4
# Private Appropriation and Common Wealth

The common wealth created by social labour comes in an infinite variety of use values, everything from knives and forks to cleared lands, whole cities, the aircraft we fly, the cars we drive, the food we eat, the houses we live in and the clothes we wear. The private appropriation and accumulation of this common wealth and the social labour congealed within it occur in two quite different ways. First, there is a vast array of what we would now consider extra-legal activities, such as robbery, thievery, swindling, corruption, usury, predation, violence and coercion, along with a range of suspicious and shady practices in the market (monopolisation, manipulation, market cornering, price fixing, Ponzi schemes etc.). Second, individuals accumulate wealth by legally sanctioned exchanges under conditions of non-coercive trade in freely functioning markets. Theorists of capital circulation and accumulation typically exclude activities of the first sort as excrescences external to the 'normal' and legitimate functioning of the capitalist market. They build their models of capital circulation and accumulation on the presumption that only the second mode of private appropriation and accumulation of social wealth is legitimate and relevant.

I think it is time we overthrew this convenient but profoundly misleading fiction promoted by the economics textbooks and recognise the symbiotic relation between these two forms of appropriation of both social labour and the products of that social labour. I make this argument in part on the simple empirical grounds that it is stupid to seek to understand the world of capital without engaging with the drug cartels, traffickers in arms and the various mafias and other criminal forms of organisation that play such a significant role in world trade. It is impossible to shunt aside as accidental excrescences the vast array of predatory practices that were so easily identifiable in the recent crash of property markets in the United States (along with recent revelations of systematic banking malfeasance – such as the falsification of asset valuations in bank portfolios – money laundering, Ponzi finance, interest-rate manipulations and the like).

But beyond these obvious empirical reasons, there are strong theoretical grounds for believing that an economy based on dispossession lies at the heart of what capital is foundationally about. The direct dispossession of the value that social labour produces at the point of production is but one (albeit major) strain of dispossession that feeds and sustains the appropriation and accumulation by private 'persons' (that is, legal entities including corporations) of large portions of the common wealth.

Bankers do not care in principle, for example, whether their profits and excessive bonuses come from lending money to landlords who extract exorbitant rents from oppressed tenants, from merchants who price-gouge their customers, from credit card and telephone companies that bilk their users, from mortgage companies that illegally foreclose on homeowners or from manufacturers who savagely exploit their workers. While theorists on the political left, inspired by their understanding of Marx's political economy, have typically privileged the last of these forms of appropriation as in some sense more foundational than all the others, the historical evolution of capital has exhibited immense flexibility in its capacity to appropriate the common wealth in all these other myriad ways. The higher wages workers may get through class struggle in the workplace can all too easily be snatched back by the landlord, the credit card companies, the merchants, to say nothing of the taxman. The bankers even construct their own shell games, from which they profit immensely, and even when they get caught it is, for the most part, the bank (that is, the shareholders) who take the hit and not the bankers themselves (only in Iceland did the bankers actually end up in jail).

At the heart of this process of private appropriation of the common wealth lies the contradictory way in which, as we have seen, money represents and symbolises social labour (value). The fact that money, as opposed to the social value it represents, is inherently appropriable by private persons means that money (provided it functions well as both a store and measure of value) can be accumulated without limit by private persons. And to the degree that money is a repository of social power, so its accumulation and centralisation by a set of individuals become critical to both the social construction of personal greed and the formation of a more or less coherent capitalist class power.

Recognising the dangers to the social world, pre-capitalist societies endeavoured to erect barriers to the reckless private appropriation and use of common wealth while resisting the commodification and monetisation of everything. They realised very well that monetisation dissolved other ways of forming community with the result, as Marx put it, that 'money became the community'.[1] We are still living with the consequences of that transition. That these older societies ultimately lost that battle should not deter us from considering ways in which this private appropriation of the common wealth might be curbed, for it is still the case that it poses immense dangers in terms of reckless appropriations and investments regardless of the environmental or social consequences, even threatening the conditions for the reproduction of capital itself.

While this may all be self-evident, there is something even more sinister at work within the monetary calculus that really puts the seal upon the politics and practices of accumulation by dispossession as the hallmark of what capital is about. In the examination of how money works, we saw how the distinction between value and price opened a gap between the realities of social labour on the one hand and the ability to hang a fictional price label on anything, no matter whether it was a product of social labour or not. Both uncultivated land and conscience can be sold for money! The gap between values and prices was therefore not only quantitative (such that prices could move instantaneously up or down in response to any disequilibrium in demand and supply) but also qualitative (such that a price could be put on even such immaterial traits as honour, allegiances and loyalties). This gap has become a yawning chasm as capital has expanded its range and depth with the passing of time.

Of all writers it was, perhaps, Karl Polanyi, an émigré Hungarian socialist economic historian and anthropologist who ended up working and writing in the United States at the height of the McCarthyite scourge, who most clearly saw the nature of this phenomenon and 'the perils to society' which it posed. His influential work on *The Great Transformation* was first published in 1944 and remains a landmark text to this day. The markets for labour, land and money are, he pointed out, essential for the functioning of capital and the production of value.

> But labor, land, and money are obviously *not* commodities …
> Labor is only another name for a human activity which goes with
> life itself, which in its turn is not produced for sale but for entirely
> different reasons, nor can that activity be detached from the rest of
> life, be stored or mobilized; land is only another name for nature,
> which is not produced by man; actual money, finally, is merely a
> token of purchasing power which, as a rule, is not produced at
> all, but comes into being through the mechanism of banking or
> state finance. None of them is produced for sale. The commodity
> description of labor, land, and money is entirely fictitious.[2]

To allow the fictions that land, labour and money are commodities to flourish without restraint would, in Polanyi's view, 'result in the demolition of society'. In 'disposing of a man's labor power the system would, incidentally, dispose of the physical, psychological, and moral entity "man" attached to that tag. Robbed of the protective covering of cultural institutions, human beings would perish from the effects of social exposure; they would die as the victims of acute social dislocation through vice, perversion, crime and starvation. Nature would be reduced to its elements, neighborhoods and landscapes defiled, rivers polluted, military safety jeopardized, the power to produce food and raw materials destroyed'; and, finally, 'shortages and surfeits of money would prove as disastrous to business as floods and droughts in primitive society'.

No society, Polanyi concluded, 'could stand the effects of such a system of crude fictions even for the shortest stretch of time unless its human and natural substance as well as its business organization was protected against the ravages of this satanic mill'.[3] To the degree that neoliberal politics and policies these last few decades have dismantled many of the protections that had been so painstakingly created through earlier decades of struggle, so we now find ourselves increasingly exposed to some of the worst traits of that 'satanic mill' which capital, left to itself, inevitably creates. Not only do we see around us abundant evidence of so many of the collapses that Polanyi feared, but a heightened sense of universal alienation looms ever more threatening, as more and more of humanity turns away in disgust from the barbarism the underpins the civilisation it has itself constructed. This constitutes, as I shall argue by way of conclusion, one of the three most dangerous, perhaps even fatal, contradictions for the perpetuation of both capital and capitalism.

How the commodification of labour, land and money was historically accomplished is in itself a long and painful story, as Marx's brief history of so-called 'primitive accumulation' in *Capital* outlines. The transformation of labour, land and money into commodities rested on violence, cheating, robbery, swindling and the like. The common lands were enclosed, divided up and put up for sale as private property. The gold and silver that formed the initial money commodities were stolen from the Americas. The labour was forced off the land into the status of a 'free' wage labourer who could be freely exploited by capital when not outright enslaved or indentured. Such forms of dispossession were foundational to the creation of capital. But even more importantly, they never disappeared. Not only were they central to the more dastardly aspects of colonialism, but to this very day the politics and policies of dispossession (administered for the most part by an unholy alliance of corporate and state power) of access to land, water and natural resources are underpinning massive movements of global unrest. The so-called 'land grabs' throughout Africa, Latin America and much of Asia (including the massive dispossessions occurring currently in China) are just the most obvious symptom of a politics of accumulation by dispossession run riot in ways that even Polanyi could not have imagined. In the United States, tactics of eminent domain, along with the brutal foreclosure wave that led to massive losses not only of use values (millions rendered homeless) but also of hard-won savings and asset values embedded in housing markets, to say nothing of the loss of pension, health care and educational rights and benefits, all indicate that the political economy of outright dispossession is alive and well in the very heart of the capitalist world. The irony of course is that these forms of dispossession are now increasingly administered under the virtuous disguise of a politics of the austerity required to bring an ailing capitalism back into a supposedly healthy state.

To isolate nature 'and form a market out of it was perhaps the weirdest of all undertakings of our ancestors,' Polanyi remarks, while 'to separate labor from other activities of life and subject it to the laws of the market was to annihilate all organic forms of existence and replace them by a different type of organization, an atomist and individualistic one.'[4] This last consequence has been crucial to how the structure of contradictions we are here examining works. Plainly, the contradictory unity between state and private property that constitutes the third foundational contradiction of capital became significant *not* as a foundational tool to facilitate accumulation by dispossession, but as a post facto legitimation and institutional rationalisation of the results of that violence of dispossession. Once land, labour and money had been objectified, pulverised and broken away from their embeddedness in the broader flows of cultural life and of living matter, then they could be resutured together under the umbrella of constitutional rights and laws founded on principles of individual rights to private property guaranteed by the state.

Land, for example, is not a commodity produced by social labour. But it was at the heart of the enclosure movement in Britain and colonising practices everywhere to divide it up, privatise and commodify it so that the land market could become a primary field for capital accumulation and wealth extraction on the part of an increasingly powerful rentier class. So-called 'natural' resources can likewise be bought up even though they are not in themselves a product of social labour. The commodification of nature has certain limits because some things (like the atmosphere and the restless oceans) are not easily privatised and enclosed. While the fish extracted from the oceans can easily be commodified, the waters in which they swim pose a different problem. Markets can, however, be created around usufructuary rights to, say, pollution of the atmosphere and the oceans or to exclusive leasing rights to fishing in certain zones (such that Spanish trawlers fish exclusively in that part of the southern Atlantic Ocean over which Argentina claims rights).

The enclosure and parcelling up of land, of labour (through extensions of both the detailed and social divisions of labour) and money power (fictitious money and credit money capital in particular) all as commodities were crucial to this transition to the system of private property rights that gives a legal basis for the operations of capital. The state–private property contradiction thus displaces a fluid and alive conception of the relation to nature, with the idea that nature is to be construed, as Heidegger once complained, as 'one vast gasoline station'.[5] It likewise displaced all those cultural assumptions that attached to common property regimes and customary rights that were more characteristic of preceding modes of production (this does not, I want to stress, warrant waxing nostalgic for the social order within which such rights and practices were embedded). It puts in place of all of this variety of being and living in the world a doctrine of the universal, self-evident and individualised 'rights of man', dedicated to the production of value, that effectively masks in universalistic and naturalised legal doctrine the lurid trail of violence that accompanied the dispossession of indigenous populations. To this day, however, opponents and dissenters to all of this – increasingly viewed as terrorists – are more likely to inhabit the prisons than live in the mini-utopia of the bourgeois suburb.

In this constructed world certain truths stand out as self-evident, chief of which is that everything under the sun must be in principle and wherever technically possible subject to commodification, monetisation and privatisation. We have already had cause to comment on how housing, education, health care and public utilities have trended in this direction and we can now add to these the activities of war-making and even government itself as more and more of these sectors get subcontracted to private companies. Those blessed with sufficient money power can then buy up (or steal) almost anything and everything to the exclusion of the mass of the population that is lacking in sufficient money power, subversive guile or political/ military influence to compete. But the fact that it is now possible to buy up proprietary rights to gene sequences, pollution credits and weather futures should surely, in the light of Polanyi's warnings, give us pause. The trouble, however, it that all of this seems to be so embedded in the 'natural' and unshakeable bourgeois order of things that it seems not only understandable but inevitable that business as usual should be able to dominate social life in spheres of social and cultural activity where it has absolutely no business to be. Exchange value is everywhere the master and use value the slave. It is in this context that the revolt of the mass of the people in the name of inadequate access to fundamental use values becomes imperative.

That imperative then couples with a systematic critique and revolt against the ongoing politics of appropriation and accumulation by dispossession. That politics sits in a puzzling and plainly contradictory relation to universal legal doctrines of private property rights that supposedly regulate state–individual relations in such a way that coercive dispossessions, thievery, robbery and chicanery ought to have no place. Capitalist constitutionality and legality, it seems, are based on a lie or at best upon confusing fictions, if events in financial and housing markets these last few years are anything to go by. Yet we lack a common sense of exactly what the nature of that lie might be. As a result, we typically reduce the problem of accumulation by dispossession to one of the inability to apply, implement and regulate market behaviours sufficiently.

There are two other insights to be taken from this formulation. First, what guarantees that the individuals who so pillage and raid the common wealth will act collectively in such a way as to ensure the reproduction of that common wealth? Private individuals or corporations acting in their own short-term self-interest often undermine, if not destroy, the conditions for their own reproduction. Farmers exhaust the fertility of their land and employers have been known to work their labourers to death or to a point of such exhaustion that they function inefficiently. This difficulty is particularly severe on the terrain of environmental damage and degradation, as the example of British Petroleum's part in the Gulf Oil Spill of 2010 suggests. Second, what incentive do individuals have to abide by the rules of good market behaviour when the profits attached to so doing are low and the rate of return on illegality, predation, thievery and cheating is very high, even after taking into account the enormous fines that might be levied for misbehaviour? The huge fines levied on financial institutions such as HSBC, Wells Fargo, CitiBank, JPMorgan and the like in recent years and the evidence of continued malfeasance in the realms of finance suggest that this too is an ongoing problem for the reproduction of the common wealth.

It is only when it is clearly understood how the 'objective' but totally fictional mediations of monetisation, commodification and privatisation of non-commodities such as land, labour and capital (all wrought and often sustained by extra-legal and coercive means) lie at the root of the hypocrisy of capitalist constitutionality that we see how that constitutionality (and its legal codes) can incorporate illegality at its very base. The fact that these fictions and fetishisms systematically advantage some individuals rather than others and so constitute the basis for the construction of capitalist class power is no longer purely incidental: it is the foundational raison d'être for the whole political and economic edifice that capital constructs. The inner relation between capitalist class power and these fictions and fetishisms is nowhere more evident than in the crucial commodification, monetisation and privatisation of labour power and it is to this that we must now turn.

# Contradiction 5
# Capital and Labour

That some human beings have appropriated and exploited the labour power of others has been a long-standing feature of human organisation. The exercise of the power to do so has entailed the construction of different social relations, from the coercions of slavery, serfdom and the trading of women (and sometimes children) as mere chattels to the willing consent of worshippers to do God's or the gods' work in theocratic societies or the submissive fealty of loyal subjects to go to war or to mobilise to build, say, pyramids, in the name of a revered leader, patriarch, monarch or local lord. That such social relations of domination, appropriation and exploitation could be racialised, ethnicised, gendered and targeted at culturally, religiously affiliated or supposedly biologically inferior beings has also been a long-standing practice. That they could be monetised and commodified is obvious. Slaves could be bought and sold directly, dowries (measured in key commodities like cattle or money) were attached to the trade in women, and mercenary armies displaced those in which religious beliefs and personal loyalties were what counted. In addition, being mired in escalating debts (debt peonage or some parallel form such as share-cropping) was, and continues to be, one of the more insidious ways in which either the labour or the products of the labour of others get appropriated by those with social, political and money power.

But what capital deals in, and this is what makes this mode of production distinctive, is labour power as a commodity. The labourer is the bearer of that commodity and sells it to the capitalist in a supposedly 'free' labour market. Trading in labour services preceded the rise of capitalism, of course, and it is entirely possible that such trading will continue long after capital has ceased to exist as a viable way to produce and consume. But what capital learned was that it could create the basis for its own reproduction – hopefully on a permanent basis – through the systemic and continuous use of labour power to produce a surplus over that which the labourer needed to survive at a given standard of living. This surplus lies at the root of monetary profit.

The remarkable thing about this system is that it does not appear to rely on cheating, theft, robbery or dispossession because labourers can be paid their 'fair' market value (the 'going rate') at the same time as they can be put to work to generate the surplus value that capital needs to survive. This 'fairness' rests on the conceit that labourers have an individualised private property right over the labour power they are capable of furnishing to capital as a commodity (a commodity which has the use value to capital of being able to produce value and surplus value) and that they are 'free' to dispose of that labour power to whomsoever they like. It is most convenient for capital, of course, that labourers be 'freed' of any access to the land or even to any means of production. They then have no option except to sell their labour power in order to live. When put to work, capitalists can see to it that labourers produce more in commodity values than the market value of their labour power. Labourers, in short, must add more value than they get if capital is to be created and reproduced. Capital pockets the added value as profit and can store that added value as an ever-increasing concentration of money power.

The commodification of labour power is the only way to solve a seemingly intractable contradiction within the circulation of capital. In a properly functioning market system, where coercion, cheating and robbery are ruled out, the exchanges should be based on a principle of equality – we exchange use values with each other and the value of those use values should be roughly the same. This contradicts the presumption that there will be more value for all capitalists because in a well-functioning capitalist system all capitalists should earn a profit. So where does the extra value come from to assure a profit when the market system in principle depends on equality of exchanges? There must exist a commodity that has the capacity to create more value than it itself has. And that commodity is labour power. And that is what capital relies upon for its own reproduction.

The effect is to transform social labour – the labour we do for others – into *alienated* social labour. Work and labour are exclusively organised around the production of commodity exchange values that yield the monetary return upon which capital builds its social powers of class domination. Workers, in short, are put in a position where they can do nothing other than reproduce through their work the conditions of their own domination. This is what freedom under the rule of capital means for them.

While the relation between the labourer and the capitalist is always an individual contractual relation (by virtue of the private property character of labour power), it is not hard to see how in both the labour market and the labour process there will arise a general class relation between capital and labour that will inevitably – like all private property relations – involve the state and the law as arbiter, regulator or enforcer. This is so by virtue of the systemic contradiction between individual private property rights and state power. Nothing stops the labourers individually or collectively agitating and fighting for more and nothing stops the capitalists from striving (also individually or collectively) to either pay the labourer less than their fair market value or reduce the value of labour power (by either trimming the market basket of goods deemed necessary to the labourer's survival or reducing the cost of the existing market basket). Both capital and labour are within their rights to struggle over these issues and, as Marx famously put it, 'between equal rights, force decides'.[1]

The more that capital is successful in the struggle against labour, the greater its profits. The more the labourers succeed, the higher their standard of living and the more options they have in the labour market. The capitalist likewise typically struggles to increase the intensity, productivity and/or length of time of the labour rendered to it in the labour process, while labourers strive to diminish both the hours and the intensity as well as the physical hazards implicit in the activity of labouring. The regulatory power of the state – for example, legislation to limit the length of the working day or to limit exposure to hazardous working conditions and materials – is often involved in these relations.

The forms and effectiveness of the contradictory relation between capital and labour have been much studied and have long played a critical part in defining the necessity of revolutionary as well as reformist political struggles. I can therefore be mercifully brief here, since I presume most of my readers are broadly familiar with what is entailed. For some analysts of a left-wing persuasion (Marxists in particular), it is this contradiction between capital and labour that constitutes the primary contradiction of capital. For that reason, it is often regarded as the fulcrum of all meaningful political struggles and the seedbed for all anti-capitalist revolutionary organisation and movement. It is also cited by some as the sole underlying source of all forms of crises. There have certainly been places and times when what is called the 'profit squeeze' theory of crisis formation seems to have been prominently at work. When workers become very powerful relative to capital, then they are likely to push wage levels up to the point where they reduce profits to capital. Under these conditions capital's typical response is to go on strike, to refuse to invest or reinvest, and deliberately create unemployment as a means to discipline labour. An argument of this kind would fit the situation in North America, Britain and Europe from the late 1960s into the 1970s.[2] But capital also just as often gets into difficulty when it dominates too easily over labour, as the unfolding situation after the crash of 2008 demonstrates.

But the capital–labour contradiction cannot stand alone as an explanation of crises either analytically or even, in the final analysis, politically. It is both embedded in and dependent upon its relation to the other contradictions of capital (even, for example, the contradiction between use and exchange values). Viewed in this light, both the nature and conception of the political task in any anti-capitalist movement have to change, because the surrounding constraints – such as the vast concentrations of money power that capital typically amasses to pursue its agenda and secure its interests – often place limits on the conditions of possibility of radical transformations in the capital–labour relation in the workplace. Even if the eventual suppression of the capital–labour contradiction and the drive to establish the conditions for unalienated (as opposed to alienated) labour are the be-all and end-all of an alternative political ambition, these objectives cannot be accomplished without addressing the other contradictions, such as that of the money form and the private capacity to appropriate social wealth, with which they are associated.

Consideration of the capital–labour contradiction certainly points to the political ambition to supersede capital's domination over labour in both the labour market and the workplace by forms of organisation in which associated labourers collectively control their own time, their own labour processes and their own product. Social labour for others does not disappear but alienated social labour does. The long history of attempts to create some such alternative (by way of worker cooperatives, autogestion, worker control and more latterly solidarity economies) suggests that this strategy can meet with only limited success for the reasons already stated. State-organised alternatives derived from the nationalisation of the means of production and centralised planning have likewise turned out to be equally problematic if not misleadingly utopian. The difficulty of successfully implementing either of these strategies derives, I believe, from the way the capital–labour contradiction is linked to and embedded in the other contradictions of capital. If the aim of these non-capitalistic forms of labour organisation is still the production of exchange values, for example, and if the capacity for private persons to appropriate the social power of money remains unchecked, then the associated workers, the solidarity economies and the centrally planned production regimes ultimately either fail or become complicit in their own self-exploitation. The drive to establish the conditions for unalienated labour falls short.

There are also some unfortunate misunderstandings of the complex terrain upon which the contradiction between capital and labour is fought out. The tendency in left thinking is to privilege the labour market and the workplace as the twin central domains of class struggle. These are therefore the privileged sites for the construction of alternatives to capitalist forms of organisation. This is where the proletarian vanguard supposedly fashions itself to lead the way to a socialist revolution. As we will see shortly, when we come to examine the contradictory unity between production and realisation in the circulation of capital, there are other terrains of struggle that can be of equal if not more compelling significance.

For example, working people in the United States typically spend about a third of their income on housing. Housing provision, as we have seen, is typically driven by increasingly speculative exchange value operations and is a site for the extraction of rents (on both land and property), of interest (largely in the form of mortgage payments) and of taxes on property, as well as profit on the industrial capital deployed in housing construction. It is also a market characterised by a great deal of predatory activity (for example, extraction of legal fees and charges). Labour, which may have won significant concessions on wages through struggles fought out in labour markets and at the point of production, may have to give back almost all of its gains to procure housing as a use value under speculatively driven housing market conditions and after unavoidable encounters with predatory practices. What labour wins in the domain of production is stolen back by the landlords, the merchants (for example, the telephone companies), the bankers (for example, credit card charges), the lawyers and commission agents, while a large chunk of what is left also goes to the taxman. As with the case of housing, the privatisation and commodity provision of medical care, education, water and sewage, and other basic services, diminish the discretionary income available to labour and recapture value for capital.

But this is not the full story. All of these practices form a collective site where the politics of accumulation by dispossession takes over as a primary means for the extraction of income and wealth from vulnerable populations, including the working classes (however defined). The stealing back of privileges once acquired (such as pension rights, health care, free education and adequate services that underpin a satisfactory social wage) has become a blatant form of dispossession rationalised under neoliberalism and now reinforced through a politics of austerity ministered in the name of fiscal rectitude. Organising against this accumulation by dispossession (the formation of an anti-austerity movement, for example) and the pursuit of demands for cheaper and more effective housing, education, health care and social services are, therefore, just as important to the class struggle as is the fight against exploitation in the labour market and in the workplace. But the left, obsessed with the figure of the factory worker as the bearer of class consciousness and as the avatar of socialist ambition, fails largely to incorporate this other world of class practices into its thinking and its political strategies.

It is also here that the complex interactions between the contradictions of *capital* and those of *capitalism* come more fully into view. I will take up this question in more detail later. But here it would be foolish as well as tactically unwise to conclude any discussion of the capital–labour contradiction without noting not only its embedded relation to the other contradictions of capital but also its clear entanglement with the contradictions of *capitalism*, particularly those associated with racialisation, gender and other forms of discrimination. Labour and housing-market segmentation and segregation along racial, ethnic or other lines, for example, are notoriously pervasive features of all capitalist social formations.

While the capital–labour contradiction is unquestionably a central and foundational contradiction of capital, it is not – even from the standpoint of *capital* alone – a primary contradiction to which all other contradictions are in some sense subservient. From the standpoint of *capitalism*, this central and foundational contradiction within the economic engine constituted by capital clearly has a vital role to play, but its tangible manifestations are mediated and tangled up through the filters of other forms of social distinction, such as race, ethnicity, gender and religious affiliation so as to make the actual politics of struggle within capitalism a far more complicated affair than would appear to be the case from the standpoint of the labour–capital relation alone.

I do not say all of this to diminish the significance of the capital–labour contradiction within the panoply of capital's contradictions, for it is indeed a key contradiction of singular character and importance. It is, after all, in the workplace and through the labour market that the force of capital impinges directly upon the body of the labourer as well as upon all those dependent on the labourer for their life chances and their well-being. The alienating and coruscating nature of that experience for many people (the often savage treatment in the labour process and the experience of raw hunger in the workers' household) is always a primary locus of mass alienation and, consequently, a flashpoint for outbreaks of revolutionary anger. But its overemphasis and its treatment as if it operates autonomously and independently of the other contradictions of capital have, I believe, been damaging to a full-blooded revolutionary search for an alternative to capital and, hence, to capitalism.

## Contradiction 6
# Capital as Process or Thing?

In years gone by physicists endlessly debated whether light should best be conceptualised in terms of particles or waves. In the seventeenth century Isaac Newton developed a corpuscular theory of light at the same time as Christiaan Huygens advocated his wave theory. Opinion thereafter fluctuated between one or other determination until Niels Bohr, the daddy of quantum mechanics, resolved the so-called 'wave–particle duality' by appeal to a principle of complementarity. Light is, under this interpretation, both a particle and a wave. Both descriptions are needed to complete our understanding, but we do not need to use both descriptions at the same time. Some physicists, however, regarded the duality as simultaneous rather than complementary. And there was considerable debate over whether the duality was inherent in nature or reflected the limitations of the observer. Whatever the case, it is clear that dualities of this sort are now accepted as foundational for theory building in many areas of the natural sciences. The mind–brain duality, to take another example, lies at the root of thinking in the contemporary neurosciences. So let it not be said that the natural sciences are inherently hostile to some kind of dialectical reasoning or immune to the idea of contradiction (though, I hasten to add, the nature of their dialectical reasoning is very different from the wooden and stultifying version of dialectics that Engels and later Stalin favoured). What a pity that conventional economics, which aspires to the status of a science, has not followed suit!

Should capital be viewed as a process or as a thing? It has to be viewed, I shall argue, as both, and I favour a simultaneous rather than a complementary interpretation of how this duality works, even though, for purposes of exposition, it is often necessary to favour one standpoint over another. The unity of the capital circulating continuously as a process and a flow on the one hand and the different material forms it assumes (primarily money, production activities and commodities) on the other make for a contradictory unity. The focus of our inquiry has to be, therefore, upon the nature of this contradiction and how it can be the locus of creativity and change as well as of instabilities and crises.

Consider a simple flow model of how a well-behaved and honest capitalist might work while respecting all the legalities that a properly regulated capitalist state might impose on market behaviours. The capitalist starts the day with a certain amount of money (whether the money is borrowed or owned outright does not matter here). That money is used to purchase means of production (use of land and all the resources that lie therein, as well as partially finished inputs, energy, machinery and the like). The capitalist also finds a labour market at hand and hires workers under contract for a given period of work (say, eight hours a day for five days for a weekly wage). The acquisition of these means of production and of labour power precedes the moment of production. The labour power is, however, usually remunerated after production has occurred, whereas the means of production are usually paid for prior to production (unless purchased on credit). Plainly, the productivity of workers depends on the technology (for example, machines), the organisational form (for example, the division of labour within the labour process and forms of cooperation) and the intensity/efficiency of the labour process as designed by the capitalist. The outcome of this production process is a new commodity (mostly things but sometimes processes, like transportation as well as services) which is taken into the marketplace and sold to consumers at a price that should yield the capitalist an equivalent sum of money to that which was initially laid out plus an additional sum that constitutes a profit.

The profit at the end of the day is the motivation for going to all the trouble to engage with this process. The following day the capitalist repeats the process all over again in order to continue to make a living.

But the next day she typically takes a part of the profit earned yesterday and uses it to expand production. She does this for a variety of reasons, including lust and greed for more money power, but also out of fear that upstart capitalist competitors may drive her out of business if she does not reinvest a part of yesterday's profits in expansion.

There are illegal versions of this process. The initial money may have been assembled through robbery and violence. Access to land and resources may be coerced and inputs may be stolen rather than purchased fairly on the open market. The conditions of contract imposed on labour may violate legally established norms, while violations of all sorts – non-payment of wages, forced extension of working hours, fines for supposed misconduct – can be widespread. Labour process conditions can become intolerable or even hazardous (exposure to toxic substances, forced increase in the intensity of work beyond reasonable human capacities). Chicanery in the marketplace through false representation, monopoly pricing and the sale of defective and even dangerous commodities can all be widespread. Competitors can be shot and monopoly prices charged. The recognition that all these things can happen has led to state policing and interventions such as regulatory laws on occupational safety and health, consumer product safety protections and the like (such protective measures have been severely weakened under the neoliberal regimes personified by Ronald Reagan and Margaret Thatcher that have prevailed these last thirty years or so).

Almost everywhere we look in the capitalist world, the evidence of widespread illegality is palpable. The definition of what is the norm for legal capital circulation is, it seems, heavily influenced, if not defined, by the field of illegal behaviours. This legal–illegal duality therefore also plays a role in how capital works. Plainly, the involvement of state power as a constraint on individual behaviours is needed. A stateless capitalism is unthinkable (see Contradiction 3). But how the state intervenes depends on class controls and influence over the state apparatus. The illegalities practised by Wall Street in recent times could not have occurred without some mix of neglect or complicity on the part of the state apparatus.

But the main point here is the definition of capital as a process, as a continuous flow of value through the various moments and across the various transitions from one material form to another. At one moment capital takes the form of money, at another it is a stock of means of production (including land and resources) or a mass of labourers walking through the factory gates. Within the factory, capital is involved in concrete labouring and the making of a commodity in which latent and as yet unrealised value (social labour) and surplus value are congealed. When the commodity is sold, then capital returns once again to its money form. In this continuous flow, both the process and the things are contingent upon each other.

The process–thing duality is not unique to capital. It is a universal condition of existence in nature, I would argue, and, since human beings are a part of nature, it is a universal condition of social activity and social life under all modes of production. I live my life as a process even as I have thing-like qualities through which the state defines who I am (name and number!). But capital confronts and mobilises this duality in a particular way and it is this that requires our close attention. Capital exists as a continuous flow of value through the different physical states we have identified (along with others yet to be considered). The continuity of the flow is a primary condition of capital's existence. Capital must circulate continuously or die. The speed of its circulation is also important. If I can circulate my capital faster than you, then I have a certain competitive advantage. There is considerable competitive pressure, therefore, to accelerate the turnover time of capital. The tendency towards speed-up is easily identifiable in capital's history. The list of technological and organisational innovations designed to speed things up and to reduce the barriers posed by physical distance is very long.

But all this presumes that the transitions from one moment to another are unproblematic. This is not, however, the case. I have money and I want to make steel, so I need to have to hand immediately all of the ingredients (labour power and means of production) to make that steel. But the iron ore and coal are still buried in the ground and it takes a lot of time to dig them out. There are not enough workers close by who are willing to sell their labour power. I need to build a blast furnace and that takes time too. Meanwhile my money capital designated for steel production sits dormant and no value is produced. The transition from money into the commodities required for production is plagued with all sorts of potential barriers of this sort and time lost is capital devalued or even capital lost. It is only when all these barriers are transcended that capital can finally flow into actual production.

Within production there are also all manner of potential problems and barriers. It takes time to produce the steel and the intensity of the work process affects how long it takes for the steel to be produced. While different organisational and technological innovations can be sought out to shorten the working time, there are physical barriers to reducing this time to zero. Workers, furthermore, are not automatons. They may lay down their tools or go slow in the labour process. Establishing control over and collaboration with the workforce is needed for continuity.

Once the steel is finished it has to be sold and again the commodity can sit on the market for some time before a buyer shows up. If everyone out there has enough steel to last a couple of years, then there can be no buyers at all for a while and the commodity capital becomes dead capital because it has ceased to circulate. The producer has a vested interest in securing and accelerating the turnover time of consumption. One of the ways to do that is to produce steel that rusts so fast that it needs rapid replacement. Diminishing the turnover time of consumption is much easier, however, in the case of cellphones and electronic devices. Planned obsolescence, innovation, shifting fashion and the like become deeply rooted in capitalist culture.

All sorts of strategies and short cuts emerge as capital desperately seeks to transcend or bypass the barriers to circulation and to smooth out and speed up its turnover time. Producers, for example, may not want to wait to sell their commodities. For them it is easier to pass the commodity on to merchants at a discount on the full value (which furnishes the merchants with an opportunity to earn their cut of the surplus). The merchants (wholesalers and retailers) take on both the costs and the risks of selling the product to final consumers. By pursuing efficiencies and economies of scale (while exploiting the labour they employ) they can connect producers with final consumers at a lower cost than would be the case if the direct producers undertook the marketing themselves. This smooths out the flow and provides producers with a more secure market. But, on the negative side, the merchants may end up exercising considerable power over the direct producers and force the latter to take lower rates of return (this is the Walmart strategy). Alternatively, producers can seek credit on unsold goods. But here too the autonomous power of the bankers, financiers and discounters may then come into play as an active factor in the circulation and accumulation of capital. Social strategies to maintain the continuity of capital flow constitute a double-edged sword. While they may succeed in their immediate aim of smoothing out and facilitating the circulation process, they simultaneously create active power blocs among the merchants (for example, Walmart) and the financiers (for example, Goldman Sachs) who may pursue their own specific interests rather than serve the interests of capital in general.

There are other more purely physical problems that exacerbate the tension between fixity and motion within the circulation of capital. These problems centre on the category of long-term investments in fixed capital. In order for capital to circulate freely in space and time, physical infrastructures and built environments must be created that are fixed in space (anchored on the land in the form of roads, railways, communication towers and fibre-optic cables, airports and harbours, factory buildings, offices, houses, schools, hospitals and the like). Other more mobile forms of fixed capital (the ships, trucks, planes and railway engines, as well as the machinery and office equipment, right the way down to the knives and forks, the plates and cooking utensils, we use on a daily basis) have a long life. The mass of all this – as we look at an urban landscape like São Paulo, Shanghai or Manhattan – is simply huge and much of it is immovable, and that part which is movable cannot be replaced during the item's lifetime without loss of value. It is one of the paradoxes of capital accumulation that as time goes on the sheer mass of this long-lived and often physically immobile capital for both production and consumption increases relative to the capital that is continuously flowing. Capital is forever in danger of becoming more sclerotic over time because of the increasing amount of fixed capital required.

Fixed and circulating capital are in contradiction with each other but neither can exist without the other. The flow of that part of capital that facilitates circulation has to be slowed down if the movement of the circulating capital is to speed up. But the value of immobile fixed capital (like a container port terminal) can be realised only through its use. A container facility to which no ships come is useless and the capital invested in it is lost. On the other hand, commodities could not find their way to market without the ships and the container terminals. Fixed capital constitutes a world of things to support the process of capital circulation, while the process of circulation furnishes the means whereby the value invested in the fixed capital is recovered.

Another layer of difficulty then arises out of this underlying contradiction between fixity and motion. When the social manoeuvres designed to smooth out capital flow (for example, the activities of merchant capitalists and even more powerfully those of the financiers) are combined with the physical problems of fixity in the land, then a space is opened up for landed property to capture a share of the surplus. This distinct faction of capital extracts rents and shapes investments on the land even as it speculates mercilessly on land, natural resource and property asset values.

Back in the 1930s Keynes happily looked forward to what he called 'the euthanasia of the rentier'.[1] That political ambition, which Keynes applied to all owners of capital, has not of course been realised. Land, for example, has become even more prominent as a form of fictitious capital to which titles of ownership (or shares of future rental income) can be traded internationally. The concept of 'land' now includes, of course, all the infrastructures and human modifications accumulated from past times (for example, the subway tunnels of London and New York built more than a century ago), as well as recent investments not yet amortised. The potential stranglehold of the rentier and the landed interest on economic activity is now an even greater threat, particularly as it is backed today by the power of financial institutions that revel in the returns to be had from escalating rents and land and property prices. The housing-price booms and crashes on which we have already commented have been typical examples. What is interesting is that these practices have not gone away. They have now morphed into the astonishing 'land grabs' going on around the world (from the resource-rich regions of north-east India to Africa and throughout much of Latin America) as institutions and individuals seek to secure their financial future by ownership of land and all the resources (both 'natural' and humanly created) embedded therein. This suggests the arrival of a coming regime of land and resource scarcity (in a largely self-fulfilling condition based on monopoly and speculative power of the sort that the oil companies have long exercised).

The rentier class rests its power on the control of fixity even as it uses the financial powers of motion to peddle its wares internationally. How this happened in housing markets in recent times is the paradigmatic case. Ownership rights to houses in Nevada were traded all over the world to unsuspecting investors who were eventually bilked of millions as Wall Street and other financial predators enjoyed their bonuses and their ill-gotten gains.

The questions, then, are: when and why does this tension between fixity and motion and between process and thing become heightened into an absolute contradiction, particularly in the form of the excessive power of the rentier class, so as to produce crises? Plainly, this contradiction can be the locus of local stresses and crises. If commodities no longer flow, then the things that facilitate the flows become useless and have to be abandoned and rental returns collapse. The long and painful history of deindustrialisation has left whole cities, like Detroit, bereft of activity and therefore sinks of lost value even as other cities, like Shenzhen or Dhaka, become hubs of activity that demand massive investments in fixed capital coupled with rental extractions and property market booms if they are to succeed. The history of capital is rife with stories of localised booms and crashes in which the contradiction between fixed and circulating capital, between fixity and motion, is strongly implicated. This is the world where capital as a force of creative destruction becomes most visible in the physical landscape we inhabit. The balance between creativity and destruction is often hard to discern, but the costs imposed on whole populations through deindustrialisation, gyrations in property values and land rents, disinvestment and speculative building all emanate from the underlying and perpetual tension between fixity and motion which periodically and in specific geographical locations heightens to the point of an absolute contradiction and, hence, produces a serious crisis.

So what kind of alternative political ambition can be derived from this analysis? One immediate and obvious target is the abolition of the powers of landed property to extract rents from the fixity they command. The capacity of rentiers to trade legal titles to immobile land and property assets fluidly across spaces, which happened as mortgages bundled into collateralised debt obligations (CDOs) were traded worldwide in recent times, must be curbed. Land, resources and the amortised built environment should be categorised and managed as a common property resource for the populations that use and rely upon them. The people as a whole gain nothing from the escalating land and property prices that have characterised recent times. The connection between financial speculation and investments in physical infrastructures and other forms of fixed capital must likewise be negated, so that financial considerations no longer dictate production and use of physical infrastructures. Finally, the use value aspects of infrastructural provision must come to the fore. This leaves the social order with no option but to explore the field of rational planning practices on the part of political collectivities to ensure that the necessary physical use values can be produced and maintained. In this way, the admittedly always complex relations between processes and things and between fixity and motion can be orchestrated for the common good rather than mobilised for the endless accumulation of capital.

## Contradiction 7
# The Contradictory Unity of Production and Realisation

As capital flows, it passes through two major checkpoints where its performance in achieving that quantitative increase which lies at the root of profit is registered. In the labour process or its equivalent, value is added through work. But this value added remains latent rather than actual until it is realised through a sale in the market. The continuous circulation of capital depends upon the successful passage (with success measured as the rate of profit) through the two moments of, first, production in the labour process and, second, realisation in the market. The unity that necessarily prevails between these two moments within the circulation process of capital is, however, a contradictory unity. So what is the main form this contradiction takes?

In the first volume of his epic analysis of capital, Marx assumes away all problems of realisation in the market in order to study how the surplus value that underpins profit is produced. Other things being equal (which, of course, we know they never are), we would expect capital to have a strong incentive to pay workers as little as possible, to work them for as many hours and as intensely as possible, to get them to bear as much of the costs of their own reproduction (through household activities and work) as possible and to keep them as docile and disciplined (by coercion if necessary) in the labour process as possible. To this end, it is mighty convenient (if not essential) for capital to have to hand a vast reservoir of trained but unused labour power – what Marx called an 'industrial reserve army' – in order to keep the aspirations of those employed in check. If such a labour surplus did not exist, then capital would need to create one (hence the significance of the twin forces of technologically induced unemployment and opening up access to new labour supplies, such as those in China, over the last thirty years). It would also be important for capital to prevent if possible all or any forms of collective organisation on the part of the workers and to hold in check by whatever means possible any drive by them to exercise political influence over the state apparatus.

The ultimate outcome of such practices on the part of capital, Marx theorised in Volume 1 of *Capital*, would be the production of increasing wealth for capital at one pole and increasing impoverishment, degradation and loss of dignity and power on the part of the working classes who actually produced the wealth at the other pole.

In the second volume of *Capital* – a volume that is little read even by accomplished leftist scholars – Marx studies the conditions of realisation, while assuming that there are no problems arising in production. A number of uncomfortable though tentative (the volume was never finished) theoretical conclusions are arrived at. If capital does all those things that it must do according to the Volume 1 analysis to ensure the production and appropriation of surplus value, then the aggregate demand exercised by the labour force in the marketplace will tend to be restricted, if not systematically diminished. In addition, if the costs of the social reproduction of the labourers are being forced back into the household, then the labourers will not be buying goods and services in the market. The irony is that the more the labourers take on the cost of reproducing themselves, the less they will have an incentive to go to work for capital. A large unemployed reserve army is, furthermore, not a source of burgeoning aggregate demand (unless propped up by generous state income subsidies), any more than falling wages (including a fall-off in state contributions to the social wage) constitute the basis for an expanding market.

Herein lies a serious contradiction:

The workers are important for the market as buyers of commodities. But as sellers of their commodity – labour power – capitalist society has the tendency to restrict them to their minimum price. Further contradiction: the periods in which capitalist production exerts all its forces regularly show themselves in periods of over-production; because the limit to the application of the productive powers is not simply the production of value, but also its realization. However, the sale of commodities, the realization of commodity capital, and thus of surplus value as well, is restricted not by the consumer needs of society in general, but by the consumer needs of a society in which the great majority are always poor and must always remain poor.[1]

Lack of aggregate effective demand in the market (as opposed to the social demand for needed use values on the part of a penurious population) creates a serious barrier to the continuity of capital accumulation. It leads to falling profits. Working-class consumer power is a significant component of that effective demand.

Capitalism as a social formation is perpetually caught in this contradiction. It can either maximise the conditions for the *production* of surplus value, and so threaten the capacity to *realise* surplus value in the market, or keep effective demand strong in the market by empowering workers and threaten the ability to create surplus value in production. In other words, if the economy does well according to the Volume 1 prescriptions it is likely to be in trouble from the standpoint of Volume 2, and vice versa. Capital in the advanced capitalist countries tended towards a demand-management stance consistent with the Volume 2 prescriptions (emphasising the conditions for realisation of value) between 1945 and the mid-1970s but in the process increasingly ran into problems (particularly those of a well-organised and politically powerful working-class movement) in the production of surplus value. After the mid-1970s it therefore shifted (after a fierce battle with labour) towards a supply-side stance more consistent with Volume 1. This emphasised cultivating the conditions for surplus value production (through reducing real wages, crushing working-class organisation and generally disempowering workers).

The neoliberal counter-revolution, as we now call it, from the mid-1970s onwards resolved the pre-eminent problems of surplus value production but it did so at the expense of creating problems of realisation in the marketplace.

This general story is, of course, a gross oversimplification, but it provides a neat illustration of how the contradictory unity of production and realisation has been manifest historically. It is clear in this instance also that the processes of crisis formation and resolution are bound together by the way crises get moved around from production to realisation and back again. There have, interestingly, been parallel shifts in economic policy and theory. For example, Keynesian demand management (broadly consistent with Marx's Volume 2 analysis) dominated economic thinking in the 1960s, whereas monetarist supply-side theories (broadly consistent with Volume 1 analysis) came to dominate after 1980 or so. I think it important to situate these histories of both ideas and public policies in terms of the underlying contradictory unity of production and realisation as represented by the first two volumes of *Capital*.

The contradiction between production and realisation can, however, be mitigated in a number of ways. To begin with, demand can be increased in the face of falling wages by the expansion of aggregate numbers in the labour force (as happened when China began to mobilise its latent labour surplus after 1980 or so), by the expansion of conspicuous consumption on the part of the bourgeoisie or by the existence and expansion of strata in the population who are not engaged in production but who have considerable purchasing power (state officials, the military, lawyers, doctors, educators and the like). There is an even more significant way that the contradiction might be countered: by resort to credit. There is nothing in principle that prevents credit being supplied to sustain in equal measure both production and realisation of values and surplus values. The clearest example of this is when financiers lend to developers to build speculative tract housing while lending mortgage finance to consumers to purchase that housing. The problem, of course, is that this practice can all too easily produce speculative bubbles of the sort that led into the crash of 2007–9 primarily in the housing markets of the United States but also in Spain and Ireland. The long history of booms, bubbles and crashes in construction testifies to the importance of phenomena of this sort in capital's history.

But the interventions of the credit system have plainly also been constructive in certain ways and played a positive role in sustaining capital accumulation through difficult times. As a result, the contradiction between production and realisation is displaced back into the contradiction between the money and the value forms. The contradiction between production and realisation is internalised within the credit system, which on the one hand engages in insane speculative activity (of the sort that animated the housing bubble) while on the other hand salving many of the difficulties of maintaining a steady and continuous flow of capital across the contradictory unity of production and realisation. Restrictions on the credit system exacerbate the latent contradiction between production and realisation, while unchaining and deregulating the credit system unleashes unchecked speculative activity particularly with respect to asset values. The underlying problem is never abolished all the time that the contradictions between use and exchange value and between money and the social labour money represents remain in place. It is out of the interconnections between these different contradictions that financial and commercial crises frequently arise.

There are a number of secondary contradictions that attach to the production–realisation relationship. While it is unquestionable that the value added arises in the act of production and that the amount of value added depends crucially on the exploitation of living labour in the labour process, the continuity of flow makes it possible for the value and surplus value to be realised at a number of different points within the circulation process. The capitalist producer who organises the production of value and surplus value does not necessarily realise that value. If we introduce the figures of the merchant capitalist, the bankers and the financiers, the landlords and property owners, and the taxman, then there are several different locations where the value and the surplus value can be realised. And the realisation can take two basic forms. By exerting immense pressure on the capitalist producers, the merchant capitalists and the financiers, for example, can reduce the return to the direct producers to the smallest of margins while racking up major profits for themselves. This is how Walmart and Apple operate in China, for example. In this case not only does realisation occur in a different sector, it also occurs across the ocean in another country (creating a geographical transfer of wealth of considerable significance).

The other path to bridge the production–realisation contradiction is to recoup from the labourers any share of the surplus that they have acquired for themselves by charging extortionate prices or imposing fees, rents or taxes upon the working classes so as to diminish their discretionary income and standard of living significantly. This practice can also occur through manipulation of the social wage such that gains made in pension rights, in educational and health care provision and in basic services can be rolled back as part of a political programme of accumulation by dispossession. This is what the current widespread appeal to a politics of austerity on the part of the state is designed to achieve. Capital may lose or concede to workers' demands at the point of production but regain what has been conceded or lost (and then some) by excessive extractions in the living space. High rents and housing costs, excessive charges by credit card companies, banks and telephone companies, the privatisation of health care and education, the imposition of user fees and fines, all inflict financial burdens on vulnerable populations even when these costs are not inflated by a host of predatory practices, arbitrary and regressive taxes, excessive legal fees and the like.

These activities are, moreover, active and not passive. The actual or attempted expulsion of low-income and vulnerable populations from high-value land and locations through gentrification, displacement and sometimes violent clearances has been a long-standing practice within the history of capitalism. It unites those residents of Rio de Janeiro's favelas subject to evictions, the former occupants of self-built housing in Seoul, those moved through eminent domain procedures in the United States and the shack-dwellers in South

Africa. Production here means the production of space, and realisation takes the form of capital gains on land rents and property values, thus generally empowering the developers and the rentiers as opposed to other factions of capital.

The contradictory unity between production and realisation therefore applies as much to the fate of the workers as it does to capital. The logical conclusion, which by and large the left has tended to sideline if not ignore, is that there is necessarily a contradictory unity in class conflict and class struggle across the spheres of working and living.

The political ambition that derives from this contradiction is to reverse the relation between production and realisation. Realisation should be replaced by the discovery and statement of the use values needed by the population at large and production should then be orchestrated to meet these social needs. Such a reversal might be difficult to accomplish overnight, but the gradual decommodification of basic needs provision is a feasible long-term project, which fits neatly with the idea that use values and not the perpetual search for augmenting exchange values should become the basic driver of economic activity. If this seems a very tall order, it is useful to remember that the social democratic states in Europe (particularly those of Scandinavia) reoriented their economies to demand-side management from the 1960s onwards as a way to stabilise capitalism. In so doing, they partially accomplished – albeit in a somewhat half-hearted way – that reversal of the production–realisation relation that the passage to an anti-capitalist economy would demand.

Part Two

# The Moving Contradictions

The foundational contradictions of capital do not stand in isolation from each other. They interlock in a variety of ways to provide a basic architecture for capital accumulation. The contradiction between use value and exchange value (1) depends on the existence of money, which lies in a contradictory relation to value as social labour (2). Exchange value and its measure, money, presume a certain juridical relation between those engaging in exchange: hence the existence of private property rights vested in individuals and a legal or customary framework to protect those rights. This grounds a contradiction between individualised private property and the collectivity of the capitalist state (3). The state has a monopoly over the legitimate use of violence as well as over the issue of fiat money, the primary means of exchange. A profound connection exists between the perpetuity of the money form and the perpetuity of private property rights (both imply the other). Private individuals can legally and freely appropriate the fruits of social labour (the common wealth) for themselves through exchange (4). This constitutes a monetary basis for the formation of capitalist class power. But capital can systematically reproduce itself only through the commodification of labour power, which solves the problem of how to produce the inequality of profit out of a market exchange system based on equality. This solution entails converting social labour – the labour we do for others – into alienated social labour – the labour that is dedicated solely to the production and reproduction of capital. The result is a foundational contradiction between capital and labour (5). Put in motion, these contradictions define a continuous process of capital circulation that passes through different material forms, which in turn implies an ever-deepening tension between fixity and motion in the landscape of capital (6). Within the circulation of capital a contradictory unity necessarily exists between production and realisation of capital (7).

These contradictions define a political terrain upon which an alternative to the world that capital creates can be defined. The political orientation must be towards use values rather than exchange values, towards a money form that inhibits private accumulation of wealth and power and the dissolution of the state–private property nexus into multiple overlapping regimes of collectively managed common property rights. The ability of private persons to appropriate the common wealth must be checked and the monetary basis for class power must be undermined. The contradiction between capital and labour has to be displaced by emphasising the power of associated labour to engage in unalienated labour, to determine its own labour process while producing needed use values for others. The relation between fixity and motion (which can never be abolished since it is a universal condition of human existence) must be managed in such a way as to counteract the powers of the rentier and to facilitate the continuous and secure fulfilment of basic needs for all. Finally, instead of production for production's sake leading the way to a forced world of manic and alienated consumerism, production should be rationally organised to provide the use values necessary to achieve an adequate material standard of living for all. Realisation should be converted into a wants-and-needs-based demand to which production responds.

These are general orientations for long-term political thinking as to how an alternative to capital might be constituted. It is against the background of these orientations that specific strategies and proposals should be evaluated.

The foundational contradictions are constant features of capital in any place and time. The only thing constant about the contradictions we will next consider is that they are unstable and constantly changing. This makes for an understanding of political economy that departs radically from the model of the natural sciences, where it can broadly be assumed that the principles being elucidated are true for all space and time. As Brian Arthur puts it in his perceptive and instructive book The Nature of Technology, the means by which the 'base laws' (or in my language 'the foundational contradictions') are expressed 'change over time, and the patterns they form change and re-form over time. Each new pattern, each new set of arrangements, then, yields a new structure for the economy and the old one passes, but the underlying components that form it – the base laws – remain always the same.'[1]

In the case of moving contradictions, the basic nature of the contradiction has first to be described, before going on to provide a general assessment of the form it now assumes. By understanding something of its evolutionary trajectory, we can then say something about future prospects and possibilities. This evolution is not predetermined. Nor is it random or accidental. But since the pace of evolutionary change tends to be relatively slow – a matter of decades rather than years (though there is evidence it is accelerating) – it is then possible to say something about future prospects as well as present dilemmas.

To capture the sense of movement is politically vital, for the instability and the movement provide political opportunities at the same time as they pose critical problems. Political ideas and strategies that make sense in one place and time do not necessarily apply at another. Many a political movement has failed because it sought to appeal to ideas and ambitions that were well past their sell-by date. We cannot shape our current political strategies and carve out our contemporary political ambitions to fit the defunct ideas of some long-dead political theorist. This does not mean there is nothing to be learned from a study of the past or that no advantage is to be had from drawing upon past memories and traditions for inspiration in the present. What it does imply is an obligation to write the poetry of our own future against the background of the rapidly evolving contradictions of capital's present.

# Contradiction 8
# Technology, Work and Human Disposability

The central contradiction that the traditional Marxist conception of socialism/communism is supposed to resolve is that between the incredible increase in the productive forces (broadly understood as technological capacities and powers) and capital's incapacity to utilise that productivity for the common welfare because of its commitment to the prevailing class relations and their associated mechanisms of class reproduction, class domination and class rule. Left to itself, the argument goes, capital is bound to produce an increasingly vulnerable oligarchic and plutocratic class structure under which the mass of the world's population is left to hustle a living or starve to death. Frustrated by this ever-increasing inequality in the midst of plenty, a self-consciously organised anti-capitalist revolutionary movement (led, in Leninist accounts, by a vanguard party) will arise among the masses to dismantle class rule before going on to reorganise the global economy to deliver the benefits promised by capital's amazing productivity to everyone on planet earth.

While there is more than a grain of truth in this analysis – we seem well on the way these days to producing a global plutocracy, for example – coupled with more than a whiff of hopeful revolutionary fervour concerning the transitional mechanism, it has always seemed to me that this formulation is too simplistic, if not fundamentally deficient. But what is clear is that the dramatic increases in productivity achieved by capital form one side of a contradictory movement that is always in danger of erupting into crises. It is not entirely clear, though, what its antithesis might rightly be. It is to this question that we now turn.

Technology can be defined as the use of natural processes and things to make products for human purposes. At its base, technology defines a specific relation to nature that is dynamic and contradictory. We will return to this all-important contradiction in depth later (see Contradiction 16). All that matters here is to recognise its existence and its fluidity and dynamism. The immediate and distinctive purpose of *capital* (as opposed, say, to the military, the state apparatus and various other institutions in civil society) is *profit*, which translates socially into the perpetual accumulation of capital and the reproduction of capitalist class power. This is capital's consuming aim. To this end, capitalists adapt and reshape the hardware of technology (the machines and computers), the software (the programming of machine uses) and their organisational forms (command and control structures over labour usage in particular). Capital's immediate purpose is to increase productivity, efficiency and profit rates, and to create new and, if possible, ever more profitable product lines.

When considering the trajectories of technological change, it is vital to remember that the software and the organisational forms are every bit as important as the hardware. Organisational forms, like the control structures of the contemporary corporation, the credit system, just-in-time delivery systems, along with the software incorporated into robotics, data management, artificial intelligence and electronic banking, are just as crucial to profitability as the hardware embodied in machines. To take a contemporary example, cloud computing is the organisational form, Word is the software and this Mac, upon which I write, the hardware. All three elements – hardware, software and organisational form – are combined in computer technology. Under this definition, money, banking, the credit system and the market are all technologies. This definition may appear unduly broad but I think it absolutely essential to keep it so.

Capital's technology was initially subject to internal transformation through competition between individual producers (at least, that was the theory). Capitalist firms, in competition with each other, sought to raise their individual efficiency and productivity so as to gain excess profits relative to their competitors. Those that succeeded flourished, while others were left behind. But competitive advantages (higher profits) from superior organisational forms, machines or, for example, tighter inventory control were usually short-lived. Competing firms could quickly adopt the new methods (unless, of course, the technologies were patented or protected by monopoly power). The outcome would be leapfrogging innovations in technologies across sectors.

I sound a note of scepticism here because the history of capital demonstrates a penchant for monopoly rather than competition and this would not be so favourable for innovation. Instead, we find a strong collective generic preference – a culture as it were – emerging among capitalists for increasing efficiency and productivity across all capitalist enterprises with or without the driving force of competition. Innovations at one point in a supply chain – for example, power loom cotton fabric production – required innovations elsewhere – for example, the cotton gin – if overall productivity was to be improved. But it sometimes took and still takes a while for a whole domain of economic activity to be reorganised on a new technological basis. Last, but by no means least, individual capitalists and corporations came to recognise the importance of product innovation as a way to earn, if only for a while, monopoly profits and, when protected by patent law, a monopoly rent.

Capital was not and is not the only agent involved in the pursuit of technological advantages. Different branches of the state apparatus have always been deeply involved. Most prominent, of course, has been the military in search of superior weaponry and organisational forms. War and threats of war (arms races) have been strongly associated with waves of technological innovation. In the early history of capitalism this source of innovation probably played a dominant role. But various other facets of state administration concerned with the levying and payment of taxes, the definition of land and property rights and legal forms of contract, along with the construction of the technologies of governance, money management, mapping, surveillance, policing and other procedures for the control of whole populations, have all along been just as if not more significantly involved as capitalist firms and corporations in developing new technological forms. Collaborations on research and development between the state and private sectors with respect to military, medical, public health and energy technologies have been widespread. The spillover benefits of innovations in the public sphere on capital's practices and vice versa have been too numerous to count.

Technological changes within capitalism, to which capital contributes and upon which capital voraciously feeds, derive, in short, from the activities of several different agents and institutions. For capital, these innovations create a vast domain of ever-changing possibilities for sustaining or increasing profitability.

The processes of technological change have altered their character over time. Technology became a special field of business. This first clearly emerged in the nineteenth century with the rise of the machine-tool industry. Generic technologies, like the steam engine and its offshoots, were developed in a way that could be applied across multiple industries. It was the profitability of the steam engine makers rather than that of the different industries using steam power (for example, transport, cotton factories and mining) that mattered, though plainly the profitability of the one could not be achieved without that of the other. The search for ever-newer and better forms of not only the steam engine but also energy and power application quickly followed.

The search for generic technologies that could be applied almost anywhere – in recent years think of fields such as computers, just-in-time delivery systems and theories of organisation – became important. A vast business of invention and innovation catering to all and sundry sprang up, providing new technologies of consumption as well as of production, circulation, governance, military power, surveillance and administration. Technological innovation became big business, not 'big' necessarily in the sense of some vast consolidated corporation (though examples of that sort now abound in fields like agribusiness, energy and pharmaceuticals) but 'big' in the sense of multiple firms, many of them small-scale start-ups and venture enterprises, exploring innovation for innovation's sake. Capitalist culture became obsessed with the power of innovation. Technological innovation became a fetish object of capitalist desire.

From the mid-nineteenth century onwards, this fetish drive for new technological forms come what may also promoted the fusion of science and technology. These two thereafter developed in a dialectical embrace. Scientific understandings had always depended upon new technologies, such as the telescope and the microscope, but the incorporation of scientific knowledges into new technologies has lain at the heart of what the business of technological innovation has been about.

This vast business became more and more adept at imposing sometimes costly technological innovations on reluctant customers, often aided by state regulation that tended to favour large firms rather than small because the costs of regulatory compliance usually diminish with scale of operation. EU regulations have, to take one example, forced small shopkeepers and restaurants to adopt electronic machines for cash transactions for tax and record-keeping purposes, putting them at a cost disadvantage relative to chain stores. The diffusion of new technologies occurs through a mix of consent and coercion. The development of military technologies, on the other hand, has become nothing short of a scandalous racket, whereby a vast military industrial complex feeds endlessly at the trough of public finance while innovating for innovation's sake.

The path of technological evolution has not been random or accidental. As Brian Arthur points out in *The Nature of Technology*, new technologies become building blocks 'for the construction of further new technologies. Some of these in turn go on to become possible building blocks for the creation of yet newer technologies. In this way, slowly over time, many technologies form from an initial few, and more complex ones form using simpler ones as components. The overall collection of technologies bootstraps itself upward from the few to the many and from the simple to the complex. We can say that technology creates itself out of itself.' Arthur calls this process 'combinatorial evolution' and I think that is a good name for it. New technologies are, however, 'created mentally before they are constructed physically' and when we look at the mental and conceptual processes involved, we see technological evolution as mental problem solving put into practice. A problem arises and is identified, a solution is demanded and the solution invariably combines earlier solutions to other problems in a new configuration. The new configuration often has spillover effects elsewhere because it creates what Arthur calls 'opportunity niches' – arenas where an innovation from one place might be meaningfully applied in another.[1]

Spontaneous development of innovation centres (some regions, cities and towns have a remarkable record for innovation) occurs because, as was long ago noted by commentators such as Jane Jacobs, the fortuitous co-presence of different skills and knowledges of the sort that Arthur regards as necessary for innovation to occur is more likely to be found in a seemingly chaotic economy characterised by innumerable small businesses and divisions of labour.[2] Such environments have historically been far more likely to spawn new technological mixes than a single-dimensional company town. More recently, however, the deliberate organisation of the research universities, institutes, think tanks and military R&D units in a given area has become a basic business model through which the capitalist state and capitalist corporations pursue innovation for competitive advantage.

But what is strange about Arthur's otherwise informative presentation on the logic of technological evolution is his avoidance of any critical discussion of the range of human purposes that technologies are supposed to serve. He waxes lyrical, for example, about the design sophistication of the F-35 Lightning II aircraft without any mention of its relation to warfare and the 'human purpose' of geopolitical domination. To Arthur the aircraft merely presents a particular set of difficult technical challenges that needed to be solved.

Similarly, there is no critique of the specific capitalistic form the economy takes and certainly no questioning of the purposive drive of capital to maximise profits, facilitate endless capital accumulation and reproduce capitalist class power. Nevertheless, Arthur's theory of relatively autonomous technological evolution has deep implications for understanding how the economic engine of capital functions. It sheds considerable light on the contradictions that technological changes now spawn for the perpetuation and reproduction of capital. There are some important transitions occurring.

The shift from a machine to an organic model of the economy has implications for economic theory. 'Order, closedness, and equilibrium as ways of organizing explanations are giving way to open-endedness, indeterminacy, and the emergence of perpetual novelty.'[3] Arthur here instinctively echoes Alfred North Whitehead's astute observation that nature itself (and human nature is no exception) is always about the perpetual search for novelty.[4] As a result, Arthur continues, 'technologies are acquiring properties we associate with living organisms. As they sense and react to their environment, as they become self-assembling, self-configuring, self-healing, and "cognitive," they more and more resemble living organisms. The more sophisticated and "high-tech" technologies become, the more they become biological. We are beginning to appreciate that technology is as much metabolism as mechanism.'

This shift from a mechanical to an organic (or chemical) metaphor is significant. The 'new economy' that Arthur sees appears more natural than the mechanical rationality superimposed on the world from the Enlightenment onwards. This is nothing short of a reversion to (perhaps 'recuperation of' would be a better phrasing) more ancient ways of understanding the relation between technology and nature. But it is not backward-looking or nostalgic and it eschews the sentimentality and mysticism of so-called 'new age' cultural thinking. The 'new principles' that must enter into economics, Arthur implies, are organic and process-based forms of thinking and theorising. Ironically (and Arthur would doubtless be shocked to hear this), this was the form of political economy that Marx long ago pioneered in *Grundrisse*! Only in this way, Arthur suggests, will we be able to grasp the 'qualities of modern technology, its connectedness, it adaptiveness, its tendency to evolve, its organic quality. Its messy vitality.'[5]

The implications of this analysis of technology for how we understand the evolving character of the economic engine that is capital are profound:

> The coming of new technologies does not just disrupt the status quo by finding new combinations that are better versions of the goods and methods we use. It sets up a train of technological accommodations and of new problems, and in so doing it creates new opportunity niches that call forth fresh combinations which in turn introduce further technologies – and further problems ... The economy therefore exists always in a perpetual openness of change – in perpetual novelty. It exists perpetually in a process of self-creation. It is always unsatisfied ... The economy is perpetually constructing itself.[6]

New technological configurations displace the old and in so doing initiate phases of what the economist Joseph Schumpeter famously dubbed 'gales of creative destruction'.[7] Whole ways of life and modes of being and thinking have to drastically alter to embrace the new at the expense of the old. The recent history of deindustrialisation and its association with dramatic technological reconfigurations is an obvious case in point. Technological change is neither costless nor painless and the cost and the pain are not evenly shared. The question always to be asked is: who gains from the creation and who bears the brunt of the destruction.

So what role do the distinctive needs and requirements of capital play in this process? Curiously, Arthur ignores the specificities of this question in his otherwise perceptive study. There are within the history and logic of capital, I would argue, five dominant but overlapping technological imperatives. Let us consider these briefly.

1. The organisation of cooperation and divisions of labour in ways that maximise efficiency, profitability and accumulation. From simple beginnings in Adam Smith's example of the pin factory, this has over time grown to encompass much of what is now covered in management and organisation theory, as well as in the articulation

of techniques of optimal corporate management. The increasing complexity and fluidity of which Arthur speaks are here everywhere in evidence and the technologies involved are in perpetual flux, with increasing emphasis upon the software and the organisational forms assumed by contemporary forms of capital. The mix of command and control and market coordinations is unstable but effective.

2. The need to facilitate speed-up and acceleration of capital circulation in all its phases, along with the need to 'annihilate space through time', has spawned an astonishing range of technological revolutions. Shortening the turnover time of capital in production and in the market and shortening the lifetime of consumer products (culminating in a shift from the production of things that last to the production of spectacles that are ephemeral) have been imperatives in capital's history, largely enforced by competition. It is here that technology's relation to the production of nature becomes most clearly apparent as sheep are bred to yield lamb in one year instead of three and hogs breed at an accelerated rate. The increasing speed of transport and communications reduces the friction and barrier of geographical distance, making the spatiality and temporality of capital a dynamic rather than a fixed feature of the social order. Capital literally creates its own space and time as well as its own distinctive nature. The mobility of the different forms of capital (production, commodities, money) and of labour power is also perpetually subject to revolutionary transformation. We will return to this topic later (see Contradiction 12).

Revolutionary transformations in the means of communication have paralleled those occurring in transportation and in more recent times have accelerated beyond belief. Instantaneous information and news availability make this a potent force for affecting policies and politics. Control over the means of communication has become a vital aspect to the reproduction of capitalist class power and the new media technologies (the social media in particular) have potentialities as well as pitfalls for the dynamics of class struggle, as has become all too apparent in recent uprisings in Cairo, Istanbul and other cities around the world.

3. Technologies of knowledge production and dissemination, for data and information storage and retrieval, are crucial for the survival and perpetuation of capital. They not only provide the price signals and other forms of information that guide investment decisions and market activity, but also preserve and promote the necessary mental conceptions of the world that facilitate productive activity, guide consumer choices and stimulate the creation of new technologies.

Capital's memory bank is indispensable. It is already vast. Its exponential growth has to be matched by the exponential growth of sophisticated technologies to handle, process and act upon it. The basic information contained in land registers, contracts, legal judgments, educational and medical records etc. has long been crucial for the functioning of capital. Information of this sort provides, in addition, the raw data out of which a working (but in many respects fictitious) model of a national economy can be built. This data (joblessness, trade deficits, stock market gyrations, growth figures, manufacturing activity, capacity utilisation and the like) permits the health of the national economy to be assessed and provides a basis upon which strategic decisions of both businesses and state agencies can (for better or for worse) be based. Agencies like the World Bank and the IMF at times seem to be drowning in the mass of data they produce. A whole host of 'experts' come into being to help us to understand the trends. The introduction of new information-processing technologies, such as computerised trading on Wall Street (and the more recent turn to nano-technologies), has had immense implications for how capital operates.

4. Finance and money form a crucial domain for the functioning of capital (see Contradiction 2). It is only in money terms that profits and losses can be exactly calculated and it is in money terms that most economic decisions are made. While the technologies of money remained fairly constant over long historical periods of time, there is no question that innovation in this domain picked up remarkably from the 1930s onwards. In recent years innovations in finance and banking have shown a tendency to explode into exponential growth with the advent of computerisation, electronic moneys and banking,

and a proliferation of a whole new range of investment vehicles. The trend to create fictitious capitals that circulate freely has accelerated remarkably alongside all manner of predatory practices within the credit system that have contributed to a wave of accumulation by dispossession and speculation in asset values. Nowhere else do we see so dramatically the acute interaction between new hardware possibilities, the creation of new organisational forms (private equity firms and hedge funds and a host of complicated state regulatory agencies) and, of course, an astonishing rate of software development. The technologies of the world's monetary and financial system are an acute source of stress at the same time as they are a field of capitalist endeavour unsurpassed in these times in importance and in 'messy vitality'.

5. Finally, there is the question of work and labour control. This is a crucial arena for capital and I will take it up in detail shortly.

Did technologies have to evolve in the way they did? There clearly were choices made that liberated technological innovation from the kinds of constraints that had inhibited the deployment of new technologies in earlier places and times (the failure to deploy technological discoveries in China being the most conspicuous example). And there have certainly been examples of intense resistance to new technological configurations on moral and ethical grounds, everything from the struggle of the Luddites against the introduction of machines to the revolt of the physicists against the possibility of nuclear weapons. Current controversies rage over the ethics and inadvisability of genetic engineering and genetically modified foods. Such questions, however, do not seem to deter the evolutionary trajectory of technological change. This is why I designate this kind of contradiction as 'moving' – it is not stable or permanent but perpetually changing its spots. For this reason it becomes crucial to evaluate where the processes of technological change are at right now and where they might move to in the future.

Arthur asks, for example, 'Could this process of constant evolution of technology and remaking of the economy ever come to a halt?' His answer is yes in principle. But the actual prospects for a halt are exceedingly remote. The decentralised dynamic of technological evolution is too strong and the field of possible discoveries of the perpetual novelty in nature far too wide for any halt to technological and economic evolution to occur in the immediate future.

> The pipeline of technologies coming in the next decade is reasonably predictable. And current technologies have future improvement paths that will be followed more or less predictably. But overall, just as the collection of biological species in the far future is not predictable from the current collection, the collective of technology in the economic future is not predictable. Not only can we not forecast which combinations will be made, we also cannot forecast which opportunity niches will be created. And because potential combinations grow exponentially, this indeterminacy increases as the collective develops. Where three thousand years ago we could say with confidence that the technologies used a hundred years hence would resemble those currently in place, now we can barely predict the shape of technology fifty years ahead.[8]

So where, in this process of 'combinatorial evolution', lies *the* contradiction or contradictions that might threaten profitability and endless capital accumulation? There are, I want to suggest, two contradictions of huge import for the future prospects of capital. The first concerns technology's dynamic relation to nature. This will be the subject of Contradiction 16. The second concerns the relationship between technological change, the future of work and the role of labour in relation to capital. This is the contradiction we will examine here.

Control over the labour process and the labourer has always been central to capital's ability to sustain profitability and capital accumulation. Throughout its history, capital has invented, innovated and adopted technological forms whose dominant aim has been to enhance capital's control over labour in both the labour process and the labour market. This attempted control encompasses not only physical efficiency but also the self-discipline of the labourers employed, the qualities of labour supplied in the marketplace, the cultural habits and mentalities of workers in relationship to the work they are expected to do and the wages they expect to receive.

Many industrial innovators have had labour control as their primary goal. A Second Empire French industrialist renowned for his innovations in the machine-tool industry openly proclaimed that his three goals were increasing precision in the labour process, increasing productivity and disempowering the worker. It is for this reason, doubtless, that Marx argued that technological innovation was a crucial weapon in class struggle and that many an innovation had been adopted by capital with the sole aim of breaking strikes. There certainly arose with this the fetish belief on the part of capital that the solution to ever-increasing profitability was endless technological innovation directed towards the disciplining and disempowerment of the worker. The factory system, Taylorism (with its attempted reduction of the worker to the status of a 'trained gorilla'), automation, robotisation and the ultimate displacement of living labour altogether respond to this desire. Robots do not (except in science fiction accounts) complain, answer back, sue, get sick, go slow, lose concentration, go on strike, demand more wages, worry about work conditions, want tea breaks or simply refuse to show up.

Capital's fantasy of total control over labour and the labourer has its roots in material circumstances, most particularly in the dynamics of class struggle in all of its manifestations both within and outside of the production process. The role of technologically induced unemployment in regulating the wage rate, the pursuit of ever-cheaper goods for the sustenance of the labour force (the Walmart phenomenon) to make lower wages more acceptable, the assault upon any hint of a basic social wage as encouraging idleness on the part of labour and the like form a domain of class struggle where technological interventions and mediations become crucial. This is what makes Arthur's presentation so strange, because never once do these elementary and obvious historical facts (satirised so wonderfully in Charlie Chaplin's *Modern Times*) enter into his account of the combinatorial evolution that does indeed play such a critical role in the details of technological change.

So here is the central contradiction: if social labour is the ultimate source of value and profit, then replacing it with machines or robotic labour makes no sense, either politically or economically. But we can see all too clearly what the mechanism is that heightens this contradiction to the point of crisis. Individual entrepreneurs or corporations see labour-saving innovation as critical to their profitability vis-à-vis competitors. This collectively undermines the possibility of profit.

In a recent book Martin Ford shapes an argument around exactly this problem. As the cutting edge of technological dynamism shifts from mechanical and biological systems to artificial intelligence, so we will see, he argues, a huge impact upon job availability not only in manufacturing and agriculture but also in services and even in the professions. Aggregate demand for goods and services will consequently collapse as jobs and incomes disappear. This will have catastrophic effects upon the economy unless some way is found for the state to intervene with targeted redistributive stimulus payments to those large segments of the population that have become redundant and disposable.

André Gorz had earlier made exactly this same argument though from a different political perspective:

> Micro-economic logic would want these savings in working time to be translated into savings in wages for those companies where such economies are achieved: producing at lower costs, these companies will be more 'competitive' and will be able (in certain conditions) to sell more. But from the macro-economic point of view, an economy which, because it uses less and less labour, distributes less and less wages, inexorably descends the slippery slope of unemployment and pauperization. To restrain its slide, the purchasing power of households has to cease to depend on the volume of work which the economy consumes. Though they perform a decreasing number of hours of work, the population has

to earn the wherewithal to purchase a growing volume of goods produced: the shortening of working time must not bring about a reduction in purchasing power.[9]

The details that Ford cites to back up his general claim are impressive. There is clear empirical evidence of inexorable exponential growth of computer capacity and speed. This has roughly doubled every two years over the last three decades or so. The growth of this computer capacity does not depend on the construction of a technology that has the ability to think as we do. It arises out of the fact that the computer is 'unimaginatively fast', and getting faster and faster all the time. Speed-up has always been, as we have seen, a crucial aim of technological innovation in relation to capital and the world of computers is no exception. As a result of the exponential growth in computer power, 'entire traditional job categories are at risk of being heavily automated in the not too distant future'. The idea that the new technologies will create jobs at a pace to compensate for these losses 'is pure fantasy'. Furthermore, the idea that it will only be the low-paying routine jobs that will be eliminated and not high-paying skilled jobs (radiologists, doctors, university professors, airline pilots and the like) is misguided. 'In the future, automation will fall heavily on knowledge workers and in particular on highly paid workers.' Ford concludes: 'Allowing these jobs to be eliminated by the millions, without any concrete plan to handle the issues that will result, is a clear recipe for disaster.' [10]

But what sort of disaster are we looking at? Larger and larger segments of the world's population will be considered redundant and disposable as productive workers from the standpoint of capital and will have a hard time surviving both materially and psychologically. Alienated from any prospect of a meaningful existence in the realm of necessary labour as defined by capital, they will have to look elsewhere to construct a meaningful life. On the other hand, output will be increasing, but where will the corresponding increase in demand come from? This is what bothers Ford most of all:

*Who* is going to step forward and purchase all this increased output? ... automation stands poised to fall across the board – on nearly every industry, on a wide range of occupations, and on workers with graduate degrees as well as on those without high school diplomas. Automation will come to the developed nations and to the developing ones. The consumers that drive our markets are virtually all people who either have a job or depend on someone who has a job. When a substantial fraction of these people are no longer employed, where will market demand come from?[11]

This is a typical Keynesian-style question of demand management and it threatens a crisis for capital of the sort that racked the global economy in the 1930s. What happens when we restate Ford's claims against the background of the contradictory unity between production and realisation? Marx interestingly identifies a similar difficulty, but he does so from the perspective of production. As more and more labour-saving devices are applied, so the value-producing agent – social labour – tends to decline quantitatively, ultimately destroying socially necessary labour and the production of value and with it the basis of profitability. The same result arises from both sides of the contradictory unity between production and realisation. Profitability erodes and endless capital accumulation collapses in both cases. Ford in an appendix recognises that there may be some sort of broad similarity between his argument and that of Marx, but he does not understand what it is and is, of course, at pains to distance himself from the damaging consequences of any such association. But the potential range of counteracting forces and solutions looks very different from the two perspectives within the contradictory unity.

Ford, for example, is desperately concerned to save capital from succumbing to the potential disaster that looms. He actually favours the spread of consumerism (no matter how mindless and alienating) to absorb the ever-cheapening products that a wholly automated capital can produce. He seeks to square the circle of supply and demand disparities by creating a state-mandated tax system to recuperate the productivity gains created by the new technologies. These funds are then redistributed as purchasing power to the dispossessed masses on an incentivised basis. In return for the funds people are expected to commit to creative or worthy social activities and contribute to the common good. Programmes of this sort already exist. The poverty grants in Argentina and Brazil redistribute money to poor families provided that they can prove that their children are attending school. Structuring such incentivised redistributions effectively may be difficult, but in Ford's view it is critical to avoid the culture of dependency that is often associated with straight welfare payments or a straight guaranteed income no matter whether one works or not. Nevertheless, redistributions and the creation of purchasing power are the only means to create sufficient demand to match the ever-increasing supply of goods and services. This is, concurs André Gorz, 'the only way of giving meaning to the decrease in the volume of socially necessary work'.[12]

Marx, on the other hand, saw a number of possible antidotes to the tendency of profit rates to fall as the result of labour-saving innovations: the opening up of entirely new product lines that were labour-intensive; a pattern of innovation that was devoted as much to capital saving as to labour saving; a rising rate of exploitation on the labour forces still employed; the prior existence or formation of a class of consumers who produced nothing; a phenomenal rate of growth in the total labour force which would augment the mass of capital being produced even though the individual rate of return was falling. Whether Marx thought these countervailing forces were sufficient to stave off the falling value of production and falling profits indefinitely is not clear.

Developmental paths of this sort have effectively held off falling profits for some time now. The absorption of the peasantries of China, India and much of South-East Asia (along with Turkey and Egypt and some Latin American countries, with Africa still the continent with massive untapped labour reserves) into the global labour force since 1980 or so, along with the integration of what was the Soviet Bloc, has meant a huge increase (rather than decrease) in the global wage labour force over and beyond that supplied by population growth. The rising rates of exploitation with the creation of horrific labour conditions in China, Bangladesh, Vietnam and elsewhere are also palpable, while the demand problem has largely been taken care of by way of a vast expansion of credit.

So there appears to be no immediate cause for panic from the standpoint of either production or realisation. But from the standpoint of the long-term future of capital, it does seem as if we exist at a 'last frontier' for labour absorption throughout global capitalism. In the advanced capitalist countries there has been a massive movement of women into the labour force over the last fifty years and internationally there are few areas left (mainly in Africa and South and Inner Asia) where massive reserves of labour power are to be found. Nothing on the scale of the recent huge expansion of the global labour force will ever be possible again. Meanwhile, the accelerating speed-up over the last few years of automation and the application of artificial intelligence to routine services (like airline check-ins and supermarket checkouts) appears, on the other hand, to be just the beginning. Automation is now identifiable in fields such as higher educational instruction and medical diagnostics and the airlines are already experimenting with pilotless planes. The contradiction between value production on the one hand and runaway labour-saving technological innovation on the other is headed into more and more dangerous territory. This danger confronts not only an increasingly disposable population facing no foreseeable employment opportunities but also (as even Ford clearly sees) the reproduction of capital itself.

The last three recessions in the United States, for example, beginning in the early 1990s, have been followed by what are euphemistically referred to as 'jobless recoveries'. The most recent deep recession has led to the creation of long-term unemployment on a scale not seen in the USA since the 1930s. Similar phenomena are observable in Europe and the capacity for labour absorption in China – a key Communist Party policy orientation – appears to be limited. Both the evidence of recent trends and the evaluation of future prospects point in one direction: massive surpluses of potentially restive redundant populations.

This has some serious implications, both theoretical and political, that require elaboration. Money (see Contradiction 2) is a representation of the value of social labour (the latter being understood as the quantity of that labour which we supply to others via the exchange value market system). If we are moving towards a world in which social labour of this sort disappears, then there is no value to be represented. The historical representation of value – the money form – is then entirely free from its obligation to represent anything other than itself. The neoclassical economists argued (when they bothered at all with the question) that Marx's labour theory of value is irrelevant because capital responds only to money signals and not to value relations. There was, they argued, no point bothering with the idea of value even if it was a plausible concept (which most felt it was not). They were, I believe, wrong in this judgement. But if the developments outlined above do occur, then the neoclassical argument *contra* the value theory will become more and more correct, to the point where even the most orthodox Marxists will have to give up the value theory. Conventional economists will doubtless crow with delight at this. What they do not realise is that this means the demise of the one restraint that has prevented the descent of capital into total lawlessness. The recent evidence of a contagious predatory lawlessness within capitalism is a sign of the weakening regulatory role of social labour. This weakening has been occurring for some time. One crucial break occurred with the abandonment of a metallic base to the world's monetary system in the early 1970s: thereafter the relation of the world's money to social labour became at best tangential and we have the long chain of financial and commercial crises around the world after the mid-1970s to prove it.

The money form has acquired a good deal of autonomy over the last forty years. Fiat and fictitious values created by the world's central banks have taken over. This leads us back to some reflections on the relation between the path of technological evolution we have here described and the evolution of monetary technologies. The rise of cyber moneys, like Bitcoin, in some instances seemingly constructed for purposes of money-laundering around illegal activities, is just the beginning of an inexorable descent of the monetary system into chaos.

The political problem posed by the question of technology for anti-capitalist struggle is perhaps the most difficult to confront. On the one hand we know all too well that the evolution of technologies, marked as it is by a good deal of autonomous 'combinatorial' logic of the sort that Arthur describes, is a form of big business in which class struggle and inter-capitalist and interstate competition have played leading roles for the 'human purpose' of sustaining military dominance, class power and perpetual accumulation of capital. We also see that capital's actions are steering closer and closer to the abyss of the loss of social labour as an underlying regulatory principle that prevents the descent of capital into lawlessness. On the other hand we also know that any struggle to combat worldwide environmental degradation, social inequalities and impoverishment, perverse population dynamics, deficits in global health, education and nutrition, and military and geopolitical tensions will entail the mobilisation of many of our currently available technologies to achieve non-capitalistic social, ecological and political ends. The existing bundle of technologies, saturated as they are in the mentalities and practices of capital's search for class domination, contains emancipatory potentialities that somehow have to be mobilised in anti-capitalist struggle.

In the short term, of course, the left is bound to defend jobs and skills under threat. But, as the miserable history of the noble rearguard action fought against deindustrialisation in the 1970s and 1980s demonstrates, this will likely be a losing battle against a newly emerging technological configuration from the very beginning. An anti-capitalist movement has in the current conjuncture to reorganise its thinking around the idea that social labour is becoming less and less significant to how the economic engine of capitalism functions. Many of the service, administrative and professional jobs the left currently seeks to defend are on the way out. Most of the world's population is becoming disposable and irrelevant from the standpoint of capital, which will increasingly rely upon the circulation of fictitious forms of capital and fetishistic constructs of value centred on the money form and within the credit system. As is to be expected, some populations are held to be more disposable than others, with the result that women and people of colour bear most of the current burden and will probably do so even more in the foreseeable future.[13]

Martin Ford correctly poses the question: how will the resultant disposable and redundant population live (let alone provide a market) under such conditions? A viable long-term and imaginative answer to this question has to be devised by any anti-capitalist movement. Commensurate organised action and planning to meet the new eventualities and the provision of sufficient use values must be thought through and gradually implemented. This has to be done at the same time as the left has also to mount a rearguard action against the technologies of increasingly predatory practices of accumulation by dispossession, further bouts of deskilling, the advent of permanent joblessness, ever-increasing social inequality and accelerating environmental degradation. The contradiction that faces capital morphs into a contradiction that necessarily gets internalised within anti-capitalist politics.

# Contradiction 9
# Divisions of Labour

The division of labour should, by rights, be positioned as one of the foundational features of what capital is all about. It refers to the human capacity to disaggregate complex productive and reproductive activities into specific but simpler tasks that can be undertaken by different individuals on a temporary or permanent basis. The specialised work of the many individuals is reunited into a working whole by way of organised cooperation. Throughout history, divisions of labour have been changing and evolving depending on both the internal and the external conditions affecting a particular society. The central problem the division of labour poses is the relation between the parts and the whole and who (if anyone) takes responsibility for the evolution of the whole.

Capital has seized upon the division of labour and reshaped it dramatically to its own purposes throughout its history. It is for this reason that I include this contradiction under the heading of 'moving', since it is perpetually in the course of being revolutionised in the world that capital commands. The division of labour now in place is radically different to the point of being almost unrecognisable from that which prevailed in, say, 1850. The evolution in the division of labour under capital has, however, a very special character since, as with everything else, it is oriented primarily towards sustaining competitive advantage and profitability, which have nothing necessarily to do – except coincidentally – with improving the qualities of working and living or even enhancing human welfare more generally. If fundamental improvements to living and working occur, as indeed they clearly do, then this is either a collateral effect or a consequence of political demands and pressures emanating from restive and discontented populations. After all, the vast increase in ever-cheaper physical output that more efficient divisions of labour produce has to be consumed somehow and somewhere if the value produced is to be realised. On the other hand there are plenty of collateral damages (for example, in environmental conditions) to be taken into account also.

Contradictions within the division of labour are a dime a dozen. There is, however, a general and important distinction between the technical and the social division of labour. By the former I mean a separate task within a complex series of operations that anyone in principle can do, like minding a machine or mopping the floor, while by the latter I mean a specialised task that only a person with adequate training or social standing can do, like a doctor, software programmer or hostess at a five-star restaurant. I cite this last example to emphasise that the divisions and definitions that exist often depend as much on social, cultural and interpersonal skills and the presentation of self as they do on technical expertise.

There are all sorts of other distinctions of note, such as those due to nature (for example, childbearing) or to culture (for example, the position of women in society); between city (urban) and country (rural); mental and manual; social (throughout society in general) and detail divisions (within a firm or corporation); blue collar and white collar; skilled and unskilled; productive and unproductive; domestic (household) versus wage-based; symbolic versus material and so on. There are then sectoral classifications between primary (agriculture, forestry, fishing and mining), secondary (industry and manufacturing), tertiary (services and the finance, insurance and real estate – FIRE – sectors that have surged to prominence in recent times) and what some like to refer to as a fourth sector made up of increasingly important cultural and knowledge-based industries. As if this is not enough, the classification of different industries and occupations in censuses typically run to more than 100 items.

To the degree that such distinctions and oppositions can be a source of tension and antagonism, they can become embroiled in and heightened into contradictions that play some sort of role in crisis formation and resolution. Certainly, when we consider movements of revolt it would be rare indeed not to find the causes as well as the active participants rooted in one or other of these oppositions or based in certain sectors. In socialist theory, of course, it has traditionally been the industrial proletariat (the 'productive' labourers) within the overall division of labour that has been favoured as the vanguard of revolutionary transformation. Bank clerks, domestic workers and street cleaners have never been thought of as revolutionary agents whereas miners, car workers, steelworkers and even schoolteachers have.

Most of these dualisms turn out to be crude distinctions that have limited purchase in helping us to understand an increasingly complex and intricate world that is constantly subject to revolutionary transformation. It is, however, both useful and important at the outset to register how the technical and social bases of these distinctions intersect, since the categories involved in the definition of the division of labour have always intermingled technical and social considerations in ways that are often confusing and misleading. There has been a long history, for example, of defining skilled labour in gendered terms such that any task that women could perform – no matter how difficult or complex – was classified as unskilled simply because women could do it. Worse still, women were often allocated these tasks for so-called 'natural' reasons (everything from nimble fingers to a supposedly naturally submissive and patient temperament). For this reason, men in the workshops of Second Empire Paris strongly resisted the employment of women since they knew that this would lead to the reclassification of their work as unskilled and worthy only of a lower rate of remuneration. While the issue at that time was very specific, this is almost certainly a key factor in determining differential rates of remuneration in the contemporary global labour market. The fact that there has been an extensive feminisation both of low-wage labour and of poverty worldwide testifies clearly to the importance of these sorts of judgements, for which there is no technical basis whatsoever. The question of gender has also entered into extensive debates over the proper role to be assigned to housework versus wage labour. While this is an important issue within capitalism and is doubtless implicated in many personal crises within households, it has had very little direct impact on the development of capital, except for a long-standing general trend to broaden the market by commodifying more and more domestic tasks (such as cooking, cleaning, washing one's hair and getting nails clipped and manicured). The campaign over wages for housework would, in any case, seem to be seriously askew from an anti-capitalist perspective because it merely deepens the penetration of monetisation and commodification into the intimacies of daily life rather than using household work as a lever to try to decommodify as many forms of social provision as possible.

It is here that the contradictions of capital and of capitalism intersect. It has long been the case that specific trades have often, for example, been strongly and sometimes even exclusively associated with particular ethnic, religious or racial groups in a population. It is not only gender that is involved in shaping distinctions within the division of labour. These associations which continue to be in evidence are not merely residuals from a very complicated past. Many software programmers and developers (an entirely new occupational category) come from South Asia and the Philippines specialises in the provision and export of women domestic workers to many different countries in the world (from the USA to the Gulf States and Malaysia). The extensive migrations of labour that have occurred both historically and in recent times have frequently been channelled in such a way as to link certain places of origin with specific occupations in the receiving country. The National Health Service in Britain simply could not function without the immigration of different groups from what was once the British Empire. In recent years migrant streams (mainly women) from Eastern Europe (Poland, Lithuania, Estonia and the like) have been recruited wholesale into various facets of the so-called 'leisure' industries throughout much of Europe including Britain (everything from cleaning hotels to waitressing and bartending). Mexican and Caribbean migrants specialise in harvesting the crops on both the east and the west coasts of the USA.

The allocation of different people to different tasks is associated with differential rates of remuneration. Ethnic, racial, religious and gender prejudices and discriminations become deeply embroiled in how the labour market as a whole gets segmented and fragmented and how pay gets determined. Jobs that are considered dirty and demeaning, for example, are typically low-paid and left to the most disadvantaged and vulnerable migrants (often those who have no legal status). Skilled worker status is often automatically accorded migrants with software qualifications from South Asia. What is even more invidious is that the rate of remuneration also varies according to gender, race and ethnicity for working in the same occupation and on identical tasks.

Struggles over status within the division of labour and the recognition of skills are in effect struggles over differential life chances for the worker and, by extension – and here is the core of the problem – over profitability for the capitalist. From the standpoint of capital it is useful if not crucial to have a labour market that is segmented, fragmented and internally highly competitive. This poses barriers to coherent and unified labour organisation. Capitalists can and often do deliberately operate a divide and rule politics by fostering and inciting interethnic tensions, for example. Competition between social groups jockeying for position within the division of labour becomes a primary means by which labour in aggregate gets disempowered and capital comes to exercise greater and more complete control over both the labour market and the workplace. Typical forms of trade union organisation along sectoral rather than geographical lines also inhibit unified action on the part of labour, even when the unions themselves strive to go further than simply serving the interests of their own members.

The historical dynamics of class struggles within capitalism as a whole over skills, their specification and their rate of remuneration is one of the most important histories yet to be properly written from a critical perspective. The following remarks are therefore preliminary.

When capital came upon the scene as a primary as opposed to occasional form of accumulation and found it necessary to gain control of labour processes in industrial production, it found at hand a division of labour and a skill structure that were strongly rooted in the trades, resting on artisan labour. The 'butcher, the baker and the candlestick maker' were the sorts of occupations within which labourers could hone their skills and seek to secure their future social positions. Most of the population in Europe in the early years of capitalism was employed in agriculture (as a landed or landless peasantry) or in services (primarily domestic servants and retainers) to monarchs, landed aristocracy and merchant capitalists. The labour of serving demanded its own brand of interpersonal, domestic and socio-political skills. Town-based artisan labour in the trades embraced a whole range of different occupations, some of which were regulated by a guild and the apprenticeship system. The guild system conferred monopoly power over access to a skill that was based on a specific technical expertise. Carpenters learned how to use their tools, as did jewellers, clockmakers, iron masters, weavers, blacksmiths, tapestry artists, shoemakers, nail and gun makers and the like. Through corporatist guild organisation, groups of workers could assure and maintain a higher standing in the social order and a higher rate of remuneration for their work.

Capital plainly had to do battle with this monopoly power of labour over its conditions of production and its labour process. It fought the battle on two fronts. First, it gradually asserted its own monopoly power with private property over the means of production, so depriving labourers of the means to reproduce themselves outside of the supervision and control of capital. Many different craft workers could then be brought together under the direction of the capitalist into a process of collective labour to produce anything from nails to steam engines and locomotives. While the narrow technical basis and associated skills of the individual tasks did not change that much, the organisation of production through cooperation and the division of labour brought these different tasks together to reap remarkable gains in efficiency and productivity. The costs of commodities in the marketplace fell rapidly to outcompete the traditional craft and artisanal forms of production.

This was the division of labour that was not only extensively analysed but also lauded to the heavens by Adam Smith in *The Wealth of Nations*, published in 1776. In the celebrated case of the pin factory, Smith emphasised how the organised division of labour within the production process led to immense improvements in technical efficiency and labour productivity. By taking advantage of workers' differing skills and talents, the overall increase in productivity and profitability within what Marx later called 'the detail division of labour' within the firm was assured. On this basis Smith went on to infer that the extensive resort to social divisions of labour between firms and across sectors was bound to have a similar effect. In this case, as Marx was later at considerable pains to point out, the coordinating mechanism could no longer be the individual capitalist organising cooperative activity according to rational principles of design, but a more chaotic and anarchistic set of coordinations in which volatile price signals in the market became crucial to determinations of quantitatively rational divisions of productive activity in different firms and sectors. Smith, recognising this, urged the state generally not to intervene in price fixing (except in the case of public utilities and natural monopolies) and to follow a policy of laissez-faire to ensure that the hidden hand of the market could do its work with maximal efficiency. To this day theorists and policymakers have continued to mistakenly place great faith in an 'efficient market hypothesis' for the coordination of not only production but also the financial activities that came so badly unstuck in September of 2008. Marx concluded that the chaotic anarchy of the marketplace would be a constant source of the upsetting of equilibrium in prices and that this would render the social division of labour unstable if not crisis-prone.

The other, and I think far more profound and far-reaching, attack upon the potential monopoly powers of labour arose out of the evolutionary path of capitalist-inspired technological change. Much of this evolution directly or indirectly aimed to undermine the power of labour, both in the workplace and in the labour market. The bias of technological change has all along been against the interests of labour and in particular against the kinds of power that labour acquired through the acquisition of scarce and monopolisable skills. One important direction in capital–labour relations has been towards deskilling, a phenomenon that Marx noted in *Capital* and which was brought back centre stage in Harry Braverman's influential and controversial book *Labor and Monopoly Capital*, published in 1974.[1] Braverman argued that capital, particularly in its monopoly form, had a vested interest in degrading skills and so destroying any sense of pride that might attach to working for capital, while disempowering labour particularly at the point of production. There had been a long history of struggle over this. In the nineteenth century the ideologists of capital – Charles Babbage and Andrew Ure in particular – were much cited by Marx as evidence of capital's penchant for deskilling. Braverman likewise made much of Frederick Taylor's efforts at scientific management to disaggregate production processes to the point where a 'trained gorilla' would be able to undertake production tasks. The 'science' involved here was one in which time and motion studies were brought together with techniques of specialisation to simplify all the tasks, to maximise the efficiency and minimise the costs of production in any given sector or individual firm.

Both Marx and Braverman recognised that some reskilling would be required to implement the extensive organisational and technical changes involved in deskilling the mass of the workers. The introduction of the assembly line empowered the engineers who installed it and managed it, just as the engineers involved in robotisation or the deployment of computers had to acquire new skills to undertake their tasks. Critics of Marx and of Braverman have pointed out, correctly, that the writings of Babbage, Ure and Taylor were essentially utopian tracts that were never fully implemented, in part because of intense resistance on the part of workers and in part because the evolutionary path of technological change was and is not uniquely directed to labour control.

New technologies have often called for redefinitions of skill through which certain segments of labour can be advantaged. This turns out to be much more important than either Marx or Braverman allowed. What is on capital's agenda is not the eradication of skills per se but the abolition of *monopolisable* skills. When new skills become important, such as computer programming, then the issue for capital is not necessarily the abolition of those skills (which it may ultimately achieve through artificial intelligence) but the undermining of their potential monopoly character by opening up abundant avenues for training in them. When the labour force equipped with programming skills grows from relatively small to super-abundant, then this breaks monopoly power and brings down the cost of that labour to a much lower level than was formerly the case. When computer programmers are ten-a-penny, then capital is perfectly happy to identify this as one form of skilled labour in its employ, even to the point of conceding a higher rate of remuneration and more respect in the workplace than the social average.

In the same way that the evolution of technology has trended through its own autonomous dynamic towards greater and greater complexity over time, so divisions of labour have multiplied rapidly and been qualitatively transformed. This has not been a simple linear evolution, in part because the dynamics of class struggle has been engaged, though more often than not to capital's advantage. In the US steel industry, for example, the number of specialised (and to some degree therefore monopolisable) skills was very large indeed in the 1920s but became far smaller, particularly after the labour legislation of the 1930s that created the National Labor Relations Board, which had powers to resolve interjurisdictional disputes over which skill was qualified to do what in a particular industry. The contemporary steel industry has a much simpler and more streamlined skill set than was the case in earlier times. On the other hand specialisms in, say, medicine or banking and finance have proliferated, while the emergence of whole new sectors associated with electronics and computerisation has spawned an immense range of new occupations and job specifications. The range of specialisms within the state regulatory apparatus (in the Food and Drug Administration or in all those institutions such as the Controller of the Currency and the Security and Exchange Commission) has also grown astronomically in recent times.

The rapid extension and the explosive increase in complexity of both the detail and the social divisions of labour have become *the* fundamental feature of a modern capitalist economy. This evolution has not occurred as a consequence of overall conscious design and decision (there is no Ministry of the Division of Labour to mandate anything). It has evolved in parallel with technological and organisational changes impelled by the systemic forces earlier identified. And this despite the simplifications of occupational specifications achieved in some sectors of industry (such as steel and cars) and the loss of anachronistic occupations (such as that of lamplighter and, in advanced countries, those of water carrier and rag picker). Significant increases in labour productivity and in the volume and variety of production have been achieved by these means. One further consequence has been increasing economic interdependence within larger and larger populations spread over larger and larger geographical areas and the emergence of an international division of labour that also requires consideration. This implies rising problems of coordination in the social division of labour and the increasing likelihood of cascading disruptions in response to the volatility of market signals. Coordinations through command, control and contractual supply relations back down a commodity supply chain have consequently become more common in certain lines of production: corporate demands for inputs (for example, the car industry's need for engines, parts, tyres, windscreens, electronics, etc.) are specified and contracted for outside of the market. But with increasing simplification of tasks and increasing complexity of coordinations come increasing risks of misfires and of unintended consequences. This introduces a whole new layer in the division of labour and a vast army of new occupations involving logistical, legal, financial, marketing, advertising and other business services. Questions of security and safety (in everything from airlines to pharmaceuticals and food supplies) also become more pressing, as does the apparatus for surveillance, monitoring and quality control of different activities. Proliferating divisions of labour within the economy are paralleled by proliferating bureaucratic divisions of regulatory and administrative authority not only within a typical state apparatus but also internally within many institutions, such as hospitals, universities and school systems.

The division of labour as a whole has undergone a metamorphosis over the last half-century. As a result, many of the inquiries available to us from nineteenth-century critics like Karl Marx, Ferdinand Tönnies, Emile Durkheim and Max Weber do not address some of the central contemporary issues. Studies of the division of labour in the past largely focused on industrial organisation and factory labour in particular national contexts and the findings of those studies still surely stand. But the increasing complexity and proliferating geographical range of divisions of labour entail a qualitative leap in problems of coordination. Further problems arise because of the proliferation of state surveillance and bureaucratic authority functions and the wide-ranging shifts in the forms of organisation in civil society. Many of these divisions of labour and of authority interlock and feed off each other, while still others acquire a hierarchical position vis-à-vis one another. We are also increasingly subject to what Timothy Mitchell calls 'the rule of experts'.[2] Expert knowledge has always played a critical role in the history of capital and the power of the expert is hard to challenge. Earlier signs of this – the 'organisation man', the rule of the 'mandarins' and the like – drew attention to an emerging autocratic and hierarchical streak within the division of labour. Arguably, the role of experts has increased exponentially over recent decades and this poses a serious problem for the transparency and legibility of the world in which we live. We all depend on experts to fix our computer, diagnose our illnesses, design our transport systems and ensure our security.

In the 1970s a new perspective was introduced to the discussion with the rise of a so-called 'new international division of labour'. David Ricardo, appealing to the doctrine of comparative advantage, had long ago insisted on the benefits in efficiency to be gained from specialisation within and trade between countries. The specialisations partly depended on natural factors (it is no more possible to grow bananas and coffee in Canada than it is possible to mine copper or extract oil where there is none). But they also derived from social features such as labour skills, institutional arrangements, political systems and class configurations, along with the brute facts of colonial and neocolonial plunder and geopolitical and military power.

But there is no question that after 1970 or so the global map of the international division of labour underwent a dramatic set of mutations. The industrial districts that had been the heartlands of capital's global dominance after 1850 were disrupted and dismantled. Productive capital began to move offshore and the factories of Japan, South Korea, Singapore, Taiwan and then, after 1980, even more spectacularly, China joined the new centres of factory labour in Mexico, Bangladesh, Turkey and many other parts of the world. The West became broadly deindustrialised, while the East and the global South became centres for industrial value production alongside their more traditional role of primary commodity producers and extractors of resources for the industrialising world. The curious feature of these mutations is that industrialisation, which had always been a sure pathway to rising per capita incomes in the past, was now in some instances, such as that of Bangladesh, more associated with the perpetuation of poverty than with the turn to affluence. The same was true for those countries that rose to prominence because of their natural resources in oil or mining. They were plagued by the so-called 'resource curse' in which rents and royalties were hijacked by an elite, leaving the mass of the population in abject poverty (Venezuela before Chávez being a prime example). The West became more and more focused on rent extraction through the development of finance, insurance and real estate, alongside a consolidating regime of intellectual property rights, cultural products and corporate monopolies (like Apple, Monsanto, the big energy companies, pharmaceuticals etc.). Knowledge-based activities that drew upon a labour force trained in what Robert Reich calls 'symbolic labor' (as opposed to manual labour) also became more central.[3] As all these changes occurred, so there seemed to be a slow tectonic shift in the power relations and geopolitical configuration of the global economy. The flow of wealth from East to West that had prevailed for some two centuries was reversed and China increasingly became the dynamic centre of a global capitalism as the West, after the financial crash of 2008, lost much of its momentum.

So wherein lie the central contradictions in all of this? Plainly, the reversal of wealth flows and the reconfiguration of geopolitical powers pose incidental dangers for global conflicts that were not there before. While these conflicts are rooted in economic conditions and have significant ramifications for those conditions, I do not subscribe to the view that economic and military conflicts arise out of the contradictions of capital as such. The degrees of autonomy that exist in how the territorial logic of state power works within the global state system are far too loosely arranged for any simple economic determinism to work. A major conflagration in the Middle East, for example, would undoubtedly be rooted in the facts of oil production and the different geopolitical and geo-economic interests that cluster around the exploitation of this key global resource, and it certainly could have a huge economic impact (as was the case with the oil embargo of 1973). But it would be wrong to infer from this that the contradictions of capital are in themselves a root cause of any such conflict.

To be sure, also, the increasing complexity in the division of labour opens up new vulnerabilities. Small disruptions in a supply chain can have very large consequences. A strike in a key car-parts factory in one region of the world can bring the whole production system to a halt everywhere. But it can also be more plausibly argued that the increasing complexity and geographical proliferation of ties within a global division of labour provide far stronger insurance against local calamities. In the pre-capitalist past, a failure of the grain harvest in Russia would mean local famine and starvation, but there is now a world market in grains that can be drawn upon to compensate for local failure. There are no technical reasons for local famines in our times precisely because of the way the global division of labour works. When famines do occur (as, sadly, they too often do), it is invariably due to social and political causes. The last great famine in

China, which may have killed some 20 million people at the time of the 'great leap forward', occurred precisely because China was then by political choice isolated from the world market. Such an event could not now happen in China. This should be a salutary lesson for all those who place their anti-capitalist faith on the prospects for local food sovereignty, local self-sufficiency and decoupling from the global economy. Freeing ourselves from the chains of an international division of labour organised for the benefit of capital and the imperialist powers is one thing, but decoupling from the world market in the name of anti-globalisation is a potentially suicidal alternative.

The central contradiction in capital's use of the division of labour is not technical but social and political. It is summed up in one word: *alienation*. The undoubted and astonishing gains in productivity, output and profitability that capital achieves by virtue of its organisation of both the detail and the social division of labour come at the cost of the mental, emotional and physical well-being of the workers in its employ. The worker, Marx for one suggests, is typically reduced to a 'fragment of a man' by virtue of his or her attachment to a fixed position within an increasingly complex division of labour. Workers are isolated and individualised, alienated from each other by competition, alienated from a sensual relation to nature (from both their own nature as passionate and sensuous human beings and that of the external world). To the degree that intelligence is increasingly incorporated into machines, so the unity between mental and manual aspects of labouring is broken. Workers are deprived of mental challenges or creative possibilities. They become mere machine operators, appendages of the machines rather than masters of their fates and fortunes. The loss of any sense of wholeness or personal authorship diminishes emotional satisfactions. All creativity, spontaneity and charm go out of the work. The activity of working for capital becomes, in short, empty and meaningless. And human beings cannot live in a world devoid of all meaning.

Sentiments of this sort about the human condition under the rule of capital are not unique to Marx. Similar ideas are to be found in the writings of Weber, Durkheim and Tönnies. Even Adam Smith, the great champion of the division of labour and celebrator of its contribution to human efficiency, productivity and growth, worried that the assignment of workers to a single task within a complex division of labour was likely to condemn the worker to ignorance and stupidity. Later commentators like Frederick Taylor, less concerned than Smith with 'moral sentiments', were less worried: it would be perfectly fine with him if all workers acted like trained gorillas rather than passionate human beings. Capitalists too, as the novelist Charles Dickens noted, liked to think of their workers as 'hands' only, preferring to forget they had stomachs and brains.

But, said the more perceptive nineteenth-century critics, if this is how people live their lives at work, then how on earth can they think differently when they come home at night? How might it be possible to build a sense of moral community or of social solidarity, of collective and meaningful ways of belonging and living that are untainted by the brutality, ignorance and stupidity that envelops labourers at work? How, above all, are workers supposed to develop any sense of their mastery over their own fates and fortunes when they depend so deeply upon a multitude of distant, unknown and in many respects unknowable people who put breakfast on their table every day?

The proliferation and increasing complexity in the division of labour under capital leave little scope for personal development or self-realisation on the part of the labourer. Our collective capacity to explore freely our species potential as human beings appears blocked. But even Marx, who is at his grimmest in describing the alienations that arise out of capital's use of divisions of labour, sees glimmers of possibility in the conditions that capital's division of labour dictates. It is not, he suggests, all doom and gloom on the side of labour and that in part for reasons that capital itself was bound to furnish. Rapid evolutions in divisions of labour under the influence of strong currents of technological change would require, he argued, a flexible, adaptable and to some degree educated labour force. 'That monstrosity, the disposable working population held in reserve, in misery, for the changing requirements of capitalist exploitation, must be replaced by the individual man who is absolutely available for the different kinds of labour required of him: the partially developed individual, who is merely the bearer of one specialized social function, must be replaced by the totally developed individual, for whom the different social functions are different modes of activity he takes up in turn.'[4] For this purpose capital would require an educated and adaptable rather than specific kind of labour power and if labourers must be educated who knows what this 'totally developed individual' might read and what political ideas he or she might get into their heads? The insertion of the educational clauses into the English Factory Act of 1864 was clear evidence for Marx of the need for the state to step in and on capital's behalf ensure that some moves were made towards the education of the 'totally developed individual'. Similarly, while the abuses of women's employment in the Industrial Revolution were easy to spot and dwell upon, Marx also saw progressive possibilities in the long run for the construction of a 'a new and higher form' of family life and of gender relations on the basis of what capital both offered and required of women in the workplace.

Within this formulation lies the question, of course, of what it is that a 'totally developed individual' might want or need to know and who is going to teach it to him or her. This is a question that is central to the field of social reproduction, which we will consider shortly. But it is a problem that demands at least a mention here. From the standpoint of capital, labourers will need to know only that which is necessary to follow instructions and do their job within a division of labour that capital devises. But once labourers can read, then the danger is that they will read and dream and even act upon all sorts of ideas culled from an immense variety of sources. For this reason ideological controls upon the flow of knowledge and of information become essential, along with schooling in the right ideas supportive of capital and its requirements for reproduction. But it is hard, if not impossible, for the educated and totally developed individual not to wonder about the nature of the totality of a human society in which their own activity of labouring is but a minuscule part and what it might mean to be human in a world of such fragmentation and partitioning as to make it hard to distil any direct sense of the meaning of a life. I suspect it was for this reason that even capital allowed that a mild dose of humanist education in literature and the arts, in cultural understandings and religious and moral sentiments might provide an antidote to the anxieties generated from loss of meaning at work. The fragmentations and divisions of labour necessary to the ever-expanding diversity of occupational niches offered up by capital pose serious psychological problems. But what is so stunning about the neoliberal era is how even this mild concession to human needs has been contemptuously thrust aside in the name of a supposedly necessary austerity. State subsidies to cultural activities are cynically dismantled, leaving the financial support for all such activities to the self-serving philanthropy of the rich or the equally self-serving sponsorship of the corporations. Culture sponsored by IBM, BP, Exxon and the like becomes the name of the cultural game.

It also turns out that the labourers themselves, as inherently passionate and sociable human beings, have something to say not only about their objective situation but also about their own subjective state of mind. The objective conditions of alienation can, even without capital's help, be turned around by labourers themselves as they grasp opportunities to humanise labour processes and their general conditions of employment through the struggles they engage in. They may demand and in some instances even be accorded respect by their employers at the same time as they are objectively exploited. Subjectively, the forms of social bonding and solidarity necessary for survival down in the mines or around the steel furnaces are translated into pride in a dangerous and difficult job well done. Community solidarities mirror such sentiments and help counter the individualistic isolation that free-market processes tend to emphasise. It is possible even under the iron rule of capital that workers can take pride in their work and their role and assume an identity as a worker of a certain sort. They patently do ask, just as much as anyone else, what the meaning of the kind of life to which they are condemned might be and who it is that is in charge of an evolutionary process that either casts them aside into the ranks of the unemployed as disposable beings or offers them a job title that sounds so weird as to be as incomprehensible as it is patently meaningless. Workers employed by capital do not have to feel totally alienated. But when meaningful jobs disappear, then the clear sense of being exploited is dangerously supplemented by a growing sense of total alienation as to their meaningless position in a make-work world.

This does not imply that the balance between alienation on the one hand and coping and compromise on the other is fixed. In the advanced capitalist countries, such as the United States, Britain, Germany, Canada, Japan and Singapore, the trends in the division of labour have favoured the production of an educated workforce capable of engaging flexibly in a wide range of different labour processes. This, coupled with a long history of struggle over the rights of labour and a multitude of fights against the alienations visited upon them by capital, has created a situation in which a significant proportion of the workforce in these countries is highly trained in at least elementary skills and if not handsomely at least comfortably remunerated. By way of contrast, the labour conditions in the clothing factories in Bangladesh, the electronics factories of southern China, the *maquila* factories strung along the Mexican border or the chemical complexes in Indonesia are much closer to those with which Marx was so familiar. We could insert contemporary accounts of labour conditions in and around these factories that would not seem out of place in *Capital*.

The transformations in work and social life wrought by the neoliberal counter-revolution that has gathered pace throughout the advanced capitalist world since the late 1970s has had devastating effects on large segments of the population that have been left behind and rendered disposable and dispensable by a combination of technological changes and offshoring. Lost in a world of long-term unemployment and decay of social infrastructures and loss of communal solidarities, large segments of the population are deeply alienated, largely given to passive resentments punctuated by occasional eruptions of sometimes violent and seemingly irrational protest. All it will take is for the volcanic protests from the Swedish suburbs to Istanbul and São Paulo to coalesce to reveal the vast magma of alienation bubbling underneath. Capital will then be confronted with a political crisis that will be almost impossible to manage without draconian autocratic repressions that will in turn exacerbate rather than assuage the discontent. Uneven geographical developments in the division of labour and the parallel increase in social inequality in life chances are exacerbating that sense of alienation, which, if it becomes active rather than passive, will surely pose a major threat to the reproduction of capital as it is currently constituted. Society will then have to face the stark choice between an impossible reform and an improbable revolution.

# Contradiction 10
# Monopoly and Competition: Centralisation and Decentralisation

Read any economics text or popular defence of capitalism and the word 'competition' will almost certainly very soon crop up. In popular defences as well as in more serious theoretical works, one of the great success stories of capitalism is that it supposedly takes the natural proclivity of human beings to compete, unleashes it from social constraints and harnesses it through the market to produce a dynamic and progressive social system that can function for the benefit of all. Monopoly power (of the sort that Google, Microsoft and Amazon wield these days) and its cognates like oligopoly (of the sort that the 'Seven Sisters' major global oil companies possess) and monopsony (the power that Walmart and Apple exert over their suppliers) all tend to be presented (if they are mentioned at all) as aberrations, as unfortunate departures from a state of happy equilibrium that should be achieved in a purely competitive market.

This biased view – for such I maintain it is – is supported by the existence of anti-trust and anti-monopoly legislation and commissions which proclaim how bad monopolies are and from time to time set out to break them up in order to protect the public from their negative effects. At the beginning of the twentieth century, for example, a wave of 'trust-busting' led by the indomitable figure of Teddy Roosevelt occurred in the USA. In the 1980s the break-up of AT&T's monopoly in telecommunications was mandated in the USA and now in both Europe and North America questions are being asked concerning the excessive market power of Google, Microsoft and Amazon. In the case of so-called 'natural monopolies' (mainly public utilities and transport links like canals and railways, which cannot be organised competitively) Adam Smith advised government regulation to prevent price gouging. The stated aim of public policy is to prevent monopoly pricing and to ensure the benefits of innovation, rising productivity and low prices that supposedly derive from inter-capitalist competition. The maintenance of a competitive environment through state action is generally touted as an essential policy stance for any healthy capitalist economy. In particular, achieving a competitive position in international trade is frequently cited as a major goal of public policies. If only a pure and perfect competitive market could be created, free of the distortions of monopoly power, then all, it is said, would be well.

This amazingly influential story has held sway for more than two centuries, ever since Adam Smith articulated it so persuasively and brilliantly in *The Wealth of Nations*. It constitutes *the* founding myth of liberal economic theory. The liberal political economists mounted a crusade against state interventions in price-fixing markets and against monopoly power from the late eighteenth century onwards. Keynes did not depart too much from it. Even more surprisingly, it is accepted as gospel in Marx's *Capital*, though in Marx's case the reasoning runs that if Adam Smith's utopian tale was correct, then things would not turn out to be for the benefit of all: the result would be to deepen the class divide of wealth and power and ensure that capital would become ever more crisis-prone as well as powerful.

In the wake of the crisis of 2007–9 it became very difficult for economists to stick with their customary storyline. The bankers in pursuit of their individual interests plainly did not contribute to the general welfare and in the USA the Federal Reserve bailed out the banks but not the people. This has now led to an admission that monopoly power is more than an aberration but a systemic problem that arises out of what economists refer to as 'rent seeking'. 'To put it baldly,' says the economist Joseph Stiglitz, 'there are two ways to become wealthy: to create wealth or to take wealth away from others.

The former adds to society. The latter typically subtracts from it, for in the process of taking it away, wealth gets destroyed.'[1] Rent seeking is nothing more than a polite and rather neutral-sounding way of referring to what I call 'accumulation by dispossession'.

The virtue of Stiglitz's somewhat truncated account of rent seeking or accumulation by dispossession is that it recognises the seamless way in which monopoly power in economic transactions is paralleled by monopoly power in the political process. Take the case of the United States. Regressive taxes and write-offs; regulatory capture (in which the foxes are put in charge of the henhouse); acquiring or leasing state or private assets at discount prices; inflated cost-plus contracts with state agencies; writing legislation to protect or subsidise particular interests (energy and agribusiness); buying political influence through campaign contributions – these are all political practices that give a free hand to big moneyed and monopolistic interests while permitting them to plunder the public treasury at the expense of the taxpayer. These political practices supplement conventional rent seeking in land and property markets; rents on resources and on patents, licences and intellectual property rights; plus excess returns due to monopoly pricing. Then there are all the quasi-legal ways of gaining excess profits. The creation of financial markets that lack any transparency or in which adequate information is lacking creates a fog of misunderstanding in which sharp practices are impossible to curb. Real money has been made out of fictitious accounting (as Enron showed so dramatically). When we add in the proliferation of abusive practices such as predatory lending in housing markets that transferred billions in asset values from the public to the financiers, abusive credit card practices, hidden charges (on phone and medical bills), as well as practices that skirt if not infringe the law, we end up with a vast array of practices where big corporations and big moneyed interests add to their wealth hand over fist even as the economy as a whole collapses and then stagnates. As Stiglitz remarks, 'Some of the most important innovations in business in the last three decades have centered not on making the economy more efficient but on how better to ensure monopoly power or how better to circumvent government regulations intended to align social returns and private rewards.'[2]

What is missing from Stiglitz's account of rent seeking as a strategy (though not from his account of the social outcomes) is the demolition of a wide range of democratic rights, including economic rights to pensions and health care, and free access to vital services such as education, police and fire protection, and state-funded programmes (like nutritional supplements and food stamps in the case of the USA) that have hitherto helped to support low-income populations at an adequate standard of living. The neoliberal assault on all these rights and services is a form of dispossession that passes the public expenditure savings on to the 'not needy but greedy' class of corporate heads and billionaires. And all of this has been accomplished by resort to a consolidated class power that monopolises both the economy and the political process while monopolising most of the media, reducing a supposed 'free market in ideas' to a series of factional squabbles about trivia. And yet economic orthodoxy still insists that the free market is the god in whom we must necessarily trust and monopoly an unfortunate aberration that we could, if we put our minds to it, avoid.

The view I shall take here, however, is that *monopoly power is foundational rather than aberrational to the functioning of capital and that it exists in a contradictory unity with competition.* This is a rather unusual stance to take and it goes well beyond Stiglitz's account, but there is good reason to believe that it is the correct formulation. Not only does it accord with the singular fact that most capitalists if given the choice prefer to be monopolists rather than competitors and that they persistently go out of their way to try to procure as much monopoly power as they possibly can. It also gets to the core of the contradictory unity between competition and monopoly in the history of capital.

So how are we to understand this contradictory unity? The most obvious place to begin is at that point where the two are indistinguishable or, to be more exact, where they are fused and the contradiction is latent rather than antagonistic. This point lies in the nature of private property, which confers a monopoly over the use of a commodity upon its owner. The monopoly power inherent in private property forms the basis for exchange and by extension for competition. This may seem elemental, trivial even, but it becomes far less so when it is recognised that the class power of capital rests entirely on the assemblage of all of these individual monopolistic property rights into a social order where the capitalist class can be defined vis-à-vis labour by its *collective monopoly over the means of production (or, in its updated version, the means of financing)*. What is lacking in the usual discussion of monopoly is the concept and the reality of *class* monopoly power (the collective power of capital), including class monopoly rents, as applied to both economic and political processes.

The role of the standard story in which competition features so large and monopoly not at all then becomes clearer. It obscures the monopoly basis of class power in private property and conveniently evades questions of class power and class struggle (as is the case in almost all economics textbooks). Capital is ideally construed as a wondrous series of molecular and competitive collisions of individual capitalists moving freely and hunting for profitable opportunities within a chaotic sea of economic activity. The reality of the international competition that is touted as so beneficial to all is that it exerts a downward pressure on wages to the benefit of capital!

Unlike the case of technological change more generally, which can plausibly be depicted as progressive and irreversible, the balance between monopoly and competition oscillates erratically back and forth. It sometimes seems cyclical over time rather than unidirectional and is subject to the political whims and leanings of state management and intervention. Marx thought that the end point of competition was bound to be monopoly power and that there might be distinctive laws governing the centralisation of capital, but he did not elaborate. Lenin famously saw capital moving into a new phase of monopoly power associated with imperialism at the turn of the twentieth century when the big industrial cartels combined with finance capital to dominate the leading national economies (these were the trusts that Teddy Roosevelt strove to break up). This view re-emerged in the 1960s with Paul Baran and Paul Sweezy's book *Monopoly Capitalism* in the United States and in the work of various theoreticians of communist parties in Europe.[3] The rising power of monopolies was again associated with strong currents of a centralised imperialism. In the 1960s it was the large corporations (such as the big three car manufacturers in Detroit or state-run enterprises in Europe) that dominated national markets and were thought to exercise excessive monopoly power. It was the large corporations, like United Fruit in Central America or ITT in Chile, that exercised monopoly power internationally and stood behind coups and the military regimes like that in Chile that did the bidding of the imperialist powers.

Capital oscillates, as Giovanni Arrighi pointed out, between the two extremes of the supposedly ruinous effects of unregulated competition and the excessive centralising powers of monopolies and oligopolies.[4] The crisis of the 1970s (that on the surface exhibited a peculiar combination of stagnation and inflation) was widely interpreted as a typical crisis of monopoly capital, whereas the deflationary crisis of the 1930s, it can be said, was produced by ruinous competition. The state of the contradictory unity between monopoly and competition at any one historical phase has to be established, not presumed. While the neoliberal turn that began in the 1970s opened up new forms of international competition though globalisation, the current situation in many sectors of the economy (pharmaceuticals, oil, airlines, agribusiness, banking, software, the media and social media in particular, and even box retailing) suggests strong tendencies towards oligopoly if not monopoly. It is, perhaps, testimony to the moving character of this contradiction that a degree of monopoly power (such as that exercised by Google) is now deemed in certain circles a worthy departure from a state of pure competition. It allows for rational calculation, standardisation and advance planning rather than the chaos of unstable market coordinations in an uncertain world. On the other hand, Google's abuse of its monopoly position (allowing the National Security Administration access to its data on private individuals) illustrates the negative potentialities that go with such a concentration of power.

The example of private property as monopoly power is particularly instructive in the case of land and property ownership. What are monopolised are not only the land and the property but a unique spatial location. No one else can put their factory down where mine is already located. An advantageous location (with privileged access to transport links, resources or markets) gives me a certain monopoly power in competition with others. The result, conventional economists ultimately had to concede when forced to study the matter, was a peculiar kind of competition called 'monopolistic competition'. The term is apt since it describes a condition in which all economic activity is competitively grounded in particular spaces with unique qualities. Naturally, this form of competition is treated as a footnote in economic theory rather than as basic to economic life, even though all productive economic activity is ultimately grounded in space. Standard economic thinking prefers a model in which all economic activity occurs on the head of a pin and no monopoly due to spatial location exists. Differential spatial qualities – more fertile land, better-quality resources, superior locational advantages – do not apparently matter. Nor does the perpetually changing structure of spatial relations primarily brought about by infrastructural investments in things like transport systems.

These absences have serious consequences for understanding how the contradictory unity of competition and monopoly works. It is often presumed, for example, that multiple small enterprises producing a similar product indicate a state of intense competition. This is not the case under certain spatial conditions. Two bakeries 300 yards apart might suggest intense competition. But if there is a deep and fast-flowing river between them, then each baker will have monopoly power on their side of the river. This monopoly power will disappear if the king builds a bridge across the river, but it will then be reinstated if a local lord imposes a steep toll on the bridge or if the river becomes a political boundary and stiff tariffs on bread are placed upon commerce across it. For this reason, the eighteenth-century political economists waged a campaign against tolls and tariffs, understanding that they were a hindrance to competition. The global regime of free trade sought by the USA after 1945 and culminating in the World Trade Organization agreements is a continuation of this policy.

But the role of transport costs as a form of 'protection' for local monopolies has long been diminishing. The reduction of these costs has been crucial to capital's history. Containerisation from the 1960s onwards played a vital role in changing the geographical range of competition, as did reductions in political barriers to trade. The US car industry, with its big three companies located in Detroit, appeared to constitute an all-powerful oligopoly in the 1960s, but by the 1980s its power had been undermined by foreign competition from West Germany and Japan as the spatial conditions of trade relations changed dramatically both physically and politically. The 1980s saw the advent of the global car as parts could be produced all over the world and merely assembled somewhere like Detroit. The advent of fierce international competition plus automation left Detroit a wasteland. The history of the brewing trade is another of my favourite examples. Highly localised in the eighteenth century, it became regionalised thanks to the railways in the mid nineteenth century, before going national in the 1960s and global, thanks to containerisation, in the 1980s.

The field of monopolistic competition has clearly been changing and, as in the case of uneven geographical development, the spatial and geographical organisation of production, distribution and consumption is itself a way of orchestrating the contradictory relation between monopoly and competition. I now eat vegetables from California in Paris and drink imported beers from all over the world in Pittsburgh. As spatial barriers diminished through the capitalist penchant for 'the annihilation of space through time', many local industries and services lost their local protections and monopoly privileges. They were forced into competition with producers in other locations, at first relatively close by, but then much further away.

Capitalists should presumably welcome such a restoration of competition. But as has already been noted, it is a peculiar fact that most capitalists, given the choice, prefer to be monopolists. They have therefore had to find other ways to construct and preserve a much-coveted monopoly position.

The obvious answer is to centralise capital in mega-corporations or to set up looser alliances (as in airlines and cars) that dominate markets. And we have seen plenty of that. The second path is to secure ever more firmly the monopoly rights of private property through international commercial laws that regulate all global trade. Patents and so-called 'intellectual property rights' have consequently become a major field of struggle through which monopoly powers more generally get asserted. The pharmaceutical industry, to take a paradigmatic example, has acquired extraordinary monopoly powers in part through massive centralisations of capital and in part through the protection of patents and licensing agreements. And it is hungrily pursuing even more monopoly powers as it seeks to establish property rights over genetic materials of all sorts (including those of rare plants in tropical rainforests traditionally collected by indigenous inhabitants). The third path is by 'name branding' so that a monopoly price can be charged for a shoe with a swoosh on it or a wine with a certain château name on the label.

As monopoly privileges from one source diminish so we witness a variety of attempts to preserve and assemble them by other means. There continue to be, however, some spatially circumscribed markets that facilitate monopoly pricing for certain activities: a hip operation in Belgium costs $13,360 (including the round-trip airfare from the USA) while an identical procedure in the USA costs over $78,000! There is, obviously, a lot of monopoly pricing going on in the US case relative to that of Belgium (almost certainly due to different state regulatory policies). Personal services of this sort have remained partially immune from spatial competition in spite of the rise of medical tourism and the outsourcing of many services to call centres like those in India. These protected markets may crumble, however, in the face of the application of artificial intelligence.

Capital is, we can conclude, in love with monopoly. It prefers the certainties, the quiet life and the possibility of leisurely and cautious changes that go with a monopolistic style of working and living outside of the rough and tumble of competition. For this reason also, capital loves commodities that are unique, so particular that they can command a monopoly price. Capital goes out of its way to appropriate such commodities and to foster their production, frequently garbing them in the raiments of pure aesthetic pleasure. The capitalist class builds an art market as an investment sphere where monopoly pricing reigns supreme, just as it does with investments in professional sports like football, hockey and baseball. It even commodifies, if it can, the unique qualities of nature and gives them monetary value subject to the regime of private property. As the anarchist geographer Elisée Reclus complained as long ago as 1866:

> At the seashore, many of the most picturesque cliffs and charming beaches are snatched up either by covetous landlords or by speculators who appreciate the beauties of nature in the spirit of a money changer appraising a gold ingot … Each natural curiosity, be it rock, grotto, waterfall, or the fissure of a glacier – everything, even the sound of an echo – can become individual property. The entrepreneurs lease waterfalls and enclose them with wooden fences to prevent non-paying travelers from gazing at the turbulent waters. Then, through a deluge of advertising, the light that plays about the scattering droplets and the puffs of wind unfurling curtains of mist are transformed into the resounding jingle of silver.[5]

The same applies to unique cultural objects and cultural and historical traditions. The commodification of history, culture and tradition may appear obnoxious but it underpins a vast tourist trade in which authenticity and uniqueness are highly valued, even as they are subject to the hegemony of market valuations. And more significant is the systematic branding of many consumer commodities as unique and special (even when such claims are dubious at best) so as to allow a monopoly price to be put upon them. The items or effects produced cannot be so unique or special as to be entirely outside of the monetary calculus of course, so even Picassos, archaeological artefacts and aboriginal art objects must have their price. For more common commodities, the aim is to set one brand apart as a superior toothpaste, shampoo or car. The idea is to use product differentiation as a way to secure a monopoly price. The reputation and the public image of a commodity becomes just as if not more important than its material use value. From this arises the immense importance of advertising, which is nothing more than an industry struggling to squeeze monopoly prices out of an otherwise competitive situation. Nearly one-sixth of the jobs in the United States are now in advertising or selling, an industry that is dedicated to the production of monopoly rents through the production of image and reputation of particular commodities.

There is an interesting geographical version of this same phenomenon. Cities like Barcelona, Istanbul, New York and Melbourne get branded, for example, as tourist destinations or as hubs for business activities by virtue of their unique characteristics and special cultural qualities. If there are no particularly unique features to hand, then hire some famous architect, like Frank Gehry, to build a signature building (like the Guggenheim Museum in Bilbao) to fill the gap.[6] History, culture, uniqueness and authenticity are everywhere commodified and sold to tourists, prospective entrepreneurs and corporate heads alike, yielding monopoly rents to landed interests, property developers and speculators. The role of the class monopoly rent that is then gained from rising land values and property prices in cities like New York, Hong Kong, Shanghai, London and Barcelona is hugely important for capital in general. The gentrification process that is then unleashed is, worldwide, a critical part of an economy based as much on accumulation through dispossession as on creating wealth through new urban investments.

In cultivating monopoly power, capital realises far-reaching control over production and marketing. It can stabilise the business environment to allow for rational calculation and long-term planning, the reduction of risk and uncertainty. The 'visible hand' of the corporation, as Alfred Chandler terms it, has been and continues to be just as important to capitalist history as Adam Smith's 'invisible hand'.[7] The 'heavy hand' of state power exercised broadly in support of capital also plays its part.

Monopoly power is strongly associated with the centralisation of capital. On the other hand competition generally entails decentralisation. It is useful here to consider this cognate relation between the centralisation and decentralisation of political-economic activities as a subset of the contradictory unity between monopoly and competition. In this instance it is also vital to see the relation between centralisation and decentralisation in terms of a contradictory unity. It has often proved the case, for example, that decentralisation is one of the best means to preserve highly centralised power, because it masks the nature of this centralised power behind a veneer of individual liberty and freedom. In a way this was what Adam Smith was advocating: a centralised state could amass far greater wealth and economic power by liberating decentralised individualised market freedoms. This is something that the Chinese state has recognised over the last few decades. In this case the decentralisation has been political (the decentralisation of powers to regions, cities down to townships and villages) as well as economic (the liberation of state and village enterprises and the banking system in both wealth creation and rent seeking). Giovanni Arrighi's book *Adam Smith in Beijing* dwells on this point at length.[8] But in this instance the crude assumption that decentralisation is inherently more democratic has to be seriously questioned, since there is no sign of the centralised Communist Party relinquishing any of its powers.

There are two ways in which we can think about the contradictory unity between decentralisation and centralisation in political-economic life. The first is sectoral. It focuses primarily on the power of associated capitals – the visible hand of the capitalist corporation in particular – and the massing of money capital as 'the common capital of the class' (in Marx's words), particularly within the credit and financial system.[9] The latter cannot function, however, without the singular backing of state power. The 'state–finance nexus' (the unity of the Central Bank and the Treasury Department in the case of the USA) sits at the apex of this structure. It is endowed with supreme monopoly power designed to support the banking industry and the financial system at the expense, if necessary, of all else, including the people. It is backed ideologically by the innumerable think tanks (the Heritage Foundation, the Manhattan Institute, the Cato Institute, the Ohlin Foundation) that promote pro-capitalist and right-wing views. Critiques of this vast centralisation of class monopoly power abound on both left and far-right wings of the political spectrum. That the Federal Reserve and the IMF have been totally dedicated to the protection of the class monopoly power of a financial oligarchy is now undeniable. Although the evidence for this is overwhelming, the mask such think tanks and the media construct around these institutions as the grand protectors of individual market freedoms goes a considerable way to successfully hiding their class character from the general public. The organisation of 'the common capital of the class' through the centralisation of the financial system takes us back to the central contradictions in the money form.

The second sphere in which the powerful forces of centralisation and decentralisation collide is geographical, resulting in uneven geographical development and the projection of economic, political and ultimately military power of class alliances in one space upon those in another. Hence the inner relation between monopoly, centralisation, imperialism and neocolonialism. We will probe further into this angle when we consider uneven geographical development explicitly.

The two ways in which the decentralising and centralising tendencies of capital play out are not independent of each other. The massing of centralised financial powers in the major centres of global finance (New York, London, Tokyo, Shanghai, Frankfurt, São Paulo etc.) is of significance, as is the long history of the flourishing of innovations in new territories like Silicon Valley, Bavaria, the so-called 'Third Italy' in the 1980s and so on, where the seeming liberty of manoeuvre and lack of regulatory control allow things to happen that might otherwise get constrained by stifling and dominant powers of state and corporate capital grown obese. So pervasive and palpable has this tension been that policymakers now seek to capture the possibilities of knowledge-based, cultural and creative economies by centralised initiatives that support the decentralisation and deregulation of economic and political power. This is what the central state's creation of 'special economic zones' in China and India is supposed to be about. Elsewhere, development is left to local initiatives on the part of increasingly entrepreneurial local state or regional metropolitan apparatuses. The hope is to replicate the conditions that sparked the innovations behind the digital revolution and the rise of the so-called 'new economy' of the 1990s, which, in spite of the way it crashed and burned at the close of the century, left in its wake a radical reordering of capitalist technologies. This is what the geographical concentration of venture capital in regions such as Silicon Valley is supposed to accomplish. While the chequered success of such policies should give us pause, this is, nevertheless, a fine illustration of how capital seizes upon certain contradictions, like that between centralisation and decentralisation or between monopoly and competition, and turns them to its own advantage.

So what, then, are the political implications of these findings for anti-capitalist politics? We first must recognise how successful capital has generally been in managing the contradictions between monopoly and competition, as well as between centralisation and decentralisation, to its own advantage, even as it uses crises to do so. It is, I think, clear that no feasible alternative future social order will be able to abolish these contradictions. The only interesting question is how to work with them. But we should beware the trap of thinking of the oppositions as being independent rather than contradictory unities. It is false to presume, for example, that decentralisation is democratic and centralisation is not. By pursuing the chimera of pure decentralisation (as some on the left are these days wont to do), there is a strong possibility of opening the way to a hidden centralised monopoly control. By pursuing the other chimera of totally rationalised centralised control, others on the left point the way to an unacceptable and totalitarian stagnation. Capital has organically arrived at a way to balance and rebalance the tendencies towards a monopolistic centralisation and decentralised competition through the crises that arise out of its imbalances.

It has also learned something else of considerable importance. Capital changes the scale at which it operates in such a way as to locate powers and influence at that scale which are most advantageous for the reproduction of its own powers. When, in the United States, the cities and the states were too strong in the first half of the twentieth century, capital looked mainly to the federal level for support, but by the end of the 1960s when the federal government was proving too interventionist and prone to regulation, capital gradually moved to support state rights and it is in the states that the Republican Party is now most fiercely waging its populist pro-capitalist agenda. In this regard the anti-capitalist left has much to learn from capital at the same time as it combats it. Interestingly, much of the anti-capitalist as opposed to social democratic left prefers in these times to wage its war at the micro scale, where autonomista and anarchist formulations and solutions are most effective, leaving the macro level almost bare of oppositional powers. An inordinate fear of centralisation and of monopolisation predominates in such a way as to hamstring anti-capitalist opposition. The dialectical but contradictory relation between monopoly and competition cannot be effectively mobilised for anti-capitalist struggle.

# Contradiction 11

# Uneven Geographical Developments and the Production of Space

Capital strives to produce a geographical landscape favourable to its own reproduction and subsequent evolution. There is nothing odd or unnatural about this: after all, ants do it, beavers do it, so why shouldn't capital do it? The geographical landscape of capitalism is, however, rendered perpetually unstable by various technical, economic, social and political pressures operating in a world of immensely changeable natural variation. Capital must perforce adapt to this wildly evolving world. But capital also has a key role in shaping that world.

The contradictions between capital and labour, competition and monopoly, private property and the state, centralisation and decentralisation, fixity and motion, dynamism and inertia, poverty and wealth, as well as between different scales of activity, are all writ large and given material form in the geographical landscape. Among all these diverse forces, though, priority has to be accorded to a combination of the molecular processes of endless capital accumulation in space and time (the daily ebb and flow of competitive entrepreneurial and corporate activity engaging in the circulation and accumulation of capital) and the attempt to organise the space of the landscape in some systematic way through the exercise of state powers.

The geographical landscape that capital makes is not a mere passive product. It evolves according to certain rough and ready rules which – like those that govern the combinatorial evolution of technologies – have their own autonomous but contradictory logic. How the landscape evolves affects capital accumulation as well as how the contradictions of capital and of capitalism are manifest in space, place and time. The independent manner in which the geographical landscape evolves plays a key role in crisis formation. Without uneven geographical development and its contradictions, capital would long ago have ossified and fallen into disarray. This is a key means by which capital periodically reinvents itself.

Capital and the capitalist state play a leading role in producing the spaces and places that ground capitalist activity. It takes a lot of capital to build a railway, for example. If the railway is to be profitable, then other capitals must use it, preferably for the lifetime of the investment fixed in it. If this does not happen, then the railway goes bankrupt and the capital invested in it is lost or at least devalued. So capital needs to use the railway once it is built. But why does capital need a railway?

Time is money for capital. Traversing space takes both time and money. Economy of time and money is a key to profitability. A premium is therefore placed on innovations – technical, organisational and logistical – that reduce the costs and time of spatial movement. The producers of new technologies are well aware of this. They concentrate a lot of their autonomous effort upon developing new ways to reduce costs or time of capital circulation. Technologies that accomplish these goals will command a ready market. What Marx called the 'annihilation of space through time' is one of the holy grails of capital's endeavours.

Cost and time reductions can be accomplished in two ways. The first entails continuous innovations in transport and communications technologies. The history of such innovations under capitalism (from canals to jet aircraft) has been outstanding. The impacts depend, however, on the kind of capital being moved around. Money in its credit form now flits around the world instantaneously. It was not always so. Our own era is marked by the far superior mobility of money capital due to information technologies. Commodities are generally less mobile. There is a huge difference between, say, the live transmission of a World Cup football match and lugging around bottled water, steel girders, furniture or perishable items like soft fruit, hot pork pies, milk and bread. Commodities are variably mobile depending upon their qualities and transportability. Production, with some exceptions like transportation itself, is the least mobile form of capital. It is usually locked down in place for a time (in some instances, like shipbuilding, the time may be considerable). But the sewing machines used in sweatshop shirt production are more easily moved around than a steel or car plant. The locational constraints in primary sectors like agriculture, forestry, mining and fishing are very special for obvious reasons.

Lower costs in transport and communications can facilitate dispersal and decentralisation of activity across larger and larger geographical spaces. The near-elimination of transport costs and times as a factor in location decisions permits capital to explore differential profit opportunities in widely disparate places. Divisions of labour within a firm can be decentralised to different locations. Offshoring becomes possible and the monopolistic element in competition is reduced. Regional specialisations and divisions of labour become even more marked because small differences in costs (such as local taxes) translate into higher profits for capital.

New geographical patterns to production typically arise out of the sharpened spatial competition facilitated by cheaper and more efficient transport and communications. Start-ups in, say, South Korea – where steel production is much cheaper because of lower-cost labour, easier access to raw materials and markets, and the like – drive out the more costly and the less efficient industries in older regions such as Pittsburgh and Sheffield. In the car industry it was not only the introduction of foreign competition that undermined Detroit, but also the setting up of new plants in Tennessee and Alabama, where labour costs were lower and trade union power weaker. In the nineteenth century cheap food grains from North America inflicted severe damage on UK and European agricultural interests. This happened because the newly minted railways and steam ships greatly reduced the cost and time of movement of agricultural commodities after 1850 or so, much as containerisation did for world trade after 1970. Deindustrialisation (the nether side of geographical expansion) has been going on for a very long time.

The second way to reduce the time and cost of movement is for capitalists to locate so as to minimise their costs of procuring means of production (including raw materials) and labour supplies and of getting to market. What are called 'agglomeration economies' arise when many different capitals cluster together (for example, the car parts and tyre industries locate close to car plants). Different firms and industries can share facilities, access to labour skills, information and infrastructures. Positive benefits arise which all firms can take advantage of (one firm trains workers that other firms can then hire right away without having to train them first, for example). Labour is likewise drawn to the opportunities of dynamic centres, even in the absence of the forces that push them off the land. Urban agglomerations are in effect constructed spatial environments favourable to collectively sustaining particular sets of productive activities.

Agglomeration produces geographical centralisation. The molecular processes of capital accumulation converge, as it were, on the production of economic regions. The boundaries are always fuzzy and porous, yet the interlocking flows within a territory produce enough structured coherence to mark the geographical area off as somehow distinctive. In the nineteenth century cotton meant Lancashire (Manchester), wool meant Yorkshire (Leeds), stainless steel meant Sheffield and metalworking meant Birmingham. Structured coherence usually extends well beyond economic exchanges to encompass attitudes, cultural values, beliefs and even religious and political affiliations. The necessity to produce and maintain collective goods requires that some system of governance be brought into existence and preferably formalised into systems of administration within the region. If the state did not already exist, then capital would have to create something like it to facilitate and manage its own collective conditions of production and consumption. Dominant classes and hegemonic class alliances can form and lend a specific character to political as well as to economic activity within the region.

Regional economies form a loosely connected mosaic of uneven geographical development within which some regions tend to become richer while poor regions get poorer. This happens because of what Gunnar Myrdal calls circular and cumulative causation.[1] Advanced regions draw new activity to themselves because of the vibrancy of their markets, the greater strength of their physical and social infrastructures and the ease with which they can procure their necessary means of production and labour supplies. Resources exist (in the form of an increasing tax base) to invest further in physical and social infrastructures (such as public education) and these attract even more capital and labour to come to the region. Transport routes are created that focus on the region because this is where the traffic is. As a result, even more capital is attracted. Other regions, by contrast, are underserved if not increasingly bereft of activities. They get caught in a downward spiral of depression and decay. The result is uneven regional concentrations of wealth, power and influence.

There are, however, limits to continuous centralisation through agglomeration. Overcrowding and rising pollution, administrative and maintenance costs (rising tax rates and user fees) take a toll. Rising local costs of living lead to wage demands that may ultimately make a region uncompetitive. Labour may become better organised in its struggles against exploitation because of its regional concentration. Land and property prices escalate as a rentier class cashes in on their command over increasingly scarce land. New York City and San Francisco are dynamic but high-cost locations, while Detroit and Pittsburgh now are not. Labour is better organised in Los Angeles now than it is in Detroit (in the 1960s it was the other way round).

When local costs rise rapidly, capitalists look for other spaces in the global economy to ply their trade. This is particularly so when new technological and production mixes are emerging and labour struggles are acute. From the late 1960s onwards, for example, Silicon Valley steadily displaced Detroit as an epicentre of the US capitalist economy. Bavaria likewise displaced the Ruhr in Germany and Tuscany displaced Turin in Italy, while new global players like Singapore, Hong Kong, Taiwan, South Korea and, eventually, China moved far ahead in the global stakes for competitive pre-eminence in certain lines of production. These moves generated crises of devaluation that reverberated throughout other regions of the global labourers are reproduced in Mexico but end up working in the fields of California, women workers raised in the Philippines play a large part in furnishing domestic labour in New York City, mathematical engineers trained under communism in what was once the Soviet Union end up in Cape Canaveral, while software engineers educated in India go to Seattle.

Social reproduction is not only about labour skills and the organisation of consumer habits. 'The reproduction of the labour force calls forth a range of cultural forms and practices that are also geographically and historically specific,' says Katz, and this includes all those associated with knowledge and learning, mental conceptions of the world, ethical and aesthetic judgements, relations to nature, cultural mores and values, as well as the sense of belonging that underpins loyalties to place, region and nation. Social reproduction also inculcates 'the practices that maintain and reinforce class and other categories of difference' and 'a set of cultural forms and practices that works to reinforce and naturalize the dominant social relations of production and reproduction'. Through these social practices 'social actors become members of a culture they simultaneously help to create and construct their identities within and against'.

'The questions of social reproduction are,' concludes Katz, 'vexed and slippery, but the arena of social reproduction is where much of the toll of globalized capitalist production can be witnessed.'[10] It is the field where the creative destruction of capital is at its most insidious, promoting, as it does, an alien consumerism and individualistic ways of life conducive to what amounts to little more than crass and competitive selfish greed, while pinning responsibility on its victims for their own plight when they fail (as they inevitably must) to build up their own supposedly human capital. It is the sphere where the reproduction of inequality begins and, lacking any powerful subsequent counterforce, ends. In the United States, for example, social mobility is almost at a standstill, so everything rests on a social reproduction process that is highly unequal and tightly channelled, if not outright discriminatory. Where once upon a time the populace at large fended for itself to reproduce itself without one economy. The Midwest 'rust belt' that was once the heart of industrial capital in the USA contrasts with a rising 'sun belt'. Regional crises of employment and production typically signal crucial moments when power shifts are occurring within the forces producing the geographical landscape of capital. This, in turn, usually signals a radical shift in the evolution of capital itself.

Capital must be able to withstand the shock of the destruction of the old and stand ready to build a new geographical landscape on its ashes. Surpluses of capital and labour must be available for this purpose. Fortunately, capital, by its very nature, perpetually creates such surpluses, often in the form of mass unemployment of labour and an overaccumulation of capital. The absorption of these surpluses through geographical expansion and spatial reorganisation helps resolve the problem of surpluses lacking profitable outlets. Urbanisation and regional development become autonomous spheres of capitalist activity, requiring large investments (usually debt-financed) that take many years to mature.

Capital typically turns to these avenues for the absorption of capital and labour surpluses at times of crisis. State-funded infrastructural projects are set in motion during crises to re-kindle economic growth. The US government tried to mop up surplus capital and unemployed labour in the 1930s by setting up future-oriented public works projects in hitherto undeveloped locations. Some 8 million people were employed in the WPA programmes in the 1930s in the United States. The Nazis built the autobahns in Germany for similar reasons at the same time. The Chinese, after the financial crash of 2008, spent billions on urban and infrastructural projects to absorb surpluses of both capital and labour in order to compensate for the crash in export markets. Whole new cities were designed and built. The Chinese landscape has been radically and dramatically transformed as a result.

In this way, capital develops what I call 'spatio-temporal fixes' to the capital and labour surplus absorption problem.[2] 'Fix' here has a double meaning. A certain portion of the total capital gets fixed literally and physically in and on the land for a relatively long period of time. But 'fix' also refers metaphorically to how long-term invest-ments in geographical expansions provide a solution (a 'fix') for crises of overaccumulation of capital. So how and when do these two meanings collide?

The organisation of new territorial divisions of labour, of new resource complexes and of new regions as dynamic spaces of capital accumulation all provide new opportunities to generate profits and to absorb surpluses of capital and labour. Such geographical expansions often threaten, however, the values already fixed in place elsewhere. This contradiction is inescapable. Either capital moves out and leaves behind a trail of devastation and devaluation (for example, Detroit). Or it stays put only to drown in the capital surpluses it inevitably produces but cannot find profitable outlets for.

Resort to credit financing heightens this contradiction at the same time as it purports to solve it. Credit makes territories vulnerable to flows of speculative capital that can both stimulate and undermine capitalist development. Territorial indebtedness became a global problem after 1980 or so, and many of the poorer countries (and even some major powers, like Russia in 1998 and Argentina after 2001) found it impossible to repay their debts. Many poor countries, like Ecuador and even Poland (behind the Iron Curtain), were lured into becoming 'sinks' for surplus capitals for which they were then held liable. The indebted country has to bear the cost of any subsequent devaluation of capital while the creditor country is protected. The resources of indebted countries can then be plundered under the draconian rules of debt repayment. The current case of Greece is a horrible example of this process carried to extremes. The bondhold-ers are prepared to rip to shreds and feed relentlessly upon whole states that have been rash enough to fall into their clutches.

The export of capital typically has longer-term effects relative to the movement of 'hot' credit moneys. Surpluses of capital and labour are sent elsewhere to set capital accumulation in motion in the new regional space. Surpluses of British capital and labour generated in the nineteenth century found their way to the United States and to the settler colonies, like South Africa, Australia and Canada, creating new and dynamic centres of accumulation which generated a demand for goods from Britain.

Since it may take many years for capitalism to mature in these new territories (if it ever does) to the point where they too begin to produce surpluses of capital, the originating country can hope to benefit from this process for a not inconsiderable period of time. This is particularly the case with investments in railways, roads, ports, dams and other infrastructures that mature slowly. But the rate of return on these investments eventually depends upon the evolution of a strong dynamic of accumulation in the receiving region. Britain lent to the United States in this way during the nineteenth century. Much later, the United States, via the Marshall Plan for Europe (West Germany in particular) and Japan, clearly saw that its own economic security (leaving aside the military aspect of the Cold War) rested on the active revival of capitalist activity in these other spaces.

Contradictions arise because these new dynamic spaces of capital accumulation ultimately generate surpluses and need to find ways to absorb them through further geographical expansions. This can spark geopolitical conflicts and tensions. In recent times we have witnessed cascading and proliferating spatio-temporal fixes primarily through-out East and South-East Asia. Surplus capital from Japan started to course around the world in the 1970s in search of profitable outlets, followed shortly thereafter by surplus capital from South Korea and then Taiwan in the mid-1980s. While these cascading spatio-temporal fixes are recorded as relationships between territories, they are in fact material and social relations between regions within territories. The formal territorial difficulties between Taiwan and mainland China appear anachronistic beside the growing integration of the industrial regions of Taipei and Shanghai.

Capital flows from time to time get redirected from one space to another. The capitalist system remains relatively stable as a whole, even though the parts experience periodic difficulties (such as dein-dustrialisation here or partial devaluations there). The overall effect of such interregional volatility is to temporarily reduce the aggregate dangers of overaccumulation and devaluation even though localised distress may be acute. The regional volatility experienced since 1980 or so seems to have largely been of this type. At each step, of course, the issue arises as to which will be the next space into which capital can profitably flow and why and which will be the next space to be abandoned and devalued. The general effect can be misleading: since capital is always doing well somewhere, the illusion arises that all will be well everywhere if we only readjust the form of capital to that predominant in Japan and West Germany (the 1980s), the United States (the 1990s) or China (after 2000). Capital never has to address its systemic failings because it moves them around geographically.

A second possible outcome, however, is increasingly fierce international competition within the international division of labour as multiple dynamic centres of capital accumulation compete on the world stage in the midst of strong currents of overaccumulation (lack of markets for realisation) or under conditions of competing scarcities for raw materials and other key means of production. Since they cannot all succeed, either the weakest succumb and fall into serious crises of localised devaluation or geopolitical struggles arise between regions and states. The latter take the form of trade wars, currency and resource wars, with the ever-present danger of military confrontations (of the sort that gave us two world wars between capitalist powers in the twentieth century). In this case, the spatio-temporal fix takes on a much more sinister meaning as it transmutes into the export of localised and regional devaluations and destruction of capital (of the sort that occurred on a massive scale in East and South-East Asia and in Russia in 1997–8). How and when this occurs will depend, however, just as much upon the explicit forms of political action on the part of state powers as it does upon the molecular processes of capital accumulation in space and time. The dialectic between the territorial logic and the capitalistic logic is then fully engaged.

So how does the relative spatial fixity and distinctive logic of territorial power (as manifest in the state) fit with the fluid dynamics of capital accumulation in space and time? Is this not the locus of an acute and abiding contradiction for capital, perhaps the apogee of the contradiction between fixity (the state) and motion (capital)? Recall: 'In order for capital to circulate freely in space and time, physical infrastructures and built environments must be created that are fixed in space.' The mass of all this fixed capital increases over time relative to the capital that is continuously flowing. Capital has periodically to break out of the constraints imposed by the world it has constructed. It is in mortal danger of becoming sclerotic. The building of a geographical landscape favourable to capital accumulation in one era becomes, in short, a fetter upon accumulation in the next. Capital has therefore to devalue much of the fixed capital in the existing geographical landscape in order to build a wholly new landscape in a different image. This sparks intense and destructive localised crises. The most obvious contemporary example of such devaluation in the USA is Detroit. But many older industrial cities in all the advanced capitalist countries and beyond (even north China and Mumbai) have had to remake themselves as their economic bases have been eroded by competition from elsewhere. The principle here is this: capital creates a geographical landscape that meets its needs at one point in time only to have to destroy it at a later point in time to facilitate capital's further expansion and qualitative transformation. Capital unleashes the powers of 'creative destruction' upon the land. Some factions benefit from the creativity, while others suffer the brunt of the destruction. Invariably, this involves a class disparity.

So where is state power in all of this and by what distinctive logic does it intervene in processes of landscape formation? The state is a bounded territorial entity formed under conditions that had little to do with capital but which is a fundamental feature of the geographical landscape. Within its territory it has a monopoly of the legitimate use of violence, sovereignty over the law and the currency, and regulatory authority over institutions (including private property), and it is blessed with the power to tax and redistribute incomes and assets. It organises structures of administration and governance that at the very minimum address the collective needs of both capital and, more diffusely, the state's citizens. Among its sovereign powers perhaps the most important is defining and conferring rights of citizenship under the law upon its inhabitants and thereby introducing the category of illegal alien or 'sans-papiers' into the equation. This creates a separate population vulnerable to unthinkable and unrestricted exploitation by capital. As a bounded entity, the question of how the state's borders were established and how they are patrolled in relation to the movements of people, commodities and money becomes paramount. The two spatialities of state and capital sit awkwardly with and frequently contradict each other. This is very clear in the case, for example, of migration policies.

The interests of the capitalist state are not the same as those of capital. The state is not a simple thing and its various branches do not always cohere, although key institutions within the state do typically play a directly supportive role in the management of capital's economy (with treasury departments usually in alliance with central banks to constitute the state–finance nexus). The governance of the state depends upon the nature of its political system, which sometimes pretends to be democratic and is often influenced by the dynamics of class and other social struggles. The practices that constitute the exercise of state powers are far from monolithic or even coherent, which means that the state cannot be construed as a solid 'thing' exercising distinctive powers. It is a bundle of practices and processes assembled together in unbounded ways since the distinction between the state and civil society (for example, in a field like education, health care or housing) is highly porous. Capital is not the only interest to which the state must respond and the pressures upon it come from a variety of interests. Furthermore, the ruling ideology behind state interventions (usually expressed as an economic and policy orthodoxy) can vary considerably. There is, also, an interstate system. Relations among states can be hostile or collaborative as the case may be, but there are always geo-economic and geopolitical relations and conflicts that reflect the state's distinctive interests and lead state practices into forms of action that may or may not be consistent with capital's interests.

The logic that attaches to the territoriality of state power is very different from the logic of capital. The state is, among other things, interested in the accumulation of wealth and power on a territorial basis and it was Adam Smith's genius to advise and generally persuade statesmen that the best way to do this was to unleash and rationalise the forces of capital and the free market within its territory and open its doors to free trade with others. The capitalist state is one that broadly follows pro-business policies, albeit tempered by ruling ideologies and the innumerable and divergent social pressures mobilised through the organisation of its citizens. But it also seeks to rationalise and use the forces of capital to support its own powers of governmentality over potentially restive populations, all the while enhancing its own wealth, power and standing within a highly competitive interstate system. This rationality contrasts with that of capital, which is primarily concerned with the private appropriation and accumulation of social wealth. The constructed loyalty of citizens to their states conflicts in principle with capital's singular loyalty to making money and nothing else.

The kind of rationality the state typically imposes is illustrated by its urban and regional planning practices. These state interventions and investments attempt to contain the otherwise chaotic consequences of unregulated market development. The state imposes Cartesian structures of administration, law, taxation and individual identification. The technocratic and bureaucratic production of space in the name of a supposedly capitalist modernity has been, however, the focus of virulent critiques (most notably that of Henri Lefebvre[3]). What tends to be produced is a soulless, rationalised geographical landscape against which populations periodically revolt. But the application of state powers to these purposes never did run smooth. They are all too easily subverted, co-opted and corrupted by moneyed interests. Conversely, the foundational interests of the state in, for example, the case of national security can be subverted by capital and turned into a permanent feeding trough for capitalist ambitions – hence the historical role of the infamous 'military–industrial complex' in the development of capital.

States can use their powers to orchestrate economic life not only through their command over infrastructural investments but also through their powers to create or reform basic institutions. When, for example, local banking was supplanted by national banks in Britain and France in the nineteenth century, the free flow of money capital across the national space altered regional dynamics. More recently, the abolition in the United States of restrictive local banking laws, followed by a wave of takeovers and mergers of regional banks, changed the whole investment climate in the country away from local and into a more open and fluid construction of regional configurations. Reforms in the organisation of international banking coupled with information technologies have over the last forty years revolutionised the global mobility of finance capital.

There has been a long-standing impulse towards the transformation of the geographical scale at which capitalist activity gets defined. Just as the coming of the railways and the telegraph in the nineteenth century completely reorganised the scale and diversity of regional specialisations, so the more recent round of innovations (everything from jet transport, containerisation and the internet) has changed the scales at which economic activity gets articulated. In the 1980s much was made of the 'global car', with parts produced almost anywhere in the world being assembled rather than produced at the final factory. This is now normal practice in many lines of production so that labels like 'made in the USA' no longer make much sense. The corporate shift to the global scale is far more emphatic now than it was in the past.

The sovereign powers of the state over capital and money flows have definitively been eroded over the last few decades. This does not mean the state is powerless, but rather that its power is more contingent on that of finance capital and the bondholders. State powers and practices have been more and more directed to satisfying the demands of corporations and bondholders, often at the expense of citizens. This entails strong state support for the creation of a good business climate favourable to capital. The result in many instances is that states can be doing very well while their populations fare poorly. This even applies, somewhat surprisingly, to countries like Germany, where wage repression contains working-class consumption at the same time as German-based capital and the country's financial state look to be in very good shape.

Changes in the molecular movement of capital are also putting strong pressures upon the scale at which state power might be constructed. Political reterritorialisations such as the European Union become not only more practicable but more and more of an economic necessity. These political shifts are not a simple function of material transformations in space relations: matters are far more complicated than that. But changing space relations on the part of capital circulation and accumulation do have transformative implications for the new political configurations (for example, the formation of NAFTA, Mercosur, the European Union, as well as the expansion of what used to be the G7 to the G20 as a decision-making body).

The geographical landscape of capitalism (as opposed to that of capital) is plainly shaped by a multitude of interests as individuals and groups seek to define spaces and places for themselves against the background of the macroeconomic processes of uneven geographical development that the rules of capital accumulation and state power jointly effect. Capital has to be somewhat sensitive to the wants and needs of the populations it exploits, of course, and even if it were not, social and class struggles would surely force it to the table to compromise with critics and tamp down on some of its wilder ambitions. It is, however, all too easy to blame the victims for what happens when capital leaves town. The ruling narrative is that it was greedy unions, profligate politicians, bad managers and the like who forced capital out. But it was capital and not people that abandoned and deindustrialised Detroit, Pittsburgh, Sheffield, Manchester, Mumbai and the like. While there have been obvious examples of mismanagement and heightened class conflicts in this or that region or city, it is preposterous to claim that these can account for the total devastation of industrial regions that had for generations been the backbone of capital accumulation in so many different parts of the world. For this we have to thank the neoliberal counter-revolution that began in the 1970s and has intensified to this day.

Uneven geographical developments conveniently mask the true

nature of capital. Hope can spring eternal because there is always a successful neighbourhood, region or state where things are going right even in the midst of multiple calamities. Macro crises get disaggregated into localised events that others elsewhere care or even know very little about. Major crises in Indonesia or Argentina pass by but the rest of the world says 'Too bad' or 'So what?' Particular rather than systemic explanations of crises dominate thinking. Argentina, Greece or Detroit should reform their ways, it is said, but capital gets off scot-free.

There is something else remarkable about the landscape of capital that plays a vital ideological role in contemporary life and politics. The capitalist city, for example, is built as a work of art in its own right, replete with fabulous architecture and competing iconic meanings. The mansions and penthouses of the 'masters of the universe' working now in palatial offices in gleaming skyscrapers in global financial centres contrast with the older industrial architecture of the traditional factories. Spectacular palaces of consumerism and the perpetual creation of postmodern urban spectacle contrast with suburban sprawl and gated communities, which in turn contrast with tenement housing, working-class and immigrant neighbourhoods and, in many cities of the world, large tracts of self-help housing. The capitalist city is the high point of capital's attempt to appear civilised and to represent the grandest of human aspirations.

There is a sense in which this claim is effective. We can marvel at the product and admire the views of Paris, Barcelona, Hong Kong and Shanghai in part because this urban spectacle hides the processes and the human labour that went into its production. Capital does not, apparently, want to have its own distinctive image. Judging from anti-capitalist cartoons, it would be far from flattering! The city landscape of capitalism exists as a diversionary image of another world closer to some transcendental sense of human longing and desire. To look upon Venice, Rome, Istanbul, San Francisco, Brasilia, Cairo or Lagos is to look upon the hopes, achievements and chronic failures of that human endeavour. And it is not only the great cities that we are talking of here. The different rural landscapes that have been carved out around the world can inspire as much affection, loyalty and admiration as any city. The English countryside, the French *paysage*, the Tuscan villages, the Argentinian pampas, the rolling plains of the Tigris valley in Anatolia, the endless cornfields of Iowa, the soya bean plantations of Brazil, all form palimpsests of the human endeavour increasingly though by no means uniquely mobilised by and for capital.

How powerful a force has uneven geographical development been for challenging capital to reinvent itself? Without uneven geographical development capital would surely have stagnated, succumbed to its sclerotic, monopolistic and autocratic tendencies and totally lost legitimacy as the dynamic engine of a society that has pretences to being civilised even as it is in danger of heading towards barbarism. Unleashing interurban, interregional and international competition is not only a primary means whereby the new comes to supplant the old, but a context in which the search for the new, billed as the search for competitive advantage, becomes critical to capital's capacity to reproduce itself. Above all, uneven geographical development serves to move capital's systemic failings around from place to place. Those failings are a perpetually moving target.

The homogeneity now being imposed by an international order dominated by the central banks and a few international institutions, such as the IMF, is from this perspective potentially devastating for capital's future chances of survival. Capital could not long survive the advent of a strong centralised global government unless, as has happened in China, that government not only orchestrated but liberated interregional and interurban competition. Given the constraints now imposed upon them by the international disciplinary apparatus, there is no chance that Greece, Portugal, Spain and Italy can rise from the ashes as did West Germany and Japan after the Second World War to reinvigorate the capitalist dynamic. They may recover somewhat, but it cannot be anything other than an anaemic recovery. Whether unchaining uneven geographical development can today work by itself as a panacea for capital's malaise is doubtful, given the storm clouds of systemic stagnation that are gathering strength and darkening the future. Instead, we see an emergent unholy alliance between state powers and the predatory aspects of finance capital to create a form of 'vulture capitalism' that is as much about cannibalistic practices (economies of dispossession) and forced devaluations as it is about achieving harmonious global development. The vultures, like the hedge funds and the private equity funds, will feed off the destruction of ways of life in whole territories if necessary.

Capital survives not only through a series of spatio-temporal fixes that absorb the capital surpluses in productive and constructive ways, but also through the devaluation and destruction administered as corrective medicine to those who fail to keep up and who fail to pay off their debts. The very idea that those who irresponsibly lend should also be at risk is, of course, dismissed out of hand. That would require calling the wealthy property-owning classes everywhere to account and insisting that they look to their responsibilities rather than to their inalienable rights to private property and accumulation without limit. The sinister and destructive side of spatio-temporal fixes (just look at how Greece is being pillaged and devastated) becomes just as crucial to capital as its creative counterpart in building a new landscape to facilitate the endless accumulation of capital and the endless accumulation of political power.

So what, then, should an anti-capitalist movement make of all this? It is first vital to recognise that capital is always a moving target for opposition because of its uneven geographical development. Any anti-capitalist movement has to learn to cope with this. Oppositional movements in one space have often been defanged because capital moved to another. Anti-capitalist movements must abandon all thoughts of regional equality and convergence around some theory of socialist harmony. These are recipes for an unacceptable and unachievable global monotony. Anti-capitalist movements have to liberate and coordinate their own dynamics of uneven geographical development, the production of emancipatory spaces of difference, in order to reinvent and explore creative regional alternatives to capital. Different social movements and resistances are emerging from within the framework of capital's uneven geographical development, from Stockholm and Cairo to São Paulo, Shanghai, Paris and London. These constitute a mosaic of different but loosely interconnected seedbeds for transformations of capitalism towards an anticapitalist future. How they might be put together is the question. We live in chaotic and volatile times, particularly with respect to uneven geographical developments. It is not unreasonable to expect that resistances and oppositions will be equally chaotic, volatile and geographically specific.

# Contradiction 12
# Disparities of Income and Wealth

An analysis of the Internal Revenue Service income tax returns for New York City in 2012 showed that the average income of the top 1 per cent in that year was $3.57 million, while half of the population in this extremely high-rent and high-cost-of-living city were trying to get by on $30,000 a year or less. In three days the ultra rich made more money than most New Yorkers made in a year. By any standards, this level of income inequality is astonishing, surely making New York City one of the most unequal cities in the world. On the other hand these figures should not surprise anyone, given the enormous earnings of the leading hedge fund managers (five of whom earned, in the wake of the crisis, more than $3 billion each in 2009) and the huge bonuses customarily doled out by the leading banks in the city. Nationally, as might be expected, the income disparities are nowhere near as dramatic, even though they had been increasing markedly since the 1970s or so.

There is no point here in attempting anything other than a highly simplifed account of aggregate global trends in inequalities of wealth and income. Struggles over distribution of the social wealth have been incessant throughout the history of capitalism. Outcomes have varied greatly from one state, region or city to another, as different groups have struggled for advantage against others as well as against dominant groups and classes for what they regard as their fair and proper share of the product of social labour. Given the powers of the state to extract taxes and to redistribute wealth and income, much has depended on which faction or political alliance holds state power and what it does with it.

Struggles over distributional shares have often been fierce and the outcomes hard to predict. In the wake of a coup, such as that which occurred in Chile in 1973, it was to be expected that distributional shares would shift dramatically towards greater inequality as the elites that backed the coup cashed in. In Russia, a small band of oligarchs collared, in an astonishing act of pillage, most of the natural resource wealth of the country after the collapse of 1989. The ex-Soviet Union now boasts one of the highest concentrations of billionaires – an authentic oligarchy – in the world. In Britain after 1945, however, a Labour government built a welfare state that supported the least affluent for a whole generation, much as the Scandinavians had done before them. The strong influence of communism during the Cold War over social policies in the capitalist world, coupled with strong social democratic impulses within that world (deriving from a history of working-class organisation and a sharpened class consciousness), meant capitalist states in general had to put a floor under conditions of life for whole populations. The welfare state that resulted was far from being socialist. It had strong elements of gender bias and was paternalistic and even pro-capitalist to the extent that it became demeaning, punitive and bureaucratic in its approach to its own clientele. To be a ward of the welfare state was more often than not unpleasant and inhuman, even as some state benefits (like social security and old age pensions) brought more security to everyone. This was the kind of state that was criticised by the progressive left and then later obligingly abolished during the Thatcherite neoliberal counter-revolution of the 1980s. The collapse of communism in 1989 removed the external pressure on states to either look to the well-being of their populations or face strong political opposition.

Even in the absence of such dramatic realignments, the to and fro of social struggles between classes and ethnic/racial groupings, along with the fluctuating conditions of boom and slump in the economy, have impacts on distributional arrangements that vary a great deal from one part of the world to another. The distribution of income and wealth in Nordic countries, for example, has until recently been much more egalitarian than that in the United States, even before the Reagan revolution started to shift the balance of concern away from labour and the poor towards subsidising and rewarding capital. But both the USA and Sweden are solidly capitalist. Capital seems to work just fine in a variety of distributional settings.

This variability and adaptability of capital to complex configurations of distribution does double duty when inserted into the incredible complexity and diversity of social groupings that can exist throughout capitalism in general. Gender, sexual, racial, ethnic, religious, cultural, national and place-bound distinctions are everywhere in evidence and questions of status, skills, talents, respect and admiration for achievements and values confer differential opportunities and life chances both for individuals and for distinctive ethnic, racial, sexual and religious social groups within capitalist social formations. To the degree that these characteristics are associated with differential access to and remunerations in, for example, labour markets, wide-ranging differentiations in economic and political power result.

Not all economic distinctions within capitalism are attributable to capital. But neither is capital innocent when it comes to fomenting conflict within and among social groups. This is one of the crucial levers it has to consolidate its control over labour. On the other hand capital often appears indifferent as to which particular social differentiations to support and which to discriminate against. It tends to support whatever form of social emancipation gains traction (such as gay rights and multiculturalism in recent years) provided that this does not challenge overall strategies of labour control and provided that it forms a distinctive niche market to be exploited. But the fact that these social distinctions take on economic and material forms leads inevitably to fierce competition over distributional shares among social groups within a population. We are here positioned at one of those key and sometimes confusing and confounding points of interaction where capital and capitalism cannot be kept clearly asunder. This is particularly the case with regards to questions of race. Racial issues in many parts of the world (such as the United States) have long been so intertwined with questions of class as to make the two mutually reinforcing if not sometimes indistinguishable categories.

A good deal also depends on dominant ideas as to what might constitute 'just' or 'ethically acceptable' disparities in wealth and income and by what means injustices might be rectified. Concerns of this sort are not confined to workers alone. There has been a long tradition of bourgeois reformism in which the presence of appalling misery and poverty, even when it is no threat to public health (as it was in cholera epidemics that did not stop at class boundaries), is judged unacceptable in any civilised society. Polls repeatedly show, for example, that most Americans have strong egalitarian views and that they are committed not only to equality of opportunities (as the right wing ritualistically maintains) but also to equality of outcomes. In a 2005 survey of more than 5,000 people in the United States, the respondents, irrespective of political party or of income, said they believed on average that the top 20 per cent should own no more than 32 per cent of the wealth. When shown (without attribution) the wealth distribution from Sweden (where 38 per cent of the wealth is held by the top 20 per cent) and parallel data from the United States (where 84 per cent of the wealth is held by the top 20 per cent), 92 per cent of respondents preferred the Swedish distribution. The repondents, it turned out, had little or no idea of what the actual distribution of wealth in the USA actually was. They believed that the top 20 per cent controlled 58 per cent of the wealth rather than the 84 per cent which was actually the case. Either way, this was a far cry from the 32 per cent they thought would be fair.[1]

So why is there so little political movement in the USA to rectify this lopsided distribution in the face of their beliefs as to what should be? The answer mainly lies in the intense popular hostility towards state interventions. This prevents the one institution capable of rectifying income and wealth disparities from doing very much about it. In the debate over Obama's health care law, for example, Republicans did not oppose the principle of universal access to decent health care, but violently denounced the right of the 'nanny' state to mandate it or to mandate individual behaviours. And so it goes with any tax proposals to redistribute from the rich to the poor. In recent times the redistributions have actually been in the other direction in the name of austerity, budget deficit reduction, tax cutting and mandating a smaller and less intrusive government. It is hard not to conclude that capital's intense interest in putting a downward pressure on wages lies behind these budgetary and fiscal manoeuvres.

Struggles over the distribution of wealth and income are not the only kinds of distributional struggles that matter. Struggles for recognition, respect, true equality before the law, over citizenship rights and cultural and religious freedoms, over proper political representations, educational opportunities and access to job opportunities and even over the right to be lazy are ongoing. Many of these struggles are collectively waged by particular segments of the population seeking redress or advantage as the case may be (for example, women, LGBT groups, racial, ethnic or religious minorities, senior citizens, trade unions, chambers of commerce, to say nothing of the social and political institutions that seek to defend the interests of labour). The flux and flow of these social struggles produces diverse outcomes, many of which have side implications for the distribution of wealth and income. Access to educational opportunity, for example, has clear impacts on future income distributions.

Capitalism, taken as a whole, is riven with such conflicts and struggles. But the questions I wish to pose here are far narrower. In what ways does capital, understood as the organisation of the economic engine of capital circulation and accumulation, rest upon certain basic principles for the distribution of wealth and income? Are the identifiable large-scale shifts in income distributions that have occurred over the last forty years attributable to the way the internal contradictions of capital have been reconfigured? Finally, does the plainly intensifying contradiction between poverty and wealth pose a threat to the reproduction of capital?

The statistical evidence confirms the adaptability of capital to wildly disparate distributional arrangements. But while there clearly is no unique distribution of income and wealth that might be considered optimal from the standpoint of the reproduction and growth of capital, no one believes that perfect equality of distribution is possible. It has been suggested, on the other hand, that grossly lopsided

distributions might spell trouble not only because of the social instability and unrest they may provoke (a fear the IMF and the Davos
conferences of the global capitalist elites frequently invoke), but
because the historical evidence suggests gross inequalities might be
a harbinger of a macroeconomic crisis to come. This is so because the
contradictory unity between production and realisation becomes far
harder to keep in balance when realisation depends on the vagaries
and discretionary habits of wealthy people as opposed to the solid
and reliable non-discretionary demands of the working poor. The
last time the USA experienced equivalent levels of inequality to those
now prevailing was the 1920s and this clearly played an important
role in fomenting if not triggering the depression of the 1930s. The
situation today seems broadly comparable. Can we hope to get out
of the current stagnation without radically reordering distributional
arrangements?

Consider some recent trends in distribution. An Oxfam media
briefing offers the following capsule description:

> Over the last thirty years inequality has grown dramatically in
> many countries. In the US the share of national income going
> to the top 1% has doubled since 1980 from 10 to 20%. For the
> top 0.01% it has quadrupled to levels never seen before. At the
> global level, the top 1% (60 million people) and particularly for
> the more select few in the top 0.01% (600,000 individuals – there
> are around 1200 billionaires in the world) the last thirty years has
> been an incredible feeding frenzy. This is not confined to the US,
> or indeed to the rich countries. In the UK inequality is rapidly
> returning to levels not seen since the time of Charles Dickens.
> In China, the top 10% now take home nearly 60% of the income.
> Chinese inequality levels are now similar to those in South Africa,
> [the most unequal country on earth, where incomes are] signifi-
> cantly more unequal than at the end of apartheid. Even in many of
> the poorest countries, inequality has grown rapidly. Globally the
> incomes of the top 1% have increased 60% in twenty years. The
> growth in income for the top 0.01% has been even greater.

The crisis of 2007–9 onwards made matters worse: 'The top 100 billionaires added $240 billion to their wealth in 2012 – enough to end world poverty four times over.'[2] Billionaires have erupted all over the place, with large numbers now recorded in Russia, India, China, Brazil and Mexico, as well as in the more traditionally wealthy countries in North America, Europe and Japan. One of the more significant shifts is that the ambitious no longer have to migrate to the affluent countries to become billionaires – they can simply stay at home in India (where the number of billionaires has more than doubled over the last few years), Indonesia or wherever. As Branko Milanovic concludes, we are witnessing the rise of a global plutocracy in which global power 'is held by a relatively small number of very rich people.'[3] The threat to the contradictory unity between production and realisation in the global economy is palpable.

Yet by other measures the world is a much more equal place than it once was. Millions of people have escaped from poverty. Much of this has been due to the phenomenal growth of China, along with substantial bursts of growth in the other so-called BRIC countries (Brazil, Russia and India). Disparities in the global distribution of wealth and income *between* countries have been much reduced with rising per capita incomes in many developing parts of the world. The net drain of wealth from East to West that had prevailed for over two centuries has been reversed as East Asia in particular has risen to prominence as a powerhouse in the global economy. The recovery of the global economy (anaemic though it was) from the traumas of 2007–9 had largely been based by 2013 on the rapid expansions in so-called 'emerging' markets (mainly the BRIC countries). This shift had even extended to Africa, which was the one part of the world that seemed to have escaped almost entirely from any effects of the crisis. The uneven impact of the crisis within Europe, however, meant rapidly widening disparities in economic well-being between southern and northern countries. But none of these trends seemed very stable. At the mere mention of a shift in Federal Reserve monetary policy in mid-2013, for example, there was an immediate outflow of capital from emerging markets such that the latter went into a swoon, only to revive when the Fed announced it was rethinking its policies.

There has been a double movement over the last forty years: on the one hand a general trend towards a levelling up in per capita wealth and incomes across states (apart from those, like Greece, hit hard by the recent crisis) and on the other dramatic increases in income and wealth disparities among individuals and social groups in almost every country of the world. Very few states or regions have bucked this trend and for the most part in backwaters of the global economy (for example, a country like Bhutan or, for a while, the state of Kerala in India). Only in Latin America have we seen some reductions in social inequality as a result of state policies. Disparities in monetary wealth are far harder to get a handle on compared to incomes. But in some respects monetary wealth is more important, since it has a long-standing rather than a volatile relation to political power. The monetary measure of wealth is difficult because the valuation of certain assets – everything from art collections to expensive jewellery and property – is often a matter of guesswork and in any case fluctuates wildly, as in the case of the market value of stocks and shares. In most countries the distribution of monetary wealth seems even more lopsided than the distribution of incomes.

Why these general global trends? Has there been something going on within the contradictory evolution of capital that would make them inevitable, or even necessary for the survival and reproduction of capital? Do increasingly lopsided wealth and income distributions within so many countries signal the existence of a moving contradiction and, if so, what sort of movement is it (for example, cyclical or linear)? Does this movement account for rising levels of unrest and social instability (as witnessed in 2013 from Stockholm to Istanbul and a hundred or so cities in Brazil)? Is it a harbinger of a grumbling and still unfolding macroeconomic crisis?

To answer these questions requires first that we establish how inequality is foundational for capital. The inequality derives from the simple fact that capital is socially and historically constructed as a class in dominance over labour. The distribution of income and of wealth between capital and labour has to be lopsided if capital is to be reproduced. Distributional equality and capital are incompatible. Certain distributional disparities actually precede the rise of capital. Workers must be dispossessed of ownership and control over their own means of production if they are to be forced into wage labour in order to live. This distributional condition precedes the production of surplus value and it must be maintained over time. Once capital circulation and accumulation become general, the wage level has to be kept within limits that permit profit making. Any drive to maximise profits means driving down wage rates or increasing labour productivity. Fierce competition between capitals leads to a general reduction in wages no matter whether individual capitalists will it or not. The distributional share between wages and profits is a product of some mix of labour scarcities and the state of class struggle. The resultant configuration is geographically uneven.

A sufficient share of the total output of social value must flow to the capitalist class to (a) incentivise the capitalists by showering them with conditions of consumption worthy of some leisure class and (b) provide them with sufficient surplus to keep the economic engine of capital working and expanding powerfully and smoothly. The 'Faustian dilemma' that lurks within the breast of every capitalist between personal enjoyment and reinvestment can be resolved only with considerable surplus generation and appropriation. A disproportionate amount of the surplus must always flow to capital at the expense of labour. This is the only way for capital to be reproduced.

The superior economic resources that accrue to capital allow it and it alone to invest and create jobs in a purely capitalist economy. This provides the right-wing rationale for public policies (taxation arrangements in particular) that favour capital over labour. While the uneven income distribution may appear unfair, it is said, it actually is advantageous to labour because capital is in command of job creation and the more the capitalist class possesses the more job creation there will be. Unfortunately, this is not the whole story. Capital reinvests in job creation only when that activity is profitable. The last three recessions in the United States have been followed by jobless recoveries because profitable opportunities were lacking even though wage rates were falling and labour surpluses were everywhere in evidence. Capital either 'warehoused' its cash or used its surplus incomes for speculative gains on the stock market, in property, in asset purchases (resources and land in particular) or in playing a casino game with new and unstable financial instruments. If it invested in production at all, it was more likely to invest in labour-saving technologies that increased unemployment rather than in job creation.

Meanwhile, the increasing concentration and centralisation of incomes and wealth within a capitalist class permitted it to exercise disproportionate influence and control over the media (public opinion) and the capitalist state apparatus. Capital procured privileged access to protection by a state which claims a monopoly over the legitimate use of violence and a monopoly over the means of money creation. It uses these privileges to protect its interests and perpetuate its power. Central banks always bail out banks but they never bail out the people. This is what the drift towards the formation of a global plutocracy and the incredible increases in the disparity of wealth and income in most countries around the world signal.

On the other side of the class divide, the neediness of workers accounts for very little or nothing as far as capital is concerned, except when the total aggregate demand exercised by workers is insufficient for the realisation of capital accumulation in the market. Capital is most immediately interested in keeping wage rates as low as possible. This defines a central contradiction, as we earlier saw, between realisation and production. The capitalist ability to manage the wage rate rests upon the availability of an 'industrial reserve army' of surplus workers. The function of this reserve is to supply the labour power required for future expansion of capital while acting as a dead weight upon the aspirations of those already employed as they struggle to improve rates of remuneration and working conditions. The industrial reserve army is of two sorts. First, there are the unemployed workers. Technological changes that enhance labour productivity produce layoffs and unemployment. Capital thus acquires considerable power over the supply of surplus labour at the same time as it manages its own level of demand. In other words, capital is committed as much to the production of unemployment as it is to job creation. Providing tax incentives to capital to reinvest can just as easily lead to the elimination of jobs as to their creation (a fact that is rarely mentioned in political discussions on the subject even though it is as plain as a pikestaff to any worker who has been laid off for technological reasons).

Second, there were and still are latent reserves in the form of extensive peasant populations, the self-employed, women and children who have yet to be subjected to wage labour. The recent vast increase of wage labour in China has entailed a transformation of this kind. Africa still constitutes a vast potential reserve of labour that has yet to be mobilised. Much of the growth that has occurred in the BRIC countries and elsewhere has entailed a mobilisation of this latent reserve. In the advanced capitalist countries the mobilisation of women into the labour force earlier performed an analogous function even as the pool of surplus rural labour was early on drained dry. This latent reserve is not necessarily available in situ. From the 1960s onwards, the Germans turned to Turkey, the French to the Maghreb, the Swedes to the former Yugoslavia, the British to their former Empire and the USA to Mexico for immigrant labour. When a rising anti-immigrant fervour among the working classes grabbed hold, capital migrated to the Mexican *maquilas*, the Chinese and Bangladeshi factories, in a mass movement to wherever surplus labour was to be had. Even when capital does not migrate, the very threat that it might do so often serves to keep labour quiescent in its demands.

The intricate details of this need not detain us. All that matters is that we clearly register by what general means capital can keep the distributive share of labour in check and can manage it, even in the face of strong currents of organised opposition and the danger of triggering a realisation crisis by stifling workers' effective demand. That it has done so over the last forty years by some mix of labour-saving technological changes and an alleatory globalisation is obvious even as conditions of fiercer international competition have put downward pressures upon profit rates in spite of rising rates of exploitation of labour power. The net effect has been a global trend towards the reduction in the share of labour in the social product. This is what underpins increasing disparities in the individual distribution of wealth and income almost everywhere we look.

There is, however, another piece of the puzzle that has to be put in place. The obvious advantage that capital derives from the presence of a vast reserve of surplus labour poses the problem of how does the reserve population live when it is unemployed? In the case of latent reserves, this problem is often dealt with by what is called 'partial proletarianisation'. Where labour reserves are drawn from rural regions, then workers can return to their rural base when thrown out of work and eke out a living there as they have always traditionally done. Much of the cost of reproduction and child rearing is also borne in the rural areas on the basis of remittances sent home by urban workers. This has been true of China, for example. It also applies to migrant (particularly undocumented) workers in the USA who return to Mexico, where they were born, when they are laid off or get sick (from excessive exposure to pesticides, for example). But, obviously, this does not work when whole families migrate into the city and cut their rural ties. Informal economies spring up (including those that entail criminal activities) to sustain life on marginal terms in low-cost accommodation in shacks, shanty towns and favelas. The unemployed eke out a living however they can in the urban slums. What this does, of course, is to define a way and standard of life and, even more importantly for capital, a cost of living that defines a lower bound for wage levels in the formal sector. That lower bound can be approached to the degree that workers can easily be recruited from the surplus that survives in the informal sector.

In the advanced capitalist countries this lower bound to wage levels is fixed by the level of social welfare and unemployment insurance established out of a long history of class struggle. This has led right-wing theorists to argue that unemployment arises because the standard of living available to the unemployed is too generous.

The best way to attack unemployment is to reduce unemployment benefits! Employers who cannot profitably produce because wage levels are too high will then increase employment opportunities at these lower wage levels. There is some evidence that something like this can indeed happen. The problem, of course, is that wage levels throughout the whole labour force diminish without necessarily generating much new employment, thus contributing to the rising rate of exploitation of labour and, other things being equal, higher profits for capital and widening income disparities. This was one of the effects of President Clinton's reform of the welfare system in the United States and the introduction of 'workfare' requirements in 1995. The far more punitive conditions of welfare for the unemployed end up, of course, increasing the vast pool of poverty-ridden unemployed who cannot find a job because none are being generated in the face of the twin forces of globalisation (and competition with massive latent reserves) and labour-saving technological changes. Clinton has been handsomely rewarded since by business organisations, earning some $17 million in 2012 from speaker's fees mainly from business groups.

The neoliberal approach to labour force management takes this tack. It comprises a broad offensive against all those institutions – such as trade unions and socialist political parties – that had for long struggled to protect labour from the worst impacts of periodic bouts of widespread unemployment. The conditions prevailing within the labour reserve have, as a consequence, deteriorated markedly since the 1980s for political and strategic reasons. Capital in effect has been deepening income inequalities and poverty in order to sustain itself.

This story is a gross oversimplification, but it provides a neat illustration of how the contradictory unity of production and realisation has been manifest historically through the cyclical movement in income disparities from relatively narrow to explosively expansive. It was also paralleled by shifts in economic orthodoxy. Keynesian demand management dominated economic thinking in the 1960s, as we earlier remarked, whereas monetarist supply-side theories came to dominate after 1980 or so.

This brings us back to the question of what level of social inequality is acceptable and desirable within capitalism. Complete economic egalitarianism is plainly impossible, in contrast to liberal political theory, which advocates (in theory) for equality in political, legal and citizenship rights. The separation between economic and political rights is palpable. But at what point does the contradiction between the production of wealth and poverty here identified as foundational for capital sharpen and become the locus of crisis formation? There are two ways in which crises might be produced.

Chronic inequalities produce imbalances between production and realisation. The lack of effective demand among the masses slows down or blocks the easy circulation of capital. The politics of austerity, widely being applied throughout much of the capitalist world in recent times, reduces effective demand and hinders the creation of profit opportunities. This explains the current situation in the USA, where business profits have been at an all-time high, while reinvestment has been weak. The second way is for unacceptable levels of inequality to fuel social discontent and revolutionary movements. This threat is not confined to situations of absolute deprivation. It can arise out of relative deprivation, particularly when that deprivation is tied to the inferior economic condition of some specific religious, ethnic, gendered or racial group. The labour unrest and the urban uprisings of the 1960s in the United States were of this sort. The social unrest in Brazil in 2013 arose at a time of modest reductions in inequality and could partially be attributed to rising expectations among hitherto marginalised populations and the failure of public services and facilities to keep up with their demands.

None of this explains the astonishing concentrations of wealth among an emergent global plutocracy at the top of the income distribution. But there is a structural explanation for this and it pivots around the rising role of merchant, media and financial capital. Rapidly evolving information technologies and space–time revolutions in communications have revolutionised the possibilities for the geographical mobility of money capital in particular. The emphasis within capital has shifted as a result towards global financialisation.

The dynamic shifts occurring across several of capital's contradictions have in effect interacted in such a way as to widen disparities in income and wealth via this financialisation. Let me elaborate.

There have been several bouts of financialisation throughout capital's history (the latter half of the nineteenth century, for example). What makes the current phase special is the phenomenal acceleration in the speed of circulation of money capital and the reduction in financial transaction costs. The mobility of money capital relative to that of other forms of capital (commodities and production in particular) has dramatically increased. Capital's penchant for the annihilation of space through time here has a large role to play. This, says Craig Calhoun in a recent essay, 'facilitates the "creative destruction" of existing structures of capital (e.g. specific modes of industrial production) and spurs the development of new technologies', which in turn spurs 'the development of new products, production processes and new sites of production'. Uneven geographical developments become even more pronounced as capital searches out and moves to newer and lower-cost locations. The pressure asserted by finance 'drives investment towards ever more short-term profits and undercuts long-term and deeper growth. It also produces speculative bubbles and busts. It increases market pressure on firms bringing less than median returns to capital, driving disinvestment from still-profitable older businesses and thus driving down wages and reducing the tendency of industrial capitalism to share profits through rising wages. *It intensifies inequality*' (my emphasis). But rapid-fire financialisation also 'leads to returns on invested wealth that far outstrip returns on employment. It rewards traders more than material producers ... It makes all other sorts of businesses pay more for financial services. The 2010 bonus pool for securities industry employees in New York City alone was $20.8 billion; the top 25 hedge fund managers earned $22.7 billion. And this was after the market meltdown revealed the damage that financialisation was doing to the larger economy.'[4] Traders of all sorts benefit, not only those trading in money. Those trading in information and all the accoutrements of the economy of spectacle and the manufacturing of images and fetish desires are also part of the deal, as well as all those who trade in futures, no matter how fictitious these turn out to be. The merchants and the rentiers as well as the financiers are repositioned as the arbiters of capital accumulation relative to industrial capital. This is how the distribution of wealth and income became so distorted from the 1970s onwards.

But this has made capital itself less secure, more volatile and more crisis-prone, because of the resultant tensions between production and realisation of social value when the main arbiters of capital accumulation have little or nothing to do with actual production. The engine of capitalism has been groaning under the strain. The engine could easily blow up (China would almost certainly be the epicentre for that) or grind to a halt (as seems to be the more likely outcome in contemporary Europe and Japan).

There is, in all of this, a deep irony. Historically, industrial capital waged a mighty struggle to free itself from the chains of the landlords who extracted rent, the usurious financiers and the merchants who looked to rob or buy cheap and sell dear in unevenly constructed markets. Twenty-first-century capitalism seems to be busy weaving a net of constraints in which the rentiers, the merchants, the media and communications moguls and, above all, the financers ruthlessly squeeze the lifeblood out of productive industrial capital, to say nothing of the workers employed. It is not that industrial capital disappears. It has merely become subservient to capital in its other more fantastic and virulent forms.

A form of capital has emerged that is ruthlessly dynamic in the field of technological changes and in the globalisation of social relations, yet which not only pays no mind to the conditions under which social labour produces but even seems not to care too much whether production takes place at all. However, if all capitalists seek to live off rents, interest, profit on merchant's and media capital, or even worse just on speculating in asset values or living off capital gains (as most of the top 1 per cent of income earners do in the USA), without producing social value, then the only possible outcome is a calamitous crisis. A political economy of this kind also betokens the concentration and centralisation of immense economic wealth, power and privilege among the merchant and media capitalists, the financiers and the rentiers. The emergence of such a plutocracy is, sadly, all too plain to see. The fact that it does so well while the mass of the people does so badly is hard to disguise. The big question is if and when a mass political movement of the dispossessed might arise to repossess that which has been lost.

This leaves us with one critical residual question: if the immense disparities of wealth and income now emerging are a reflection of the rise of this new form of capital, then what were the contradictions that made for the rise of this new form of capital? This is a crucial question that will be taken up later in the context of the dangerous contradictions. It was not, I shall hope to show, a mere accident of history.

The political implications of all this for an anti-capitalist strategy are simple enough but far-reaching. If, for example, the poll data for the United States is at all emblematic, then there will be massive public support for a reform movement that produces far more egalitarian outcomes than is currently the case, even as it demands that the state not be the vehicle to accomplish this. There would be and is widespread support for worker-control initiatives, solidarity economies and autonomous communitarian and cooperative structures. The example of Mondragon, the largest and most long-lasting workers' cooperative in Europe, with its collective management bragging, until very recently, an income disparity of no more than three to one (compared to the 350 to one in a typical US corporation) is appealing.

In this case we also see the potential value of a very important category of political action. This is the idea of 'revolutionary reform'. Plainly, the reduction of wealth and income disparities from their current levels would not challenge the reproduction of capital one wit. Indeed, such a reduction, it can be plausibly argued, is absolutely necessary for capital to survive in the present conjuncture because the current disparities threaten to become an absolute contradiction by virtue of escalating imbalances between the capacity to manage the contradictory unity between production and realisation.

But, if the theory of capital's necessary inequalities is correct, then there will come a point where a programme to reduce wealth and income inequalities will threaten the reproduction of capital. Once a move towards a profit squeeze gets under way, then it can ultimately threaten to squeeze the lifeblood out of capital to compensate for the way capital systematically sucks the lifeblood out of labour. Nobody knows exactly where the breaking point might lie, but it will surely be well before the levels of equality preferred in the US public opinion polls are reached. A reform movement around reducing social inequality can become the cutting edge for revolutionary transformation.

# Contradiction 13
# Social Reproduction

Once upon a time it could reasonably be said that capital cared not a wit about the neediness of the worker, leaving it to the initiative and ingenuity of the workers to reproduce themselves biologically, psychologically and culturally on the basis of the pittance of a wage that capital provided. The workers for the most part conveniently obliged because they had no option. This was the situation that Karl Marx encountered and it was probably for this reason that he left the question of the social reproduction of the labour force to one side in his theorising of capital's political economy. But plainly, if labourers do not reproduce themselves or are overworked to a premature death down the mines and in the factories (or commit suicide from overwork, as has been regularly happening in Chinese factories) and if capital's easy access to a labour surplus is somehow blocked, then capital cannot reproduce. Marx recognised this danger when he clearly saw that limits had to be put upon the exorbitant length of the working day and murderous rates of exploitation and that state legislation on this point was just as important to protect the reproduction of capital as it was to protect the lives of the labourers. The contradiction between the conditions required to ensure the social reproduction of the labour force and those needed to reproduce capital has always been latently present. But over the last two centuries it has evolved to become a far more prominent and complex contradiction, loaded with dangerous possibilities and full of far-reaching but uneven geographical manifestations and consequences.

This contradiction became more prominent with the rise of the factory system and the increasing complexity and roundaboutness of capital's production systems. While traditional artisanal skills were of diminishing importance, capital became much more interested in the procurement of a modestly educated workforce, one that was literate, flexible, disciplined and complicitous enough to fulfil the variety of tasks demanded of it in the machine age. The insertion of education clauses in the English Factory Act of 1864 was a sign of this increasing interest of capital in the workers' capacities and powers and this entailed limited interventions in the life of workers outside of the factory. Within capitalism as a whole, this concern for the reproduction of labour power of adequate qualities coincided in many parts of the world with a political project on the part of a reformist bourgeoisie to create a 'respectable' working class that would refrain from riot and revolution and succumb to the blandishments that capital could offer. The growth of public education, along with the 'gas and water' socialism that prevailed politically in many parts of the capitalist world, certainly eased the lot of the regularly employed worker and did so in such a way as to permit the extension of political representation (the right to vote and thereby influence public policies) to the point of universal suffrage.

The increasing interest in the education of the workforce and the mobilisation of financial resources to accomplish this task has been a major feature in capital's history. But it has not been a disinterested history nor has it evolved without complications deriving from the dynamics of class struggle between capital and labour. For what has been at stake here, as earlier noted, is what it is that capital wishes the working classes to be educated in and what it is that the working classes themselves want and desire to know. In early English and French history, for example, the autodidact, the self-educated labourer, was a permanent thorn in capital's side, given to often wildly divergent socialist utopian ideas about alternatives to the form of life that capital offered and prepared to take political if not revolutionary action to bring some anti-capitalist alternative into existence. The incredible flourishing of emancipatory and utopian tracts and sects in France during the 1830s and 1840s (associated with names like Fourier, Saint-Simon, Proudhon, Cabet, etc.) was paralleled across the English Channel by a more sober but nonetheless persistent literature on worker rights and the necessity to construct institutional solidarities such as trade unions and various modes of political agitation (Chartism) and organisation, some of which was supported by utopian thinkers and practitioners such as Robert Owen. If this was what constituted the education of the working classes, then capital wanted none of it. But faced with the persistent pursuit of self-education on the part of at least an influential segment of the working classes, capital had to come up with something to put in its place. As Mr Dombey put it in Charles Dickens's *Dombey and Son*, he had no objection to public education provided it taught the worker his proper place in society. Marx, for his part, while critical of much of the socialist utopian literature, learned mightily from it and likewise sought to create a whole anti-capitalist knowledge field that would provide a fount of ideas for anti-capitalist agitation. Heaven forbid that the workers would read such stuff.

While public education has done much to meet capital's demand for ideological conformity combined with the production of skill sets appropriate to the state of the division of labour, it has not eradicated the underlying conflict. And this is so in part because state interests also enter in to attempt to forge a sense of cross-class national identity and solidarity that is at war with capital's penchant for some form of rootless cosmopolitan individualism, to be emulated by both capital-ist and worker alike. None of these contradictions of the content for public education can easily be settled, but this does not detract from the simple fact that investment in education and training is a sine qua non for capital's competitiveness. Massive investment in education has, for example, been a striking feature of China's recent develop-ment, as it was earlier in Singapore and other East Asian states. This was so because the profitability of capital rested more and more on the increasing productivity of increasingly skilled labour.

But, as so often happens within the history of capital, education ultimately became a 'big business' unto itself. The stunning inroads of privatisation and fee paying into what had traditionally been public and free education have placed financial burdens on the populace such that those desirous of education have to pay for this key aspect of social reproduction themselves. The consequences of creating a heavily debt-encumbered educated labour force may take a considerable time to work out. But if the street battles between students and authorities in Santiago in Chile that began in 2006 and have continued to this day over the expensive privatisation of both high school and advanced education are anything to go by, then this too will likely be a simmering source of discontent wherever it has been implemented.

The creation of a highly productive labour force gave rise to what is called 'human capital' theory, which is one of the weirdest widely accepted economic ideas that could ever be imagined. It found its first expression in the writings of Adam Smith. The acquisition of productive talents on the part of labour, he argued, through 'education, study or apprenticeship, always costs a real expense, which is a capital fixed and realized as it were in his person. Those talents, as they make a part of his fortune, so do they likewise that of the society to which he belongs. The improved dexterity of a workman may be considered in the same light as a machine or instrument of trade which facilitates and abridges labour, and which, though it costs a certain expense, repays that expense with a profit.'[1] The question, of course, is who foots the bill for the creation of such talents – labour, the state, capital or some institution in civil society (like the Church) – and who gets the benefits (or 'profits' in Adam Smith's parlance)?

To be sure, skilled and highly trained labour might reasonably expect a higher rate of remuneration than unskilled labour, but that is a far cry from accepting the idea that the higher wage is a form of profit on the workers' investment in their own education and skills. The problem, as Marx pointed out in his acerbic criticism of Adam Smith, is that the worker can only realise the higher value of those skills by working for capital under conditions of exploitation such that it is, in the end, capital and not the worker that reaps the benefit from the higher productivity of labour.[2] In recent times, for example, worker productivity has surged but the share of output going to labour has declined, not increased. In any case, if what the worker truly possessed in bodily form was capital, Marx pointed out, then he or she would be entitled to sit back and just live off the interest of his or her capital without doing a single day's work (capital as a property relation always has that option at hand). As far as I can tell, the main point of the revival of human capital theory, at the hands of Gary Becker in the 1960s, for example, was to bury the significance of the class relation between capital and labour and make it seem as if we are all just capitalists earning different rates of return on our capital (human or otherwise).[3] If labour was getting very low wages, it could then be argued that this was simply a reflection of the fact that workers had not invested enough effort in building up their human capital! It was, in short, their fault if they were low-paid. Hardly surprisingly, all the major institutions of capital, from economics departments to the World Bank and the IMF, wholeheartedly embraced this theoretical fiction for ideological and certainly not for sound intellectual reasons. These same institutions have more recently similarly embraced the wondrous fiction that the informal sector of social reproduction which dominates in many cities of the developing world is in fact a seething mass of micro-enterprises that need only a dose of microfinance (at usurious rates of interest pocketed at the end of the trail by major financial institutions) in order to become fully fledged card-carrying members of the capitalist class.

For exactly the same reasons, I have profound objections to Bourdieu's characterisation of personal endowments (which are undeniably of great importance in social life) as a form of capital called 'cultural capital'.[4] While it is perfectly fine to emphasise the role of such endowments in confirming status position in our society and thereby contributing to the replication of class distinctions in the course of social reproduction, to treat this as a form of capital in the sense we are using this term here is confusing if not perverse. It would propose that there is some way of accumulating monetary wealth and income by learning to appreciate Scarlatti (if you are French) and Snoop Dogg if you are American. Where the idea of cultural capital does enter in (but this is not Bourdieu's point) is in the branding and marketing of goods and places in such a way as to command a monopoly rent (as in the case of fine wines and perfect tourist destinations). But what we are dealing with here is the manufacture of symbols of distinction which, if they stick, can be a source of permanent monopoly rents and monetary gain. Product differentiation to emphasise that my brand of toothpaste is unique and special has always been a way to avoid the levelling effect of market exchange. Who invents the symbolic world that lies behind the branding of goods and places – a manipulative work that lies at the heart of contemporary advertising and the tourism industry – then becomes critical to the manipulation of human desires for monetary gain. It is, of course, the capitalists who take the monetary gain and who pay for the branding of their products. And in some instances they certainly do not hesitate to attach signs of class and even more emphatically seductive gender images to the qualities of their products. Capital undoubtedly uses such signs of distinction in its sales practices and pitches, but that does not mean that distinction is a form of capital, as Bourdieu proposes, though it does often give rise to monopoly rents if the distinction is unique and original (like a Picasso painting).

Capital and the capitalist state (though mainly the latter) have in recent times taken a deep interest in aspects of social reproduction that affect the competitive qualities of the labour force. If any country is desirous of becoming wealthier by moving up the value-added chain of production into fields of research and development, thereby garnering the wealth to be tapped from command over intellectual property rights, then this depends on having at one's disposal a well-educated and scientifically qualified labour force which must be either trained at home (hence the immense significance of the research universities in countries such as the USA) or imported from abroad. The education of such a workforce has to begin early in life, which puts the whole educational system in the cross-hairs of capital's concerns, although, as usual, capital is inclined not to pay for any of it if it can possibly help it. In countries like Singapore and now China strong state investment in education at all levels has been key to their economic success.

The rapidly changing technological context, particularly the progress of robotisation and artificial intelligence already noted, has radically altered the kinds of skills that are advantageous to labour and educational systems have often lumbered awkwardly to keep up with the new demands. More than twenty years ago, for example, Robert Reich pointed out an emergent division between knowledge-based 'symbolic-analytic' services, routine production and 'in-person' services. The 'symbolic analysts' included engineers, legal experts, researchers, scientists, professors, executives, journalists, consultants and other 'mind workers', who were primarily engaged in collecting, processing, analysing and manipulating information and symbols for a living. This group of workers, which Reich estimated made up roughly 20 per cent of the labour force in the USA, occupied a privileged position in part because they could practise their trade almost anywhere in the world. They needed, however, to be well educated in analytic and symbolic skills and much of this begins in the home, where, loaded down with electronic gadgets, children learn at an early age how to use and manipulate data and information adequate for an emergent 'knowledge-based' economy.[5] This group forms the core of a relatively affluent though highly mobile upper middle class within capitalism and one that increasingly tends to segregate itself (and to enclose its processes of social reproduction) in privileged enclaves away from the rest of society. By way of contrast, traditional production workers (for example, in steel and car production) and ordinary service workers have very little future, in part because those are the jobs most likely to disappear and in part because even those jobs that remain are likely to be low-wage with very scant benefits simply because of the massive labour surpluses now available.

The long-standing interest in increasing labour productivity among at least a certain segment of the workforce did not initially encompass all of the worker's cultural and affective life. Aspects of social reproduction, such as the raising of children or caring for the sick and elderly, continued in many instances and places to be very much the individual worker's affair and outside of market considerations, as were many of the particular trappings of cultural life. But with the complexities of capitalist industrialisation and urbanisation, the capitalist state increasingly found itself necessarily embroiled in the regulation and provision of public health, of education, social control and even the cultivation of certain habits of heart and mind conducive to self-discipline and citizenship among the populace at large.

While the whole field of social reproduction is, as Cindi Katz puts it, 'the fleshy, messy, and indeterminate stuff of everyday life', it is 'also a set of structured practices that unfold in dialectical relation with production, with which it is mutually constitutive and in tension'. The contradictory unity between social reproduction and the reproduction of capital crystallises out as a moving contradiction of singular interest throughout the history of capital. What it is about now is light years away from what it was in 1850. 'Social reproduction', Katz continues, 'encompasses daily and long term reproduction, both of the means of production and the labour power to make them work. At its most basic, it hinges on the biological reproduction of the labour force, both generationally and on a daily basis.' It also encompasses the production and reproduction of manual, mental and conceptual skills.[6] All of this is achieved on the basis of the individual wage plus the social wage provided by various state agencies (for example, education and health care) and key institutions of civil society (for example, the Church and a wide range of philanthropically supported NGOs).

From the standpoint of labour, social reproduction has a very particular meaning. The labourers receive a money wage and it is their choice how they spend it. What they spend it on and why were, in the early days, of no interest to capital. But that is by no means true today, as we shall see. How much labourers need to survive and reproduce themselves in part depends upon how much labourers and their families and communities can do for themselves. There is a vast amount of unpaid labour absorbed in social reproduction, most of it, as feminists have repeatedly and quite correctly pointed out, traditionally and even to this day being done by women. Social reproduction is for capital a large and convenient sphere in which real costs are externalised on to households and other communal entities. Its costs weigh disproportionately on different groups in the population. In the case of partial proletarianisation, as discussed earlier for example, almost all the costs of child rearing and caring for the sick and the aged are left to the household labours of peasant or rural societies. Under conditions of social democracy, however, political movements drove capital to internalise some of these costs either directly (through pension, insurance and health care provisions in wage contracts) or indirectly (through taxation on capital to support the state provision of services via a welfare state).

Part of the neoliberal political programme and ethos in recent times has been to externalise as much as possible the costs of social reproduction on to the populace at large in order to raise the profit rate for capital by reducing its tax burden. The argument has been that the welfare state was becoming too costly and that tax relief for capital would stimulate deeper and faster economic growth, which, when the benefits were spread around, would make everyone better off. It never worked out that way, of course, because the rich took virtually all of the savings and passed on none of the benefits (except in the form of some morally questionable therapeutic philanthropy).

Households are not, however, isolated entities. They are embedded in a matrix of social interactions and social relations present in places. Their labours are often shared – in middle-class US neighbourhoods, for example, car-pooling, childcare, the staging of collective events like park picnics, street fairs and block parties are all part of daily life and there is even an associated constituency, soccer moms, who garner political attention. There is a good deal of non-monetary exchange, of mutual aid in evidence, spread across everything from helping to fix the neighbour's car to painting the patio and helping maintain common spaces for communal enjoyment. How much of this occurs and through what mechanisms can be immensely varied but it is undeniable that in many parts of the world households conjoin in a whole range of practices of mututal support to create some semblance of a common life. Such practices get formalised in the establishment of community associations, ethnic assemblies, religious organisations and the like, which pay considerable attention to defining and maintaining (sometimes repressively) the appropriate neighbourhood conditions for social reproduction. Such associations can form the basis for larger social movements and it is from them that much inspiration is drawn for the idea that another life is possible to that given by pure market and monetary transactions. While it would seem that the neoliberal assault on state provision of social services might be counteracted by an upsurge of practices of mutual aid, the evidence for the most part seems otherwise – that the individualistic and self-centred profit-maximising ethic through which neoliberalism works (along with other features such as increased geographical mobility) has if anything diminished mutual aid as a feature of a common social life except in communities that define their ties in religious or ethnic bonding terms. None of this is helped by the increasing predilection of consumers to treat their home as a short-term speculative investment rather than as a place to create a solid and settled life. It is also true that the modes of urban living that capital typically produces (particularly with respect to dependence on the car) are not very conducive to the creation of mutually supportive social networks that can encourage more adequate and fulfilling forms of social reproduction.

Behind all of this there lurks an incipient and potentially damaging contradiction that we have encountered before in different guises. Labourers and households are a significant source of effective demand and they play a significant role in the realisation of values in the market. If they are largely producing for themselves outside of the market, then they do not buy in the market and they furnish less in the way of effective demand. This is the problem with partial proletarianisation and explains why, at some point, it often gives way (usually under the pressure of capital) to full proletarianisation. If the welfare state is dismantled, then bang goes a hefty chunk of effective demand and the field for realisation of values shrinks. This is the problem with austerity politics. The contradiction between capital's rising potential profitability in production and its falling potential profitability due to insufficient effective demand intensifies as attempts to manage the contradiction between social reproduction and production lurch from one extreme to another.

In partial answer to this dilemma, there has been a long-standing trend within the history of capital for household labour to be supplanted by market-based transactions (everything from haircuts to takeaway or frozen meals, fast foods, to dry-cleaning, entertainment and child and old-age care). The privatisation of personal household labours into the market sphere, along with increasing capital intensity of household technologies (everything from washing machines and vacuum cleaners to microwaves and, of course, houses and cars) that have to be purchased with a considerable outlay (often debt-financed), has not only radically transformed the nature of household economies but also revolutionised processes of realisation of capital values in the market. The commodifications in the housing markets of the world have opened up a vast field of capital accumulation through the consumption of space for social reproduction. Capital has long been concerned, as we have seen, with promoting 'rational consumption', understood as that form of household consumerism that fuels capital accumulation irrespective of whether it meets real human wants and needs (whatever these might be) or not. Social reproduction has increasingly been infected and in some cases totally transformed by such considerations.

This elementary fact has prompted much reflection on the increasing role of capital in dominating what Jürgen Habermas calls (following the German philosopher Edmund Husserl) our 'lifeworld' or what Henri Lefebvre analyses under the rubric of 'everyday life'.[7] The systemic penetration of almost all aspects of our lifeworld by capital and its products in one form or another has, of course, provoked resistance, but for most of the world's population it has proved a losing battle, even when it was not actively welcomed. Arguments have been advanced on the progressive left (socialist feminists in particular) that wages should be paid for housework. Given that so much of that labour is performed disproportionately by women, the political reasoning is clear, but it unfortunately succeeds only in furthering the total monetisation of everything, which ultimately plays into the hands of capital. Apart from the sheer difficulty of monetisation of household tasks, it is unlikely that such a measure would benefit the people, least of all women, who will most likely continue to be excessively exploited even as they are paid for their household labours.

Whereas it was perfectly reasonable, therefore, for the eminent French historian Fernand Braudel to take the sphere of material life and material reproduction of the common people in the late medieval period as having little or nothing to do with capital or even with the market, this formulation has no relevance to our own times except in those increasingly remote areas of the world (for example, indigenous societies or remote peasant populations) where capital has yet to exert its dominant influence.[8] The commodification of daily life and social reproduction has proceeded apace and created a complex space for anti-capitalist struggle.

The sphere of social reproduction has in fact almost everywhere become the site of highly intrusive capitalist activities. The tentacles of the state's and capital's influence and power now proliferate within the spheres of social reproduction in many parts of the world in myriad ways. Not all of these interventions are pernicious, of course. Social reproduction is the site where the oppression of and violence against women flourishes in many parts of the world, where educational opportunities for women are denied, where violence and abuse of children all too frequently occur, where intolerance breeds contempt for others, where labour all too often transfers its own bitter experience of violence and oppression in the labour process back on to others in the household, where drink and drugs take their toll. It is for this reason that a modicum of social regulation and even, perhaps, state interventionism in the world of social reproduction become so necessary. But this then constitutes a bureaucratic framing of daily life and of social reproduction that leaves very little room for autonomous development. Furthermore, the deeper material embedding of all processes of production, exchange, distribution and consumption in the web of social and biological life has produced a world where a contradiction between a potentially alienating household consumerism of excess and the consumption necessary for adequate social reproduction becomes every bit as salient as the contradiction between the social reproduction of the labour force and the reproduction of capital. How much of contemporary social reproduction in, say, the United States is given over to training as many people as possible in the insane arts of conspicuous consumption and speculative finance as opposed to training them to be good and well-educated workers?

What Randy Martin calls 'the financialization of daily life' has become a conspicuous insertion into social reproduction over the last generation.[9] If we ask the elementary questions: how much social reproduction is debt-financed and what are the implications of that fact?, the answers are quite stunning. In many parts of the world the usurious moneylender has always been a significant figure and continues to be so up to this day. Social reproduction takes place in much of India under the shadow of the looming power of the usurer. This is not relieved by the arrival of the institutions of microcredit and microfinance (which in some instances have driven people – mostly women – to suicide as the only relief from their collective indebtedness). But personal indebtedness associated with social reproduction has now become a calamitous problem in one form or another almost everywhere. The huge indebtedness of students in the United States is now being mimicked in Britain, Chile and China, while borrowings to finance the conduct of everyday life have been mounting at astonishing rates. In just a few years personal debt in China has soared way beyond incomes from a base of close to zero in, say, 1980.

This generalisation is cut across, however, by the uneven geographical development of these contradictions. Some parts of the world (such as the United States, where consumption accounts for more than 70 per cent of GDP) seem to be more about furnishing the effective demand through an alien consumerism that corrupts reasonable forms of social reproduction, while others are focused more on the social reproduction of a labour force that can churn out value without cease (for example, China, where consumerism accounts for around 35 per cent of GDP). In divided cities like Lagos, São Paulo and, yes, even New York, one part of the city is given over to conspicuous consumption and the other to the reproduction of an easily exploited but largely redundant because surplus labour force. The study of social reproduction in these different environments reveals a huge gap in both the qualities and meaning of household activities, with hardly any commonalities between them. These divisions produce some curious manifestations in the realm of bourgeois morality. While moral opprobrium is cast upon the practices first in Pakistan and later in India of having young children working for pennies on a ten- or twelve-hour-day schedule to produce footballs to be kicked around by players who earn millions, these very same moralists are totally blind to the exploitation by capital of their own children as consumers in the marketplace, even as those children are also being inculcated into the dark arts of the deal, as well as stock market manipulations (money for nothing) by pushing buttons on their keyboards. Google the case of Jonathan Lebed to see what I mean. By the time he was fifteen years old he had gained several million dollars from trading in penny stocks, setting up chat rooms to promote stocks he had just bought and selling at the higher price that his favourable ratings in the chat room created. Prosecuted by the Securities and Exchange Commission, he simply maintained that this was all that Wall Street did anyway; the SEC fined him a small amount and dropped the whole project of prosecution like a hot potato because Lebed was quite right.

The contradictions of social reproduction cannot be understood outside of these geographically differentiated circumstances, even as they have also dramatically changed their general character over time. The contingencies of material activity, of cultural forms and local ways of living, are of great import in many parts of the world. As Katz notes, social reproduction 'necessarily remains mainly place-bound' in a context where capital is highly mobile. The result is that 'all sorts of disjunctures occur across space, across boundaries, and across scale, which are as likely to draw upon sedimented inequalities in social relations as to provoke new ones'. Agricultural

iota of assistance from capital or the state, the populace now has to reproduce itself in the midst of massive corruptions and interventions of both state and capital in the construction of a daily life oriented not only to fill the highly differentiated slots (including that of ne'er-do-well) in a particular kind of labour force but also to being a sink for a wide range of unnecessary and unwanted products that capital produces and markets with such flair.

There are those, of course, who see the contradiction and seek ways around it. Some long for a return to indigenous ways of thinking and of living, or at least see some hope of mounting a challenge to the crass forms of contemporary social reproduction under fully organised consumerist capitalism by building alternative communities on the basis of networked households and workers' associations. But capital's strategy to infect social reproduction with consumerism has been both persistent and long-standing, as well as generously financed by an advertising and promotional industry that will stop at nothing to get products sold. 'Get the women' was the slogan of the new department store owners in Second Empire Paris as they sought to acquire more market power. More recently it has been 'Get the kids and the younger the better' that has dominated much consumerist advertising. If children are raised sitting in front of a TV or playing computer games or with an i-Pad, then this has far-reaching implications for their psychological and cultural attitudes, their mental conceptions of the world and their possible future political subjectivities. Reproduction is a vexed problem, says Katz, in part because it is so highly focused on the reproduction of 'the very social relations and material forms that are so problematic'. For this reason, social reproduction is unlikely to be a source of revolutionary sentiments. Yet so much rests upon it, including oppositional politics.

The ubiquity of social reproduction makes it a central standpoint from which to construct a critique of capital in one of its most insidious forms. This was precisely Henri Lefebvre's project in writing his multi-volume *Critique of Everyday Life*.[11] He here set out to provide a critique of individuality (the 'private' consciousness and individualism); a critique of money (which he understood in terms of fetishism and economic alienation); a critique of needs (psychological and moral alienation from consumerism though not, of course, from necessary consumption); a critique of work (alienation of the worker); and, last but not least, a critique of the concept and ideology of freedom (the power over nature and over human nature).

This points us towards a political form of anti-capitalist responses to what has happened to daily life under capitalism and what has so transformed social reproduction. The negation of multiple alienations must be the cutting edge in any collective political response to the degradations of daily life and the loss of autonomy in social reproduction at the hands of capital and the capitalist state. This does not imply that the only response to this situation is the isolated individual household doing whatever it will. The alternative is the embedding of households in a social network for purposes of managing and advancing a common life replete with 'civilised' values. We will take up this alternative in the conclusion. Meanwhile, Lefebvre's last point – the critique of freedom – also calls for careful attention, for it lies at the crux of yet another of capital's major contradictions, as we shall see in the study of Contradiction 14.

But there is one thing that is certain. Any so-called 'radical' strategy that seeks to empower the disempowered in the realm of social reproduction by opening up that realm to monetisation and market forces is headed in exactly the wrong direction. Providing financial literacy classes for the populace at large will simply expose that population to predatory practices as they seek to manage their own investment portfolios like minnows swimming in a sea of sharks. Providing microcredit and microfinance facilities encourages people to participate in the market economy but does so in such a way as to maximise the energy they have to expend while minimising their returns. Providing legal title for land and property ownership in the hope that this will bring economic and social stability to the lives of the marginalised will almost certainly lead in the long run to their dispossession and eviction from that space and place they already hold through customary use rights.

# Contradiction 14
# Freedom and Domination

Stone walls do not a prison make,
Nor iron bars a cage;
Minds innocent and quiet take
That for an hermitage;
If I have freedom in my love
And in my soul am free,
Angels alone, that soar above,
Enjoy such liberty.

So wrote Richard Lovelace in his much-cited poem written from prison to his lover Althea. Lovelace had been thrown into prison in 1642 for petitioning Parliament to have a law regulating the clergy repealed. He was jailed for exercising his freedom to petition Parliament. The timing is important. It was during the first phase of the English Civil War that curbed the power of the established Church and culminated in the execution of King Charles I. It was a time when, as the historian Christopher Hill puts it, the world was 'being turned upside down' by political, religious and social movements that sought a way to relate powerful ideas and ideologies about individual rights and liberty and the management of collective and common interests for the supposed common good (about which there was plenty of disagreement).[1] Whatever the disagreements, the divine right of kings and of the established Church (though not of the dissenters) was under fierce attack. But what sort of body politic could and might replace it and with what freedoms?

The sentiments expressed in Lovelace's poem are very much alive and well. Most of us socialised into the ways of capital believe we are blessed with a capacity for freedom of thought no matter what walls and barriers surround us. We can easily imagine a situation or even a world that is different from that which we currently inhabit. We can even imagine active steps by which our world can be remade in a different image. And if we are free to imagine alternatives, why cannot we freely struggle to make our imaginings reality, even as we recognise that the historical and geographical circumstances may not be particularly propitious for proposing and pursuing alternatives? It is not only followers of the right-wing libertarian novelist Ayn Rand who hold to this view. Radicals of all stripes, including Marx, willingly subscribe to it. After all, says Terry Eagleton in *Why Marx Was Right*, 'the free flourishing of individuals is the whole aim of his politics, as long as we remember that these individuals must find some way of flourishing in common'.[2] What separates Rand from Marx is that the latter saw the true flourishing of individual creativity (an ideal that goes back to Aristotle's conception of the good life) as best accomplished through collaboration and association with others in a collective drive to abolish the barriers of scarcity and material necessity beyond which, Marx held, the true realm of individual freedom could begin.

But behind all this there lurks an awkward question: is there something about the contemporary meaning and definition of freedom that stops short of embracing anti-capitalist alternatives? Will I, like Lovelace, end up in jail for freely pursuing such alternatives? Do we operate, almost without knowing it, with some partial, debased and in the end imprisoning concepts of liberty and freedom that merely support the status quo and more deeply instantiate capital's warped vision of human rights and social justice? Is the economic engine of capital so powerfully committed to certain foundational but partial concepts of liberty and freedom as to preclude anything other than at worst an entrepreneurial and at best a liberal humanist approach to the crucial political question of freedom versus domination?

In almost every presidential inaugural address I have ever read, a dominant theme has been that the United States stands for liberty and freedom and will not only make any sacrifice and go to any lengths to counter threats to those freedoms, but also use its power and influence to promote the spread of liberty and freedom around the world. George Bush Jr, who repeatedly used the words liberty and freedom in all his speeches, described in stirring rhetorical terms (as the USA marched into a trumped-up war against Iraq) the US tradition this way: 'The advance of freedom is the calling of our time. It is the calling of our country. From the Fourteen Points [Woodrow Wilson] to the Four Freedoms [Theodore Roosevelt] to the Speech at Westminster [Ronald Reagan], America has put our power at the service of principle. We believe that liberty is the design of nature. We believe that liberty is the direction of history. We believe that human fulfillment and excellence come in the responsible exercise of liberty. And we believe that freedom – the freedom we prize – is not for us alone. It is the right and capacity of all mankind.' In a speech to British parliamentarians at the Mansion House in London he located the roots of his thinking as follows: 'We're sometimes faulted for a naïve faith, that liberty can change the world: if that's an error it came from reading too much John Locke and Adam Smith.'[3] While the idea of Bush actually reading these authors is mind-boggling, the rooting of his arguments in the propositions of early political economy is, as we shall see, of critical importance.

This concern on the part of the United States to protect liberty and freedom has, unfortunately, been used systematically to justify the imperial and neocolonial domination of much of the world. There has been and is no reluctance on the part of the United States to resort to coercion and violence in the pursuit of the absolute values of liberty and freedom. There is a long history of covert operations mounted by the USA to support coups against democratically elected leaders (Jacobo Arbenz in Guatemala in 1954, Salvador Allende in Chile in 1973 and more recently the failed attempt against Hugo Chávez in Venezuela). Closer to home, we now live in a world of extensive government surveillance of the private communications of citizens, the cracking of all encrypted codes by government authorities (so they have access to our bank, medical and credit card records), all in the name of keeping us free and secure from the threat of terror. The quest for liberty and freedom provides a licence, it seems, to engage in a wide range of repressive practices. The US public at large is either totally oblivious to or so deeply familiar with this contradiction that it scarcely notices how the inspiring rhetoric about liberty and freedom which it so readily embraces is so often paired with some shabby operation of domination often for narrow venal gain, to say nothing of chronic abuses of human rights, from Abu Ghraib in Iraq to Guantanamo Bay in Cuba, as well as on the ground in Afghanistan. Even Amnesty International has openly condemned the United States for 'atrocious violations of human rights' on Guantanamo, a criticism that the US government blithely ignores. There is, alas, nothing new in reversals of this kind. 'War is peace. Freedom is slavery. Ignorance is strength,' wrote George Orwell in *Nineteen Eighty-Four*, with the then Soviet Union obviously in mind.

It is tempting in the face of all this to conclude that the political rhetoric concerning the pursuit of liberty and freedom is a sham, a mask for hypocrites like Bush to pursue more venal aims of profit, dispossession and domination. But this would deny the force of that other history which, from peasant revolts to revolutionary movements (American, French, Russian, Chinese etc.), to the struggle to abolish slavery and the fight to liberate whole populations from their chains of colonial rule, has in the name of freedom wrought a seismic reworking of the contours of how our world society works. All of this has been going on while social forces have been extending the field of freedom and liberty through struggles against apartheid, for civil rights, workers' rights, women's rights and the rights of many other minorities (LGBT, indigenous or disabled populations etc.). All of these struggles have worked their way through the history of capitalism in myriad ways to transform our social world. When protesters against tyrannical rule planted liberty trees, the gesture was more than empty. When the cry demanding 'freedom now' echoes in the streets, then the ruling social order has to tremble or concede something, even if what it offers turns out to be of little more than symbolic value.

The popular desire for liberty and freedom has been a powerful motive force throughout capital's history. That quest will not easily die no matter how much it may get banalised and degraded in the rhetoric of the ruling classes and their political representatives. But there is a dark side to this coin. At some point in their trajectory (particularly the closer they come to achieving their aims) all these progressive movements have to decide who or what has to be dominated to secure the liberty and freedom that they seek. In revolutionary situations somebody's ox gets gored and the question then is whose and why? Poor Lovelace ends up in jail and that seems unfair. The Terror was launched in the French Revolution in the cause of consolidating 'liberty, equality, fraternity'. The hopes and dreams of generations of communist insurgents have crashed on the rocks of this contradiction as the promise of human emancipation crumbles into the dust of bureaucratised and sclerotic state management backed by an apparatus of police-state repression. Similarly, the denizens of post-colonial societies who truly believed that a struggle for national self-liberation and freedom would lead to an immense growth in the domain of freedom now live in a state of disillusionment if not fear for the future of their freedoms. South Africa, after years of fierce struggle against apartheid, is no better off now than it ever was in achieving basic freedoms from want and need. In some parts of the world, like Singapore, individual freedoms are strictly limited, traded away, as it were, for rapidly increasing material well-being.

There is, plainly, a whale of a contradiction here. Freedom and domination go hand in hand. There is no such thing as freedom that does not in some way have to deal in the dark arts of domination. Domination over one's own fears in the face of overwhelming odds, over cynics and doubters, to say nothing of external enemies, may be necessary to open the way to greater freedoms. This unity of freedom and domination is, as always, a contradictory unity. Unjust means may be required to prosecute a just cause.

The two polar terms of freedom and domination lie at the extremes of a contradiction that takes many subtle and nuanced, to say nothing of disguised, forms (domination can be masked as consent or be established by persuasion and ideological manipulation). But I prefer to stick with the flagrant and most disturbing language precisely because to ignore its potential consequences lies at the root of the disillusionment of millions who have faithfully struggled for freedom, sometimes at the cost of their lives, only to find their descendants swimming in the dark waters of yet another form of domination. Any struggle for freedom and liberty must be prepared to confront at the very outset that which it is prepared to dominate. It also has to recognise that the price of maintaining its freedoms is eternal vigilance against the return of either old or new forms of domination.

This is where the references to John Locke and Adam Smith are relevant. For what classical liberal political economy proposed was not only some sort of utopian model for a universalised capitalism but a certain vision of individual liberty and freedom that ultimately came to underpin, as the French philosopher Michel Foucault acutely notes, a self-regulatory structure of governance that placed limits on the arbitrariness of state power at the same time as it led and enabled individuals to regulate their own conduct according to the rules of a market society.[4] The domination and disciplining of self were internalised within the individual. This meant that the dominant conceptions of freedom and liberty were and still are deeply embedded in the social relations and codes characteristic of market exchange based on private property and individual rights. These exclusively defined the realm of freedom and any challenge to them had to be ruthlessly put down. The social order was constituted by what Herbert Marcuse called 'repressive tolerance': there were strict boundaries beyond which one was never supposed to venture, no matter how pressing the cause of furthering liberty and freedom, at the same time as the rhetoric of tolerance was deployed to get us to tolerate the intolerable.[5]

The only surprising thing about all this is that we get surprised when we notice and think about it. After all, is it not obvious that the violence and domination of the state necessarily have to stand behind the freedoms of the market? In the theory and practices of the liberal state that gradually emerged from the eighteenth century onwards, the guiding idea was that the state should be self-limiting in its interventions, that it should practise laissez-faire with respect to individual and particularly entrepreneurial practices in the market-place, not out of paternalistic benevolence but out of self-interest in maximising the accumulation of monetary wealth and power within its sovereign jurisdiction. That the state frequently overreaches in its regulatory and interventionist activities is a common complaint among inhabitants and, of course, a standard complaint from capital. And from time to time political movements such as the Tea Party in the United States arise with a clear mission to roll back state interven-tion no matter whether that interventionism is benevolent or not. It is time, say libertarian critics, for the nanny state to be gone and the true reign of individual liberty and freedom to begin.

Karl Polanyi understood these relations all too well, though from the other side of the political argument. 'The passing of market-economy,' he hypothetically wrote, 'can become the beginning of an era of unprecedented freedom. Juridical and actual freedom can be made much wider and more general than ever before; regulation and control can achieve freedom not only for the few, but for all. Freedom, not as an appurtenance of privilege, tainted at the source, but as a prescriptive right extending far beyond the narrow confines of the political sphere into the intimate organization of society itself. Thus will old freedoms and civil rights be added to the fund of new freedom generated by the leisure and security that industrial society offers to all. Such a society can afford to be just and free.'

The difficulty of achieving this extension of the realm of freedom lay in the class interests and the entrenched privileges that attach to great concentrations of wealth. The affluent classes, secure in their own freedoms, resist any restrictions on their actions, claim they are being reduced to the status of a slave to socialist totalitarianism and cease-lessly agitate for the extension of their own particular freedoms at the expense of others. 'Free enterprise and private ownership are declared to be essentials of freedom. No society built on other foundations is said to deserve to be called free. The freedom that regulation creates is denounced as unfreedom; the justice, liberty and welfare it offers are decried as a camouflage of slavery ... This means the fullness of freedom for those whose income, leisure and security need no enhancing, and a mere pittance of liberty for the people, who may in vain attempt to make use of their democratic rights to gain shelter from the owners of property.'[6] Thus does Polanyi construct a telling rebuttal to the central theses of Friedrich Hayek's *Road to Serfdom*, written in 1942–3 but to this day a bible of the libertarian right and a mightily influential text (having sold more than 2 million copies).

Clearly at the root of the dilemma lies the meaning of freedom itself. The utopianism of liberal political economy 'gave a false direction to our ideals,' notes Polanyi. It failed to recognise that 'no society is possible in which power and compulsion are absent nor a world in which force has no function'. By clinging to a pure free-market view of society it 'equated economics with contractual relationships, and contractual relations with freedom'.[7] This is the world that libertarian Republicans construct. It is also the view of individual liberty and freedom embraced by much of the anarchist and autonomista left, even as the capitalist version of the free market is roundly condemned. It is impossible to escape the contradictory unity of freedom and domination no matter what politics are espoused.

The political consequence was, Polanyi argued, that 'neither voters, nor owners, neither producers, nor consumers could be held responsible for such brutal restrictions of freedom as were involved in the occurrence of unemployment and destitution'. Such conditions were the result of natural causes beyond anyone's control and for which no one in particular was responsible. The obligation to do anything about such conditions could be 'denied in the name of freedom'.[8] The House of Representatives in the United States with its Republican majority can happily vote to cut off food stamp aid to an increasingly impoverished population (while affirming the subsidies paid out to agribusiness) in the name of supporting the cause and increasing the realm of freedom. We cannot, Polanyi concluded, approach the question of freedom without first discarding the utopian vision of classical political economy and much of its cognate libertarian politics. Only then could we come 'face to face with the reality of society' and its contradictions. Otherwise, as is today most spectacularly the case, our freedoms are contingent on the denial of social reality. This denial of reality is what most right-wing discourses, such as that of President Bush, accomplish so precisely.

The inner connection between conceptions of liberty and freedom and capital, mediated through the utopian writings of the political economists, should not be surprising. After all, the extraction of surpluses from labour presupposes the domination and the relative unfreedom of labour under the rule of capital. As Marx ironically noted, labourers are free in the double sense: they are free to sell their labour power to whomsover they like, at the same time as they have been freed from control over those means of production (for example, the land) which would permit them to make a livelihood other than that defined by wage labour. The historical divorce of labour from access to the means of production entailed a long and continuing history of violence and coercion in the name of capital's freedom of access to wage labour. Capital also required a freedom to roam the world in search of profitable possibilities and this required, as we earlier saw, the eradication or reduction of physical, social and political barriers to its mobility. 'Laissez-faire' and 'laissez-passer' became the watchwords of the capitalist order. This applies not only to mobility but also to freedom from regulatory interference, except under those circumstances where external damages to other capitalists or to the economy as a whole became so totally unacceptable or so dangerous as to mandate state interventions. The freedom to pillage resources from under the feet of local and indigenous populations, to displace and despoil whole landscapes where necessary, to stretch the use of ecosystems up to and in some instances well beyond their capacity to reproduce all became a key part of capital's necessary freedoms. Capital demands that the state protect private property and enforce contracts and intellectual property rights against the threat of expropriation, except in cases where the public interest (usually a stalking horse for capital itself) demands.

None of the freedoms that capital needs and demands has passed uncontested. Indeed from time to time the contestation has been fierce. Capital's freedoms clearly rested, many people recognised, on the unfreedom of others. Both sides, Marx noted, had right on their side, as capital sought to extract as much labour time as possible from the workforce while the workers sought to protect their freedom to live their lives without being worked to death. Between two such rights, Marx famously said, force decides. But this was the exploitative world that the political economists justified in the name of a utopian programme of universal progress that was supposed to redound to the ultimate benefit of all. But if, said Marx, the true realm of freedom begins when and where necessity is left behind, then a political economic system that is based on the active cultivation of scarcity, impoverishment, labour surpluses and unfulfilled needs cannot possibly allow us entry into the true realm of freedom, where individual human flourishing for all and sundry becomes a real possibility. The paradox is that automation and artificial intelligence now provide us with abundant means to achieve the Marxian dream of freedom beyond the realm of necessity at the same time as the laws of capital's political economy put this freedom further and further out of reach.

The corrosive power of capital's economic reasoning sadly works its way into the heart of deeply felt humanist efforts to extend the realm of freedom beyond the gated communities in which the rich and wealthy of this world are increasingly imprisoned. Consider, for example, the exemplary work of Amartya Sen, who in his book *Development as Freedom* strives mightily to push economic reason to its humanitarian limits 'in the name of freedom'. Sen understands freedom as both process and what he calls 'substantive opportunities'. The distinction is important for it harbours a critique of a traditional welfare statism that treated the workers and the populace in general as mere objects of policy rather than as subjects of history. For Sen it is just as important to mobilise the populace and to develop its capabilities as active agents in economic development as it is to bring the people to a state where they have the necessary substantive opportunities (access to material goods and services) to live a valued life. He notes, correctly I believe, the many instances in which subjects would willingly trade in substantive freedoms in order to freely participate in the active and unalienated pursuit of their own fates and fortunes. Slaves and serfs may have been substantively better off than wage workers, but the latter would be unlikely to trade away their relative freedom as wage workers for that reason. Freedom to participate and to develop one's own capabilities is crucial as a means of achieving development. This is far preferable to substantive changes, however impressive, being imposed and orchestrated by alien and often paternalistic state powers. Sen uses this perspective on freedom 'in the evaluative analysis for assessing change and in the descriptive and predictive analysis in seeing freedom as a causally effective factor in rapid change'. These processes of development work through 'a variety of social institutions – related to the operation of markets, administrations, legislatures, political parties, nongovernmental institutions, the judiciary, the media, and the community in general'. All of these, Sen argues, can 'contribute to the process of development precisely through their effects on enhancing and sustaining individual freedoms'. Sen seeks an 'integrated understanding of the perspective roles of these different institutions and their interactions', along with an appreciation of 'the formation of values and the emergence of evolution of social ethics'. The result is a diverse field of freedoms attaching to a variety of institutions and activities that cannot be reduced to some simple formula 'of accumulation of capital, or opening up of markets, or having efficient economic planning'. The unifying factor here is 'the process of enhancing individual freedoms and the social commitment to bring that about ... Development is indeed a momentous engagement with freedom's possibilities.'[9]

The problem, of course, is that Sen's vision, however attractive, is in the end yet another version of the utopianism of liberal political economy. Freedom becomes not an end but a means of what Michel Foucault calls 'governmentality'. It is *through* freedom that the self-discipline of whole populations is managed by state power and it is that self-discipline that assures conformity and compliance with bourgeois institutions and ways of life, including, of course, capitalist class domination in terms of its cumulative wealth and power. In other words, the end is not in question and does not have to be challenged in the name of freedom because freedom is incorporated in the process. This is what 'development as freedom' means.

Sen depicts a contradiction-free world. He does not recognise the overwhelming force of the class antagonisms (of the sort that Polanyi clearly notes), the tense dialectical relation between freedom and domination, the power of private persons to appropriate social wealth, the contradictions of use and exchange value, of private property and the state. To be sure, the oppositions get mentioned, but all of them, in Sen's universe, are manageable. That any of them might become absolute contradictions and the locus of crisis is ruled out by assumption or merely put down to bad management. Sen's laudable and deeply attractive attempt to ground an unalienated approach to freedom through process presumes a non-contradictory version of capital's universe. This is the utopian universe that Polanyi clearly sees we have to abandon if we are to bring society into a world where real substantive freedoms can be achieved instead of an idea of freedom that denies social reality.

I do not pick on Sen for arbitrary reasons. Of all the economists he has gone as far as possible, it seems to me, in exploring the possibilities for the extension of freedom by way of a regulated and socially responsible form of market capitalist development evaluated against noble humanist ideals as opposed to crass measures of development. But his core belief, for which he can provide no definitive evidence, lies in the idea that the market system, properly regulated and managed, is a just and efficient way of fulfilling human wants and needs and that it can produce freedom from want in a free way. The contradictions inherent in the money form are nowhere to be seen even as the moneylenders are daily ravaging the livelihoods of impoverished populations throughout his beloved India. This is the kind of liberal humanism that dominates in the world of the NGOs and philanthropic organisations seriously committed in their heads and their hearts to the eradication of poverty and disease but with no real idea of how to do it.

In an astonishing and revelatory mea culpa published in the *New York Times*, Peter Buffett, a composer of music and son of the legendary billionaire investor Warren Buffett, recounts his encounter with the world of capitalist philanthropy consequent upon receiving a donation from his father to set up a charitable foundation some years ago. Early on, he recounts, he 'became aware of something I started to call Philanthropic Colonialism ... People (including me) who had very little knowledge of a particular place would think they could solve a local problem ... with little regard for culture, geography or societal norms.' Investment managers, corporate leaders and heads of state were all 'searching for answers with their right hand to problems that others in the room have created with their left'. Even as philanthropy becomes a massive business (with 9.4 million people employed giving away $316 billion in the USA alone), the global inequalities continue to spiral out of control 'as more lives and communities are destroyed by the system that creates vast amounts of wealth for the few'. Philanthropy becomes a form of 'conscience laundering' which merely 'allows the rich to sleep better at night, while others get just enough to keep the pot from boiling over. Nearly every time someone feels better by doing good, on the other side of the world (or street), someone else is further locked into a system that will not allow the true flourishing of his or her nature or the opportunity to live a joyful and fulfilled life.'[10] The concordance of Buffett's aims with those of both Sen and Marx is striking, as is the sad history of a bourgeois reformism that never solves social problems, but just moves them around.

The work of this powerful and rapidly growing 'charitable-industrial complex' has been corroded by the application of ever-tighter principles of capitalist economic rationality. The value of philanthropy is judged, notes Buffett, 'as if return on investment were the only measure of success'. The application of principles of microfinance to an informal sector reconceptualised as microenterprises endowed with private property rights may sound economically rational. But, asks Buffett, 'what is this really about? People will certainly learn to integrate into our system of debt and repayment with interest. People will rise above making $2 a day to enter our world of goods and services so they can buy more. But doesn't all this just feed the beast?' Indeed it does. And it does so at an opportune moment when the realisation of capital is threatened by flagging effective demand elsewhere and in a way where the practices of accumulation by dispossession through debt encumbrancy and debt peonage (and less legal predatory practices) provide a lucrative supplement to boost the overall rates of return on capital. Sadly, Buffett here hits the wall of his own conditions of repressive tolerance. 'I'm really not calling for an end to capitalism,' he weakly concludes, 'I'm calling for humanism.' But the practices he is criticising are exactly what capitalist humanism is all about. The only answer, which lies well beyond the bounds of the contemporary version of repressive tolerance, is a revolutionary humanism that confronts the (capitalist) beast that feeds very well thanks to the freedom it has to dominate others with its left hand as it seeks to minister to them with its right.

Marx not only took on the partisan ways in which bourgeois conceptions of liberty and freedom were deployed against the interests of the common people. He probed further into the very depths of what true wealth might mean in a genuinely free society. As he wrote in *Grundrisse*:

> When the limited bourgeois form is stripped away, what is wealth other than the universality of human needs, capacities, pleasures, productive forces etc., created through universal exchange? The full development of human mastery over the forces of nature, those of so-called nature as well as of humanity's own nature? The absolute working-out of his creative potentialities ... i.e. the development of all human powers as such the end in itself, not as measured on a *predetermined* yardstick? Where he does not produce himself in one specificity, but produces his totality? Strives not to remain something he has become, but is in the absolute movement of becoming? In bourgeois economics – and in the epoch of

production to which it corresponds – this complete working-out of the human content appears as a complete emptying-out, this universal objectification as total alienation.[11]

Marx does not avoid in this formulation the question of domination ('mastery'). He recognised the force of the contradiction between freedom and domination in revolutionary situations. Why is it, he asks in 'On the Jewish Question', 'that the right of man to freedom ceases to be a right as soon as it comes into conflict with political life, whereas according to the theory, political life is only the guarantee of the rights of man, the right of individual man, and so must be given up as soon as it contradicts its end, these rights of man'? The example that Marx had in mind was the curbing of press freedoms in the French Revolution. This posed the 'riddle' that 'still remains to be solved of why, in the minds of the political emancipators, the relationship is turned upside down and the end appears as the means and the means as the end'.[12] Marx got to the heart of the riddle of how freedom became slavery well before George Orwell.

Marx thought he found the answer in the writings of Rousseau:

> He who dares to undertake the making of a people's institutions ought to feel capable, so to speak, of changing human nature, of transforming each individual, who is by himself a complete and solitary whole, into part of a great whole from which in a manner he receives his life and being; of altering man's constitution for the purpose of strengthening it; and of substituting a partial and moral existence for the physical existence nature has conferred on us all. He must, in a word, take away from man his own resources and give him instead new ones alien to him, and incapable of being made use of without the help of other men.[13]

In other words, a fully socialised individual acquires a different political subjectivity, a different conception of what freedom means, from that of the isolated individual.

While this answer in itself is far too glib to bear the historical weight that it would have to bear, it does point to a fertile direction for inquiry. Is human freedom for all better defended by a regime of exclusionary individual private property rights or by common rights collectively managed by associated individuals? Are we not faced with a stark choice at the end of the day between individual freedoms being mobilised in the cause of capitalist class domination or class struggle being mobilised by the dispossessed in the cause of greater social and collective freedoms?

Notice also something important about Rousseau's formulation that does double duty in Marx's thought. Revolutionary transformations involve creative destruction. Something is lost but something is gained. What was lost for Rousseau was isolated individualism (which derived from a state of nature in Rousseau's theory but which was a political product of the bourgeois revolution for Marx). Isolated individualism had to give way in the face of new but 'alien' resources. The bourgeoisie had to be alienated from its individualised past in order for the dispossessed to gain its disalienated future freedoms. This turns Marx's theory of alienation inside out: the moment of alienation is charged with both positive and negative potential at key moments of revolutionary transition. There is no such thing as a contradiction that does not generate potentially contradictory responses.

Marx does not mince words with regard to the need to overthrow (or 'dominate') individualistic bourgeois conceptions of wealth and of value in order to release the potential for creative but collective human flourishing that surrounds us latently at every turn. Curiously, even Margaret Thatcher thought there was a difference somewhere here worth noting, thereby proving that even a viciously conservative grocer's daughter with an interest in chemistry is capable of transcendental thoughts. 'It is not the creation of wealth that is wrong,' she said (though I doubt she explicitly had Marx's conception of wealth as the full realisation of all individual human capacities and powers in mind), 'but the love of money for its own sake.'

The world of true freedom is thoroughly unpredictable. 'Once the shackles on human flourishing have been removed,' Eagleton remarks, 'it is far harder to say what will happen. For men and women are then a lot more free to behave as they wish within the confines of their responsibility for one another. If they are able to spend more of their time in what we now call leisure activities rather than hard at work, their behavior becomes even harder to predict. I say "what we now call leisure" because if we really did use the resources accumulated by capitalism to release large numbers of people from work, then we would not call what they did instead leisure.' Full advantage could then be taken of automation and artificial intelligence to actually release rather than imprison people in meaningless labours. 'For Marx,' says Eagleton, 'socialism is the point where we begin collectively to determine our own destinies. It is democracy taken with full seriousness rather than democracy as (for the most part) a political charade. And the fact that people are more free means that it will be harder to say what they will be doing at five o'clock on Wednesday.'[14] But that does not imply there will then be no need for self-discipline, commitment and dedication to those complex tasks we might freely choose to undertake for our own satisfaction as well as for the well-being of others. Freedom attaches, as Aristotle long ago understood, to the good life and the good life is an active life dedicated like all of nature to the perpetual search for novelty. An unalienated version of the dialectic between freedom and domination is possible in the quest for individuals, always in association with others, to reach the summit of their potentialities and powers. But that search for unalienated relations cannot proceed without the prior experience of alienation and its contradictory possibilities.

Part Three

# The Dangerous Contradictions

The moving contradictions evolve differentially and provide much of the dynamic force behind capital's historical and geographical evolution. In some instances their movement tends to be progressive (though never without reverses here and setbacks there). Technological change has by and large been cumulative, as has the geographical production of space, though in both instances there are strong countercurrents and reversals. Viable technologies get left behind and fade away, spaces and places that were once vigorous centres of capitalist activity become ghost towns or shrinking cities. In other instances the movement is more like a pendulum, as between monopoly and competition or the balance between poverty and wealth. And elsewhere, as in the case of freedom and domination, the movement is more chaotic and random, depending upon the ebb and flow of political forces in struggle with one another, while in still other instances, such as the complex field of social reproduction, the intersections between the historical evolution of capitalism and the specific requirements of capital are so indeterminate and intermingled as to make the direction and strength of movement episodic and rarely consistent. The advances (for such they are) in the rights of women, of the handicapped, of sexual minorities (the LGBT social group), as well as of religious groupings that have strict codes on various facets of social reproduction (such as marriage, family, child-rearing practices and the like), make it hard to calculate exactly how capital and capitalism are or are not working with or against each other in terms of foundational contradictions. And if this is true of the contradictions of social reproduction, it is even more so in the complex case of domination and freedom.

The patterning of the moving contradictions provides much of the energy and much of the innovative zest in the co-evolution of both capital and capitalism and opens a wealth (and I use that word advisedly as meaning a potential flourishing of human capabilities rather than of mere possessions) of possibilities for new initiatives. These are the contradictions and spaces in which hope for a better society is latent and from which alternative architectures and constructions might emerge.

As in the case of foundational contradictions, the moving

*contradictions intersect, interact and run interference with each other in intriguing ways within the totality of what capital is about. The production of space and the dynamics of uneven geographical development have been strongly impacted by technological changes in both organisational forms (for example, of state apparatuses and territorial forms of organisation) and technologies of transportation and the production of space. It is within the field of uneven geographical development that differentiations in social reproduction and in the balance between freedom and domination flourish to the point where they in themselves become part of the production of space and of uneven development. The creation of heterotopic spaces, where radically different forms of production, social organisation and political power might flourish for a while, implies a terrain of anti-capitalist possibility that is perpetually opening and shutting down. It is here too that questions of monopoly and centralisation of power versus decentralisation and competition play out to influence technological and organisational dynamism and to animate geopolitical competition for economic advantage. And it goes without saying that the balance between poverty and wealth is constantly being modified by interterritorial competition, migratory streams and competitive innovations regarding labour productivities and the creation of new product lines.*

*It is within the framework of these interactive and dynamic contradictions that multiple alternative political projects are to be found. Many of these are constituted as distinctive responses of capital to its own contradictions and are therefore primarily directed to facilitate the reproduction of capital under conditions of perpetual risk and uncertainty if not outright crises. But even in these instances there lie innumerable possibilities for the insertion of initiatives that so modify the functioning of capital as to open perspectives on what an anti-capitalist alternative might look like. I believe, as did Marx, that the future is already largely present in the world around us and that political innovation (like technological innovation) is a matter of putting existing but hitherto isolated and separated political possibilities together in a different way. Uneven geographical developments cannot but generate 'spaces of hope' and heterotopic situations where new modes of cooperation might flourish, at least for a while, before they get reabsorbed into the dominant practices of capital. New technologies (like the internet) open up new spaces of potential freedom from domination that can advance the cause of democratic governance. Initiatives in the field of social reproduction can produce new political subjects desirous of revolutionising and humanising social relations more generally and cultivating a more aesthetically satisfying and sensitive approach to our metabolic relation to nature. To point to all these possibilities is not to say they will all bear fruit, but it does suggest that any anti-capitalist politics has to be assiduous in hunting through the contradictions and ferreting out its own path towards the construction of an alternative universe using the resources and ideas already to hand.*

*This then brings us to the dangerous, if not potentially fatal, contradictions. Marx is famously supposed to have said that capital would ultimately collapse under the weight of its own internal contradictions. I cannot actually find where Marx said this, and from my own reading of him I think it extremely unlikely that he would ever have said such a thing. It presupposes a mechanical breakdown of the economic engine of capitalism that will occur without any human agent throwing sand in the machine or militantly setting about halting its progress and replacing it. Marx's position, and I broadly follow him in this (against certain currents in the Marxist/communist tradition, as well as against the grain of the views his many critics typically attribute to him), is that capital can probably continue to function indefinitely but in a manner that will provoke progressive degradation on the land and mass impoverishment, dramatically increasing social class inequality, along with dehumanisation of most of humanity, which will be held down by an increasingly repressive and autocratic denial of the potential for individual human flourishing (in other words, an intensification of the totalitarian police-state surveillance and militarised control system and the totalitarian democracy we are now largely experiencing).*

*The resultant unbearable denial of the free development of human creative capacities and powers amounts to throwing away the cornucopia of possibilities that capital had bequeathed us and squandering the real wealth of human possibilities in the name of perpetual* augmentation of monetary wealth and the satiation of narrow economic class interests. Faced with such a prospect, the only sensible politics is to seek to transcend capital and the restraints of an increasingly autocratic and oligarchical structure of capitalist class power and to rebuild the economy's imaginative possibilities into a new and far more egalitarian and democratic configuration.

The Marx I favour is, in short, a revolutionary humanist and not a teleological determinist. Statements can be found in his works that support the latter position, but I believe the bulk of his writings, both historical and political-economic, support the former interpretation. It is for this reason that I reject the idea of 'fatal' in favour of 'dangerous' contradictions, for to call them fatal would convey a false air of inevitability and cancerous decay, if not of apocalyptic mechanical endings. Certain contradictions are, however, more dangerous both to capital and to humanity than others. These vary from place to place and from time to time. Were we writing about the future of capital and humanity fifty or a hundred years ago, we would very likely have focused on different contradictions from those which I focus on here. The environmental issue and the challenge of maintaining compound growth would not have called for that much attention in 1945, when settling the geopolitical rivalries and rationalising processes of uneven geographical development, all the while rebalancing (through state interventions) the contradictory unity between production and realisation, were far more salient questions. The three contradictions I focus on here are most dangerous in the immediate present, not only for the ability of the economic engine of capitalism to continue to function but also for the reproduction of human life under even minimally reasonable conditions. One of them, but just one of them, is potentially fatal. But it will turn out so only if a revolutionary movement arises to change the evolutionary path that the endless accumulation of capital dictates. Whether or not such a revolutionary spirit crystallises out to force radical changes in the way in which we live is not given in the stars. It depends entirely on human volition. A first step towards exercising that volition is to become conscious and fully aware of the nature of the present dangers and the choices we face.

# Contradiction 15
# Endless Compound Growth

Capital is always about growth and it necessarily grows at a compound rate. This condition of capital's reproduction now constitutes, I shall argue, an extremely dangerous but largely unrecognised and unanalysed contradiction.

Most people do not well understand the mathematics of compound interest. Nor do they understand the phenomenon of compounding (or exponential) growth and the potential dangers it can pose. Even the dismal science of conventional economics, as Michael Hudson shows in a recent trenchant commentary, has failed to recognise the significance of compounding interest on rising indebtedness.[1] The result has been to obscure a key part of the explanation for the financial disruptions that shook the world in 2008. So is perpetual compounding growth possible?

In recent times there has been a flurry of worry among some economists that faith in the long-held supposition of perpetual growth might be misplaced. Robert Gordon, for example, has suggested in a recent paper that the economic growth experienced over the last 250 years 'could well be a unique episode in human history rather than a guarantee of endless future advance at the same rate'. His case rests largely on an overview of the path and effects of innovations in the productivity of labour which have underpinned the growth of per capita incomes. Gordon joins with several other economists in thinking that the innovation waves of the past have been much stronger than the most recent wave, resting on electronics and computerisation, that began around the 1960s. This last wave has been weaker in its effects than generally supposed, he argues, and is in any case now largely exhausted (reaching its apogee in the dot-com bubble of the 1990s). On this basis, Gordon predicts that 'future growth in real GDP per capita will be slower than in any extended period since the late 19th century, and growth in real consumption per capita for the bottom 99 percent of the income distibution will be even slower than that'. The inherent weakness of the last wave of innovations is aggravated in the case of the USA by a number of 'headwinds' that include rising social inequality, problems deriving from the rising cost and declining quality of education, the impacts of globalisation, environmental regulation, demographic conditions (the ageing of the population), rising tax burdens and an 'overhang' of consumer and government debt.[2] But even in the absence of these 'headwinds', Gordon argues, the future would still be one of relative stagnation compared to the last 200 years.

A component of one of the 'headwinds', government debt, has, at the time of writing, become a political football in the USA (with many echoes elsewhere). It has been the focus of strident and exaggerated arguments and claims in the media and in Congress. The supposedly huge and monstrous burden debt will place on future generations is again and again invoked to promote draconian cutbacks in state expenditures and the social wage (as usual, of course, to the benefit of the oligarchy). In Europe the same argument is used to justify imposing ruinous austerity on whole countries (like Greece), though it does not take too much imagination to see how this might also be for the benefit of the richer countries like Germany and the affluent bondholders more generally. In Europe democratically elected governments in Greece and Italy were peacefully overthrown and for a while replaced by 'technocrats' who had the confidence of the bond markets.

All of this has made it particularly hard to get a clear-eyed view of the relation between the compounding of debt obligations, the exponential growth of capital accumulation and the dangers they pose. Gordon's concern, it should be noted, was primarily with per capita GDP. This looks rather different from aggregate GDP. Both measures are sensitive to demographic conditions but in very different ways. A casual inspection of the available historical data on total GDP suggests that while there has always been a loose relation between wealth and debt accumulation throughout the history of capital, the accumulation of wealth since the 1970s has been far more tightly associated with the accumulation of public, corporate and private debt. The suspicion lurks that an accumulation of debts is now a precondition for the further accumulation of capital. If this is the case, then it produces the curious result that the strenuous attempts on the part of the right-wing Republicans and analogous groups in Europe (such as the German government) to reduce if not eliminate indebtedness are mounting a far graver threat to the future of capital than the working-class movement has ever posed.

Compounding is, in essence, very simple. I place $100 in a savings account that pays 5 per cent annual interest. At the end of the year I have $105, which at a constant rate of interest becomes $110.25 the year after (the figures are greater if the compounding occurs monthly or daily). The difference between this sum at the end of the second year and an arithmetic rate of interest without compounding is very small (just 25 cents). The difference is so small it is hardly worth bothering with. For this reason it easily escapes notice. But after thirty years of compounding at 5 per cent I have $432.19 as opposed to the $250 I would have if I was accumulating at a 5 per cent arithmetic rate. After sixty years I have $1,867 as compared to $400 and after 100 years I have $13,150 instead of $600. Notice something about these figures. The compound interest curve rises very slowly for quite a while (see Figures 1 and 2) and then starts to accelerate and by the end of the curve it becomes what mathematicians refer to as a singularity – it sails off into infinity. Anyone with a mortgage experiences this in reverse. For the first twenty years of a thirty-year mortgage the principal still owed declines very slowly. The decline then accelerates and over the last two or three years the principal diminishes very rapidly.

There are a number of classic anecdotes to illustrate this quality of compounding interest and exponential growth. An Indian king wished to reward the inventor of the game of chess. The inventor asked for one grain of rice on the first square of the chessboard and

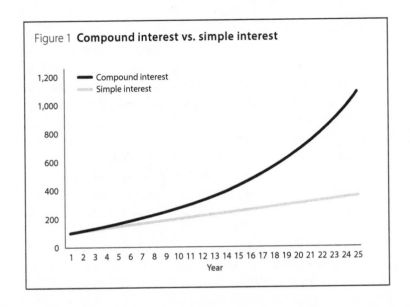

Figure 1 **Compound interest vs. simple interest**

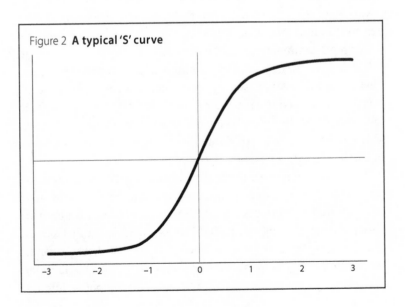

Figure 2 **A typical 'S' curve**

that the amount be doubled from one square to the next until all the squares were covered. The king readily agreed, since it seemed a small price to pay. The trouble was that by the time it came to the twenty-first square more than a million grains were required and after the forty-first square (which required more than a trillion grains) there simply was not enough rice in the world to cover the remaining squares. One version of the story has the king so angry at being tricked that he had the inventor beheaded. This version of the story is salutary. It illustrates the tricky character of compounding interest and shows how easy it is to underestimate its hidden power. In the later stages of compounding the acceleration takes one by surprise.

An example of the dangers of compound interest is illustrated by the case of Peter Thelluson, a wealthy Swiss merchant banker living in London, who set up a trust fund of £600,000 that could not be touched for 100 years after he died in 1797. Yielding 7.5 per cent at a compound rate, the fund would have been worth £19 million (far in excess of the British national debt) by 1897, when the money could be distributed to his fortunate descendants. Even at 4 per cent, the government of the time calculated that the legacy would be equivalent to the entire public debt by 1897. The compounding of interest would produce immense financial power in private hands. To prevent this, a bill was passed in 1800 limiting trusts to twenty-one years. Thelluson's will was contested by his immediate heirs. When the case was finally decided in 1859, after many years of active litigation, it turned out that the entire legacy had been absorbed by legal costs. This was the basis for the celebrated case of Jarndyce versus Jarndyce in Charles Dickens's novel *Bleak House*.[3]

The end of the eighteenth century saw a flurry of excited commentary about the power of compound interest. In 1772 the mathematician Richard Price, in a tract that later drew Marx's amused attention, wrote: 'money bearing compound interest increases at first slowly. But, the rate of increase being continuously accelerated, it becomes in some time so rapid, as to mock all the powers of the imagination. One penny, put out at our Saviour's birth to 5 per cent compound interest, would, before this time, have increased to a greater sum, than would be contained in one hundred and fifty millions of earths, all solid gold. But if put out to simple interest, it would, in the same time, have amounted to no more than seven shillings and fourpence halfpenny.[4] Notice once more the element of surprise at how compound growth can produce results that 'mock all the powers of the imagination'. Are we too about to be shocked at what compounding growth can lead to? Interestingly, Price's main point (in contrast to the current crop of alarmists) was how easy it would be to retire the existing national debt (as the Thelluson example also showed) by putting the powers of compound interest to work!

Angus Maddison has painstakingly attempted to calculate the rate of growth in total global economic output over several centuries. Obviously, the further back he goes, the shakier the data. Significantly, the data before 1700 increasingly relies on using population estimates as a surrogate for total economic output. But even in our own times there are good reasons to challenge the raw data, because it includes a number of 'gross national bads' (such as the economic consequences of traffic accidents and hurricanes). There has been significant agitation by some economists to change the basis of national accounting on the grounds that many of the measures are misleading. But if we stick with Maddison's findings, then capital has been growing at a compound rate since 1820 or so of 2.25 per cent. This is the global average figure.[5] Clearly there have been times when (for example, the Great Depression) and places where (for example, contemporary Japan) the growth rate has been negligible or negative, while at other times (such as the 1950s and 1960s) and in other places (such as China over the last twenty years) the growth has been much higher. This average is slightly below what seems to be a generally accepted consensus figure in the financial press and elsewhere of 3 per cent as a minimum acceptable rate of growth. When growth falls below that norm the economy is described as sluggish and when it goes below zero this is taken as an indicator of recession or, if prolonged, of depression conditions. Growth that goes much above 5 per cent, on the other hand, is typically taken in 'mature economies' (that is, not contemporary China) as a sign of 'overheating', which always comes with the threat of runaway inflation. In recent times, even across the 'crash' years of 2007–9, global growth kept fairly steady, close to 3 per cent or so, though most of it was in emerging markets (such as Brazil, Russia, India and China – the BRIC countries in short). The 'advanced capitalist economies' fell to 1 per cent growth or below from 2008 to 2012.

In 1820, Maddison calculates, global output was worth $694 billion in 1990 constant dollars ('billion' on the US scale, meaning 1,000 million). By 1913 it had risen to $2.7 trillion (on the US scale a trillion is 1,000 billion); in 1973 it stood at $16 trillion and by 2003 nearly $41 trillion. Bradford DeLong gives different estimates, starting with $359 billion in 1850 (in 1990 constant dollars) rising to $1.7 trillion in 1920, $3 trillion in 1940, $12 trillion in 1970, $41 trillion in 2000 and $45 trillion in 2012. DeLong's figures suggest a lower initial base and a somewhat higher rate of compound growth. While the figures are quite different (testifying to how difficult and often arbitrary these estimates are), in both cases the effect of compounding growth (with considerable temporal and geographical variation) is clearly visible.[6]

So let us take a 3 per cent compound rate of growth as the norm. This is the growth rate that permits most if not all capitalists to gain a positive rate of return on their capital. To keep to a satisfactory growth rate right now would mean finding profitable investment opportunities for an extra nearly $2 trillion compared to the 'mere' $6 billion that was needed in 1970. By the time 2030 rolls around, when estimates suggest the global economy should be more than $96 trillion, profitable investment opportunities of close to $3 trillion will be needed. Thereafter the numbers become astronomical. It is as if we are on the twenty-first square of the chessboard and cannot get off. It just does not look a feasible growth trajectory, at least from where we sit now. Imagined physically, the enormous expansions in physical infrastructures, in urbanisation, in workforces, in consumption and in production capacities that have occurred since the 1970s until now will have to be dwarfed into insignificance over the coming generation if the compound rate of capital accumulation is to be maintained. Take a look at a map of the city nearest you in 1970 and contrast it with today and then imagine what it will look like when quadrupled in size and density over the next twenty years.

But it would be a serious error to assume that human social evolution is governed by some mathematical formula. This was the big mistake made by Thomas Malthus when he first advanced his principle of population in 1798 (roughly the same time when Richard Price and others were celebrating – if that is the right word – the power of exponential growth in human affairs). Malthus's arguments are directly relevant to the issue at hand, while they also provide a cautionary tale. He argued that human populations, like all other species, had the tendency to increase at an exponential (that is, compounding) rate, while food output could at best increase only arithmetically given the conditions of agricultural productivity then prevailing. Diminishing returns on the application of labour in agriculture were likely to make the gap between rates of population expansion and food supply even greater over time. The widening gap between the two curves was taken as a measure of the increasing pressure of population on resources. As the gap increased, the inevitable result would be, Malthus argued, famine, poverty, epidemics, war and increasing pathologies of all kinds for the mass of humankind. These would act as brutal checks to keep population growth within the bounds dictated by supposedly natural carrying capacities. Malthus's dystopian predictions did not come to pass. In recognition of this, Malthus later broadened his principles to include changes in human demographic behaviour, the so-called 'moral restraints', such as later age of marriage, sexual abstinence and (tacitly) other techniques for population limitation. These would dampen if not reverse any tendency towards exponential population growth.[7] Malthus likewise failed miserably to anticipate the industrialisation of agriculture and the rapid expansion of global food production through colonisation of hitherto unproductive lands (particularly in the Americas).

By invoking the tendency towards the exponential growth of capital accumulation, are we in danger of repeating Malthus's mistake of assuming human evolution conforms to a mathematical formula, rather than reflecting fluid and adaptable human behaviours? If so, are there ways in which capital has been and is adapting to accommodate disparities between an accumulation process that is necessarily exponential (if that is indeed the case) and the conditions that might limit the capacity for exponential growth?

There is, however, a prior consideration that needs to be addressed. If population is growing exponentially (as Malthus supposed), then the economy has to grow at a parallel rate for living standards to be sustained. So what, then, is the relation between demographic trajectories and the dynamics of capital accumulation?

Currently, the only countries that are increasing their populations at a 3 per cent compound rate of growth or more are in Africa, South Asia and the Middle East. Negative population growth rates are found in Eastern Europe, while Japan and much of Europe have such low growth rates that they are not reproducing themselves. In these last cases economic problems are arising because of lack of domestic labour supply and because of the increasing burden of supporting ageing populations. A smaller and often declining workforce has to produce sufficient value to pay pensions to an increasing retired population. This relation continues to be important in certain parts of the world. Early on in capital's history, rapid population growth or a vast reserve of untapped and yet-to-be urbanised wage labour unquestionably helped to fuel rapid capital accumulation. Indeed, a plausible case can be made that population growth from the early seventeenth century on was a precondition for capital accumulation. The role of what Gordon calls 'the demographic dividend' in fostering economic growth was clearly important in the past and continues to be so. The vast inflow of women into the labour force in North America and Europe after 1945 is one case in point, but this is something that cannot be repeated. The world's labour force expanded by 1.2 billion between 1980 and 2009, nearly half of that growth coming from India and China alone. This too will be hard to repeat. But in many parts of the world this relation between rapid population growth and rapid capital accumulation is beginning to break down, as population growth conforms to an S-shaped curve that starts flat and then accelerates exponentially upwards before rapidly slowing down to become flat, with zero or even negative population growth (for example, in Italy and Eastern Europe). It is into this demographic vacuum of zero growth in some parts of the world that strong migration streams are drawn (though not without social disruptions, political resistances and a lot of cultural conflict).

While population projections even in the medium term are a particularly tricky proposition (and the projections change rapidly from year to year), the hope is that the global population will stabilise during this century and peak at no more than 12 billion or so (perhaps as low as 10 billion) by the end of the century and thereafter achieve a steady state of zero growth. Clearly this is an important issue in relation to the dynamics of capital accumulation. In the United States, for example, job creation since 2008 has not kept pace with the expansion of the labour force. The falling unemployment rate reflects a shrinkage in the proportion of the working-age population seeking to participate in the labour force. But whatever happens, it is pretty clear that capital accumulation in the long-term future can rely less and less upon demographic growth to sustain or impel its compound growth and that the dynamics of production, consumption and realisation of capital will have to adjust to these new demographic circumstances. When this might happen is hard to say, but most estimates suggest that the vast increase in the global wage labour force that occurred after 1980 or so will be hard to replicate once it exhausts itself after 2030 or so. In a way this is just as well, given that, as we have seen, technological change is tending to produce larger and larger redundant and even disposable populations among the less skilled.[8] The gap between too few high-skill workers and a massive reserve of unemployed and increasingly unemployable medium- and low-skill workers appears to be widening, while the definition of skills is evolving rapidly.

So would it be possible for capital accumulation to move beyond the exponentials it has exhibited over the past two centuries on to a similar S-shaped trajectory as has occurred in the demographics of many countries, culminating in a zero-growth, steady-state capitalist economy? The answer to this prospect is a resounding no, and it is vital to understand why. The simplest reason is that capital is about profit seeking. For all capitalists to realise a positive profit requires the existence of more value at the end of the day than there was at the beginning. That means an expansion of the total output of social labour. Without that expansion there can be no capital. A zero-growth capitalist economy is a logical and exclusionary contradiction. It simply cannot exist. This is why zero growth defines a condition of crisis for capital. If prolonged, zero growth of the sort that prevailed in much of the world in the 1930s spells the death knell of capitalism.

How, then, can capital continue to accumulate and expand in perpetuity at a compound rate? How can it do so when it seems to entail a doubling if not tripling in the size of the astonishing physical transformations that have been wrought across planet earth over the last forty years. The dramatic industrialisation and urbanisation of China over those years is a foretaste of what would have to be accomplished to keep capital accumulation going in the future. For much of the last century large parts of the world were attempting to mimic the growth path of the United States. In the coming century most of the world would have to mimic the growth path of China (with all its ghastly environmental consequences), which would be impossible for the United States and Europe and unthinkable almost everywhere else (apart from, say, Turkey, Iran and some parts of Africa). Throughout these last forty years, it is worth remembering also that there have been multiple traumatic crises, usually localised, cascading around the world, from South-East Asia and Russia in 1998 through Argentina in 2001 to the almighty global financial crash of 2008 that shook the world of capital to its very roots.

But it is here that the cautionary tale of Malthus's mistaken dystopian vision ought to give us pause. We need to ask: in what ways can capital accumulation change its spots to adapt to what appears a critical situation in order to reproduce itself? There are, in fact, a number of key adaptations that are already occurring. Can the difficulties be staved off and if so can they do so indefinitely? What behavioural adaptations, akin to Malthus's 'moral restraints' (though the term 'moral' will hardly end up being appropriate), might reshape the accumulation dynamic while preserving its necessary essence of compounding growth?

There is one form that capital takes which permits accumulation without limit and that is the money form. This is so only because the money form is now unchained from any physical limitations such as those imposed by the money commodities (the metallic moneys like gold and silver that originally gave physical representation to the immateriality of social labour and which are largely fixed in terms of their global supply). State-issued fiat moneys can be created without limit. The expansion of the contemporary money supply is now accomplished by some mix of private activity and state action (via the state–finance nexus as constituted by treasury departments and central banks). When the US Federal Reserve engages in quantitative easing it simply creates as much liquidity and money as it wants at the drop of a hat. Adding a few zeros to the quantity of money in circulation is no problem. The danger, of course, is that the result will be a crisis of inflation. This is not occurring because the Federal Reserve is largely refilling a hole left in the banking system when trust between the private banks broke down and interbank lending, which was leveraged into massive money creation within the banking system, broke down in 2008. The second reason why inflation is not on the horizon is because organised labour has almost zero power (given the disposable surplus labour reserves) in these times to raise wages and thereby influence the price level (though class struggles in China have raised labour costs there marginally).

But, plainly, the perpetual accumulation of capital at an exponential rate by way of an exponential creation of money is almost certain to end in disaster unless accompanied by other adaptations. Let's go through a number of these before deciding whether they add up to what a sustainable future for the reproduction of capital might look like under conditions of perpetual compound growth.

Capital is not only about the production and circulation of value. It is also about the destruction or devaluation of capital. A certain proportion of capital is destroyed in the normal course of capital circulation as new and cheaper machinery and fixed capital become available. Major crises are often characterised by creative destruction, which means mass devaluations of commodities, of hitherto productive plant and equipment, of money and of labour. There is always a certain amount of devaluation going on as new plants drive out old before their lifetime is over, as more expensive items are replaced by cheaper items because of technological changes. The rapid deindustrialisation of older industrial districts in the 1970s and 1980s in North America and Europe is an obvious example. In times of crisis, of war or of natural disasters, the devaluation can be massive. In the 1930s and the Second World War losses were considerable. Estimates from the IMF suggested that the net losses worldwide in the financial crisis year of 2008 added up to close to the value of one whole year's global output of goods and services. But large though these losses were, they did little more than generate a brief pause in the trajectory of compounding growth. In any case, as property values recovered, particularly in the USA and the UK, where they had been hit hard during the crisis, so a lot of asset values were recovered (though, as always, they now lay in the hands of the rich folk, thereby contributing to the massive regressive redistribution of wealth that, in the absence of revolutionary interventions, typically occurs in the course of a crisis). The devaluations would have to be vastly greater and longer-lasting than those experienced in 2008 (closer, perhaps, to those of the 1930s and 1940s) to really make much of a difference.

The problem of the uneven development of devaluation and of geopolitical struggles over who is to bear the cost of devaluation is significant, in part because it frequently relates to the spread of social unrest and political instability. So while devaluation does not work very well as an antidote to compounding growth worldwide, its geographical concentrations do have a significant bearing on the dynamics of anti-capitalist sentiment and struggle. The two 'lost decades' of development throughout most of Latin America produced a political climate of opposition to neoliberalism (though not necessarily to capital) and this has in turn played an important role in protecting the region from the worst impacts of the global crisis of devaluation that broke out in 2008. The differential imposition of losses on, for example, Greece and southern Europe more generally amounts to a geographical version of the redistributions of wealth occurring between rich and poor.

Conversely, privatisation of public assets, the creation of new markets and further enclosures of the commons (from land and water to intellectual property rights) have expanded the terrain upon which capital can freely operate. The privatisation of water provision, social housing, education and health care and even war making, the creation of carbon trading markets and the patenting of genetic materials have given capital the power of entry into many areas of economic, social and political life that were hitherto closed to it. As an outlet for compounding growth these additional market opportunities have been significant, but, as with devaluation, I do not believe they constitute enough potential to absorb compounding growth, particularly in the future (they did, I believe, play a significant role in the 1980s and 1990s). Besides, when everything – but everything – is commodified and monetised, then there is a limit beyond which this process of expansion cannot go. How close we are to that limit right now is hard to judge but nearly four decades of neoliberal privatisation strategies have already accomplished a great deal and in many parts of the world there is not much left to enclose and privatise. There are, in addition, many signs of political resistance to the further enclosure and commodification of life forms beyond where we are now and some of these struggles, against, for example, water privatisation in Italy and genetic patenting, have been successful.

Consider, thirdly, the limits that might be encountered with respect to final consumption and the realisation of capital. One of the ways that capital has adapted to compound growth has been through radical transformations in the nature, form, style and mass of final consumption (aided, of course, by population increases). Economic limits to this are set by the aggregate effective demand (roughly, wages and salaries plus bourgeois disposable incomes). Over the last forty years that demand has been strongly supplemented by private and public debt creation. I focus here, however, on one important physical limit which is set by the turnover time of consumer goods: how long do they last and how quickly do they need to be replaced?

Capital has systematically shortened the turnover time of consumer goods by producing commodities that do not last, pushing hard towards planned and sometimes instantaneous obsolescence, by the rapid creation of new product lines (for example, as in electronics in recent times), accelerating turnover by mobilising fashion and the powers of advertising to emphasise the value of newness and the dowdiness of the old. It has been doing this for the last 200 years or so and concomitantly produced vast amounts of waste. But the trends have accelerated, capturing and infecting mass consumption habits markedly over the last forty years, particularly in the advanced capitalist economies. The transformations in middle-class consumerism in countries like China and India have also been remarkable. The sales and advertising industry is now one of the largest sectors of the economy in the United States and much of its work is dedicated to the acceleration of the turnover time of consumption.

But there are still physical limits to how fast the turnover of, say, cellphones and fashions can be. Even more significant, therefore, has been the move towards the production and consumption of spectacle, a commodity form that is ephemeral and instantaneously consumed. Back in 1967 Guy Debord wrote a very prescient text, *The Society of the Spectacle*, and it almost seems as if the representatives of capital read it very carefully and adopted its theses as foundational for their consumerist strategies.[9] Everything from TV shows and other media products, films, concerts, exhibitions, sports events, mega-cultural events and, of course, tourism is included in this. These activities now dominate the field of consumerism. Even more interesting is how capital mobilises consumers to produce their own spectacle via YouTube, Facebook, Twitter and other forms of social media. All of these forms can be instantaneously consumed even as they absorb vast amounts of what might otherwise be free time. The consumers, furthermore, produce information, which is then appropriated by the

owners of the media for their own purposes. The public is simultaneously constituted as both producers and consumers, or what Alvin
Toffler once called 'prosumers'.[10] There is an important corollary here
and this broaches a theme that we will encounter elsewhere: capital
profits not through investing in production in these spheres but by
appropriating rents and royalties on the use of the information, the
software and the networks it constructs. This is just one of several
contemporary indications that the future of capital lies more in the
hands of the rentiers and the rentier class than in the hands of the
industrial capitalists.

These transformations in the field of consumption are what
Hardt and Negri seem to be after when they propose a grand shift of
capital's operations from the field of material to immaterial labour.[11]
They argue that the relation between capital and consumers is no
longer mediated by things but by information, images, messaging
and the proliferation and marketing of symbolic forms that relate
to and work on the political subjectivity of whole populations. This
amounts to an attempt by capital and the state to engage with the
biopolitical manipulation of populations and the production of new
political subjects. It has always been the case, of course, that the
kinds of people we are have been shaped by the commodity world
we inhabit. Suburbanites are a special breed of people whose political
subjectivity is shaped by their daily living experiences in the same
way that the imprisoned Italian communist leader Antonio Gramsci
envisaged what he called Americanism and Fordism producing a
new kind of human subject through factory labour.[12] The contemporary production of 'new' political subjects through everything from
subliminal advertising to direct propaganda undoubtedly forms
a vast field for capital investments. To call this 'immaterial labour'
is a bit unfortunate, given the vast amount of material labour (and
the crucial importance of material infrastructures) underpinning
activities of this sort, even when they take place in cyberspace and
produce their effect primarily in the minds and beliefs of persons. A
vast amount of material social labour is involved in the production of
spectacles (like the opening ceremonies of Olympic Games, which,

you will have noted, have become grander and grander over time in ways quite consistent with the argument being made here).

These ideas now circulating about an internal revolution in the dominant form of capital accumulation parallel much contemporary commentary about the rise of an 'information society' and the development of a 'knowledge-based' capitalism. There is, it seems, an urgent need for many commentators to demonstrate how capital has changed its spots in recent times. It is perhaps comforting to explain away the recent stresses within capital as if we are confronting the birth pangs of an entirely new capitalist order in which knowledge and culture (and biopolitics, whatever that is) are the primary products rather than things. While some of this is undoubtedly true, it would be an error to imagine any radical break with the past and a double error to presume that the new forms escape the contradictions of compound growth. Spectacle, for example, has always been an important vehicle for capital accumulation and when was there ever a form of capital in which superior knowledge and information were not a source of excess profits? When was it, furthermore, that debt and finance were irrelevant and why is this phase of financialisation so different from that which occurred at, say, the end of the nineteenth century? So while it is true that the consumption of spectacle, images, information and knowledge is qualitatively different from the consumption of material commodities like houses, cars, bread and fashionable clothes, we would err if we failed to recognise that the rapid expansion of activity in these spheres is rooted in the futile (and I will explain why I use that word shortly) necessity of escaping the material constraints to compound growth. All of these alternative forms are captive to capital's struggle to absorb the necessity of its permanent compound growth.

It was, I think, no accident that the limits on money creation set by tying it to money commodities like gold and silver broke down in the early 1970s. The pressure of exponential expansion on what was in effect a fixed global supply of metal was simply irresistible at that moment in capital's historical development. Since then we have lived in a world where the potential limitlessness of money creation can prevail. Before the 1970s the main avenue for capital was to invest in production of value and of surplus value in the fields of manufacturing, mining, agriculture and urbanisation. While a lot of this activity was debt-financed, the general presumption, which was not incorrect, was that the debt would ultimately be recuperated out of the application of social labour to the production of commodities like houses, cars, refrigerators and the like. Even in the case of the long-term financing of infrastructures (such as roads, public works, urbanisation) there was a reasonable presumption that the debt would ultimately be paid off out of the increasing productivity of the social labour engaged in production. It could also be reasonably assumed that all of this would generate increasing per capita incomes. The interstate highway system built in the United States during the three decades after 1960 had a huge impact upon aggregate labour productivity and paid off handsomely. This was, in Robert Gordon's account, the strongest innovation wave in capital's history.[13]

There have always been significant circuits of what can be called 'fictitious capital' – investments in mortgages, public debt, urban and national infrastructures and the like. From time to time these flows of fictitious capital got out of hand to form speculative bubbles that ultimately burst to form serious financial and commercial crises. The legendary railway booms and busts of the nineteenth century, as well as the land and property market boom in the United States in the 1920s, were past examples. In promoting these speculative activities, financiers frequently came up with contorted, innovative (and often shady) ways to assemble and channel fictitious capitals so as to realise short-term gains (hedge funds, for example, have long existed) even when the long-term investments went bad. All sorts of crazy financial schemes flourished as well, which led Marx to speak of the credit system as 'the mother of all insane forms', while characterising Emile Pereire, a leading banker in Second Empire France, as having the 'charming character of swindler and prophet'.[14] This is not a bad description of the masters of the universe on Wall Street, men like Lloyd Blankfein, CEO of Goldman Sachs, who claimed they were only doing God's business when being criticised by a congressional committee for not doing the people's business properly.

The liberation of money creation from its money-commodity restraints in the early 1970s happened at a time when profitability prospects in productive activities were particularly low and when capital began to experience the impact of an inflexion point in the trajectory of exponential growth. Where was all the surplus money to go? Part of the answer lay in lending it out as government debt to developing countries – a very particular form of fictitious capital circulation – because, as Walter Wriston famously put it, 'countries don't disappear, you always know were to find them'. But states are not geared up to being productive enterprises. The consequence a few years later was a grumbling Third World debt crisis that stretched from 1982 well on into the early 1990s. It is important to note that this crisis was finally taken care of by exchanging actual debt obligations that might never be repaid for so-called 'Brady Bonds' backed by the IMF and the US Treasury that would be repaid. The lending institutions, with a few exceptions, decided to take the money they could get rather than hold out for the full amount on the never-never. The bondholders in this case took a 'haircut' (usually between 30 and 50 per cent) on the fictitious capital they had circulated.[15]

The other path was to invest the surplus capital not in production but in the purchase of assets (including debt claims). An asset is simply a capitalised property title and its value is set in anticipation of either some future stream of revenue or some future state of scarcity (for example, of gold or of Picassos). The result of investment flows into these fields was a general rise in asset values – everything from land and property, and natural resources (oil in particular of course) to urban debt and the art market. This was paralleled by the creation of wholly new asset markets within the financial system itself – currency futures, credit default swaps, CDOs and a whole range of other financial instruments that were supposed to spread risk but which in fact heightened risks in a way that made the volatility of short-term trading a field for smart speculative gains. This was fictitious capital feeding off and generating even more fictitious capital without any concern for the social value basis of the trading. This disconnection could flourish precisely because the representation of value (money) became increasingly distant from the value of social labour it was supposed to represent. The problem was not the circulation of fictitious capital – that had always been important to the history of capital accumulation – but that the new channels down which fictitious capitals were moving constituted a labyrinth of countervailing claims that were almost impossible to value except by way of some mix of future expectations, beliefs and outright crazy short-term betting in unregulated markets with no prospect of any long-term pay-off (this was the famous Enron story, which was repeated in the collapse of Lehman and the global financial system in 2008).

Much of the compound growth realised until the financial crash of 2008 was achieved by way of speculative gains out of successive asset bubbles (the dot-com boom and bust of the 1990s followed by the property market boom and bust of the 2000s in the USA). This speculative froth concealed, however, some very important real transitions occurring in investment behaviours after the 1970s. Some of the assets being purchased (land and property, natural resources) were secure and grounded and could be held for long-term gain. This made the booms and the busts particularly helpful to long-term investors, who could purchase assets at fire-sale prices in the wake of a crash with the prospects of making a long-term killing. This is what many of the banks and foreign investors did during the South-East Asian crisis of 1997–8 and what investors are now doing as they buy up masses of cheap foreclosed housing in, for example, California to rent out until the property market revives. This is what the hedge funds do, though under very different conditions, when they short-sell in fictitious capital markets.

But what this means is that more and more capital is being invested in search of rents, interest and royalties rather than in productive activity. This trend towards a rentier form of capital is reinforced by the immense extractive power that increasingly attaches to rents on intellectual property rights to genetic materials, seeds, licensed practices and the like. Small wonder that the US government has fought so fiercely through international institutions to protect and forcibly impose an intellectual property rights regime on others (by way of the so-called TRIPS agreement within the framework of the World Trade Organization).

But is all this really sufficient to absorb compound growth? Theories that rest on a wholesale shift to immaterial production sell a dangerous illusion that endless compound growth can be accommodated without any serious material difficulties. Increasing quantities of capital now circulate in fictitious form and the creation of electronic moneys is in principle limitless (it is just numbers on a screen). So there is no barrier to limitless growth there. The economy of spectacle and of knowledge production as a form of realisation of capital plainly reduces the rate of expansion of demand for material goods and resources. But the extensive physical infrastructures required, along with the need to generate more and more energy in usable form, militate against the idea that production can ever become immaterial. If consumption is limited to this immaterial form, then money power cannot be released to low-income populations, who require basic material goods in order to live. It has to be concentrated within a relatively small fraction of the population able to consume in this fictitious way. A repressive oligarchy would likely be the only political form that capital could assume. This is where emerging markets, of the sort that flourished in the wake of the financial crash of 2008, have a distinctive advantage: the markets that form consequent upon rising output and incomes in middle-income countries focus far more on tangible wants and needs of an expanding population. The turn towards immaterial production and spectacle is, as André Gorz long ago remarked, more like a last gasp of capital rather than the opening of a new horizon for endless accumulation.

So where does this leave us, faced with the necessity of compound economic growth for ever without any clear material basis to support that growth? There are, as we have seen, various adjustments under way, but the more closely these are examined the more they appear as symptoms of the underlying problem rather than as signs of or paths towards long-term solutions. Of course, capital can construct an economy (and to some degree has already done so) based on a fetish world of fantasy and imagination built upon pyramiding fictions that cannot last. One final Ponzi scheme to eclipse all others is a possible scenario. Ironically, the innovations that are available to us in these times are most easily applied to increase rather than dampen speculative activity, as the case of nano-trading on the stock exchange illustrates. Such an economy will, before any ultimate denouement, be subject to periodic volcanic eruptions and crashes. Capital will not, under this scenario, end with either a bang or a whimper but with the sound of innumerable asset bubbles popping across the uneven geographical landscape of an otherwise listless capital accumulation. Such disruptions will almost certainly merge with the outbreaks of popular discontent that bubbles just beneath the surface of capitalist society more generally. Episodic volcanic eruptions of popular anger (of the sort seen in London, 2011; Stockholm, 2013; Istanbul, 2013; a hundred Brazilian cities, 2013; etc.) are already much in evidence. The discontent, it must be remarked, does not simply focus on the technical failings of capital to deliver on its promises of a consumer paradise and employment for all, but increasingly objects to the degrading consequences for anyone and everyone who has to submit to the dehumanising social rules and codes that capital and an increasingly autocratic capitalist state dictate.

There is, however, one particularly dark side to this account that rests upon the contagious impact that compound growth will most likely have on many if not all the other contradictions here identified. The impact upon environmental contradictions is likely to be huge, as we shall shortly see. The ability of capital to rebalance relations between production and realisation, as well as between poverty and wealth, becomes less agile, while the gap between money and the social labour it supposedly represents becomes ever wider as more and more fictitious capital has to be created at a far higher risk premium to sustain the compounding growth. It will likewise be extremely hard, if not impossible, to reverse the commodification, monetisation and marketisation of all use values without severely curtailing the terrain for capital accumulation. The reckless push towards speed-up and consequent devaluations through increasing volatility in uneven geographical developments will be harder to contain. And so it goes! Far from constraining each other's excesses, as has sometimes happened in the past, the contradictions are far more likely to explode contagiously with the rising pressure of a necessary compounding growth at their back. Use values are bound to become an even more trivial consideration against the background of an explosion of exchange value considerations in speculative fevers. And from this some rather surprising results may derive.

There is, for example, one thread of a threat that may be a minor footnote to my argument, but which has a curious resonance with the fears expressed about the future of capital by the political economists of long ago. Capital will end, said Ricardo, when land and natural resources become so scarce that all revenues will be absorbed either by the wages needed to cover the high price of food or (what in the end amounts to the same thing) as rents by an all-powerful but unproductive rentier class. This unproductive class will so squeeze industrial capital as to make the latter's productive operations impossible. A parasitic class of rentiers will suck industrial capital dry, to the point where no social labour can be mobilised and no value produced. Without the production of social value, capital will come to an end. In making this prediction, Ricardo relied heavily on Malthus's erroneous assumptions of diminishing returns to labour on the land. For this reason later economists generally dismissed the idea of a falling rate of profit (though Marx tried to keep it alive by appeal to a quite different mechanism). Keynes, for example, living under very different circumstances, optimistically looked forward to the euthanasia of the rentier and the construction of a state-supported regime of perpetual growth (the possibilities of which were partially realised in the period after 1945).

What is now so striking is the increasing power of the unproductive and parasitic rentiers, not simply the owners of land and all the resources that reside therein, but the owners of assets, the all-powerful bondholders, the owners of independent money power (which has become a paramount means of production in its own right), and the owners of patents and property rights that are simply claims on social labour freed of any obligation to mobilise that social labour for productive uses. The parasitic forms of capital are now in the ascendant. We see their representatives gliding through the streets in limousines and populating all the upmarket restaurants and penthouses in all the major global cities of the world – New York, London, Frankfurt, Tokyo, São Paulo, Sydney ... These are the so-called creative cities, where creativity is measured by how successfully the 'masters of the universe' can suck the living life out of the global economy to support a class whose one aim is to compound its own already immense wealth and power. New York City has a huge concentration of creative talent – creative accountants and tax lawyers, creative financiers armed with glitteringly new financial instruments, creative manipulators of information, creative hustlers and sellers of snake oil, creative media consultants, all of which makes it a wondrous place to study every single fetish that capital can construct. The fact that the only class in the world to benefit from the so-called economic recovery (such as it is) after 2009 is the top 1 per cent, and that there is no visible protest on the part of the rest of the population left behind in the economic doldrums, is testimony to the success of their project. The parasites have won the battle. The bondholders and the central bankers rule the world. The fact that their success is bound to be illusory and that they cannot possibly win the war for capital's survival scarcely raises a sliver of doubt. After days spent 'conscience laundering' with their philanthropic colleagues in attempts to correct, as Peter Buffett puts it, with their right hand the damage they had earlier created with their left, the oligarchs may sleep well at night. Their inability to see how close they are sailing to the edge of disaster reminds one of King Louis XV of France, who is reported to have prophetically said: '*Après moi, le déluge.*' Capital may not end with a deluge. The World Bank is fond of reassuring us that a rising tide of economic development is bound to lift all boats. Maybe a truer metaphor would be that exponentially rising sea levels and intensifying storms are destined to sink all boats.

# Contradiction 16
# Capital's Relation to Nature

The idea that capitalism is encountering a fatal contradiction in the form of a looming environmental crisis is widespread in certain circles. I consider it a plausible but controversial thesis. Its plausibility largely derives from the accumulating environmental pressures arising from capital's exponential growth. There are four main reasons to cast doubt on the idea.

First, capital has a long history of successfully resolving its ecological difficulties, no matter whether these refer to its use of 'natural' resources, the ability to absorb pollutants or to cope with the degradation of habitats, the loss of biodiversity, the declining qualities of air, land and water, and the like. Past predictions of an apocalyptic end to civilisation and capitalism as a result of natural scarcities and disasters look foolish in retrospect. Throughout capital's history far too many doomsayers have cried 'wolf' too fast and too often. In 1798 Thomas Malthus, as we have seen, erroneously predicted social catastrophe (spreading famine, disease, war) as exponential population growth outran the capacity to increase food supplies. In the 1970s Paul Ehrlich, a leading environmentalist, argued that mass starvation was imminent by the end of the decade, but it did not occur. He also bet the economist Julian Simon that the price of natural resources would soon dramatically increase because of natural scarcities: he lost the bet.[1] Because such predictions – and there have been many of them – turned out wrong in the past does not guarantee, of course, that a catastrophe is not in the making this time. But it does give strong grounds for scepticism.

Second, the 'nature' we are supposedly exploiting and exhausting and which then supposedly limits or even 'takes revenge' on us is actually internalised within the circulation and accumulation of capital. The ability of a plant to grow is incorporated, for example, into agribusiness in its pursuit of profit and it is the reinvestment of that profit that has the plant growing again the next year. Natural features and elements are active agents at all points in the process of capital accumulation. Money flow is an ecological variable and the transfer of nutrients through an ecosystem may also constitute a flow of value.

While matter can neither be created nor destroyed, its configuration can be radically altered. Genetic engineering, the creation of new chemical compounds, to say nothing of massive environmental modifications (the creation of whole new ecosystems through urbanisation and the fixing of capital in the farms, fields and factories on the land), now go well beyond what has been a long history of humanly induced environmental modifications that have remade the earth in aggregate into a far more hospitable place for human life and, over the last three centuries, for profitable activity. Many organisms actively produce a nature conducive to their own reproduction and humans are no exception. Capital, as a specific form of human activity, does the same, but increasingly in the name of capital and not of humanity.

The 'domination of nature' thesis that has broadly held sway both in scientific writings and in the popular imagination since the Enlightenment (from the writings of Descartes onwards) has no place in this conceptual scheme. This poses some problems for thinking through the capital–nature relation. Cartesian thinking wrongly constructs capital and nature as two separate entities in causal interaction with each other and then compounds this error by imagining that one dominates over (or, in the case of nature, 'takes revenge' upon) the other. More sophisticated versions incorporate feedback loops. The alternative way of thinking proposed here is at first not so easy to grasp. Capital *is* a working and evolving ecological system within which both nature and capital are constantly being produced and reproduced. This is the right way to think of it.[2] The only interesting questions then are: what kind of ecological system is capital, how is it evolving and why might it be crisis-prone?

The ecosystem is constructed out of the contradictory unity of capital and nature, in the same way that the commodity is a contradictory unity between use value (its material and 'natural' form) and exchange value (its social valuation). Recall, also, the definition of technology as a human appropriation of natural things and processes to facilitate production. The nature that results is something that is not only evolving unpredictably of its own accord (because of the autonomous random mutations and dynamic interactions built into the evolutionary process in general) but actively and constantly being reshaped and re-engineered by the actions of capital. This is what Neil Smith has called 'the production of nature' and these days it is production 'all the way down' into the level of molecular biology and DNA sequencing.[3] The direction this production of nature takes is an open and not a closed question. It has long been apparent, also, that it is full of unintended consequences. The refrigerators that facilitated the delivery of non-contaminated food supplies to burgeoning urban populations were many years later identified as the source of the chloro-fluorocarbons – CFCs – that were destroying the stratospheric ozone layer that protects us from excessive solar radiation!

The third main point is that capital has turned environmental issues into big business. Environmental technologies are now a big-ticket item on the world's stock exchanges. Once this happens, as with the case of technologies in general, the engineering of the metabolic relation to nature becomes an autonomous activity relative to actual existing needs. Nature becomes, again in Neil Smith's words, 'an accumulation strategy'. When, for example, a new medicinal drug is invented or a new way to reduce carbon emissions is devised, then uses have to be found for them. This may entail need creation rather than need satisfaction. A drug like Prozac initially had no disease available for it to address so one had to be invented, giving rise to the so-called 'Prozac generation'. The same 'combinatorial evolution' as prevails in the case of technological change comes into play. New drugs create side effects that require other drugs to control them and new environmental technologies create environmental problems that call forth other technologies.

For its own profit, capital seeks to capture the dialectics of how we can only change ourselves by changing the world (and vice versa). All ecological and environmental projects are socio-economic projects (and vice versa). Everything then depends on the purpose of the socio-economic and ecological projects – the well-being of people or the rate of profit? In fields like public health and clean water, this dialectic has worked for the benefit of people, sometimes at the expense of profits. Popular support for big business environmentalism has consequently been helpful both to capital and to environmental politics. Some of this politics is, unfortunately, symbolic rather than substantive. This is known as 'greenwashing' – disguising a profit-driven project as a project to enhance human welfare. Al Gore's great gift to the environmental movement as it sought to do something about global warming was to create a new market in carbon trading that has been a grand source of speculative gain for hedge funds but done little to curb total global carbon emissions. The suspicion lurks that this was what it was designed to do all along. New organisational forms developed to conserve fish stocks entail a mode of privatisation that privileges large-scale financial and corporate capital at the expense of small-scale fishing.

Fourth, and this is perhaps the most uncomfortable thought of all, it may be perfectly possible for capital to continue to circulate and accumulate in the midst of environmental catastrophes. Environmental disasters create abundant opportunities for a 'disaster capitalism' to profit handsomely. Deaths from starvation of exposed and vulnerable populations and massive habitat destruction will not necessarily trouble capital (unless it provokes rebellion and revolution) precisely because much of the world's population has become redundant and disposable anyway. And capital has never shrunk from destroying people in pursuit of profit. This was true of the recent appalling tragedies of fires and building collapses in the textile mills of Bangladesh that have claimed the lives of more than a thousand workers. Toxic waste disposal is highly concentrated in poor and vulnerable communities (some of the worst sites in the USA are in Indian reservations) or in impoverished parts of the world (toxic batteries are taken care of in China in insalubrious conditions and old ships dismantled at considerable human cost on the shores of India and Bangladesh). Deteriorating air quality in northern China is reported to have reduced life expectancy in the population by more than five years since 1980. Unfair distributions of environmental damages of this sort may add fuel to an environmental justice movement. But the resultant social protests do not, as of now, constitute any major threat to the survival of capital.

The big underlying question is: under what circumstances might these internal difficulties be dangerous, if not fatal, for the reproduction of capital? To answer this question we have to understand more fully how the contradictory unity between capital and nature works. It is helpful here to look at how the seven foundational contradictions of capital affect matters. Nature is necessarily viewed by capital – and I must stress that it may be and is viewed very differently within capitalism as a whole – as nothing more than a vast store of potential use values – of processes and things – that can be used directly or indirectly (through technologies) in the production and realisation of commodity values. Nature is 'one vast gasoline station' (to cite Heidegger) and natural use values are monetised, capitalised, commercialised and exchanged as commodities. Only then can capital's economic rationality be imposed upon the world. Nature is partitioned and divided up as private property rights guaranteed by the state. Private property entails enclosure of nature's commons. While some aspects of nature are hard to enclose (such as the air we breathe and the oceans we fish in), a variety of surrogate ways can be devised (usually with the help of the state) to monetise and make tradable all aspects of the commons of the natural world. State interventions are also often developed to correct for market failures. While these interventions may seem progressive, their effect is to further promote the penetration of market processes and market valuations into all aspects of our lifeworld. This is the case with carbon trading and the growing market in pollution rights and ecological offsets. When the natural commons are privatised, then all things, objects and processes therein are assigned a value (sometimes arbitrarily by bureaucratic fiat) no matter whether any social labour has been expended on them or not. This is how capital creates its own distinctive ecosystem.

Private individuals are then free to extract social wealth from their ownership of a commodified nature. They can even capitalise it as monetary wealth. This creates a basis for the formation of a potentially powerful rentier (including landowning) class, which regulates access to the store of use values by virtue of its class monopoly power and the rents it extracts from the land. This class 'owns' the nature we need in order to live and it can threaten the perpetuation of capital by monopolising all wealth for itself. Ricardo (following Malthus) thought that capital was doomed, as we saw earlier, because profit rates would inevitably fall as rental extractions and food prices rose. The power of rentiers is magnified by the fact that many resources, being found in geographically specific locations, are subject to monopolistic competition and therefore open for the extraction of monopoly rents. Urban land and property markets as well as the world of so-called 'natural' resources are fecund sites for a flourishing rentier class to amass more and more wealth and power. This power of the rentier carries over to that aspect of nature which is internalised within the circulation of capital as technology. Patents and ownership rights have been established at the behest of those producing nature in the form of new technologies. Privately owned genetic materials (for example, seeds), new methods and even new organisational systems are privately licensed out to others in return for a monopoly rent. Intellectual property rights have become a vital field of accumulation over the last few decades.

The stranglehold that the rentier class (for example, landlords and owners of mineral, agricultural and intellectual property rights) has over so-called 'natural' assets and resources allows it to create and manipulate scarcities and to speculate on the value of the assets they control. This power has long been in evidence. It is now generally accepted, for example, that almost all famines over the last 200 years have been socially produced and not naturally ordained. Every time rising oil prices provoke a chorus of commentary on the natural limits of 'peak oil' it is followed by a period of rueful remorse as it is realised that it was the speculators and the oil cartel who together pushed the oil prices up. The 'land grabs' now going on around the world (particularly in Africa) have more to do with escalating competition to monopolise the food chain and resources with an eye to extracting rents than with fear of impending natural limits to food production and mineral extractions. The rising food prices that have sparked so much unrest in recent times (including the revolutions in North Africa) are mostly attributable to the ways the exchange value system is being manipulated for reasons of profitability.

Capital's conception of nature as a mere objectified commodity does not pass unchallenged. A perpetual battle ensues between how capital conceptualises and uses the metabolic relation to nature to construct its own ecosystem and the different concepts of and attitudes towards nature held in civil society and even within the state apparatus. Capital cannot, unfortunately, change the way it slices and dices nature up into commodity forms and private property rights. To challenge this would be to challenge the functioning of the economic engine of capitalism itself and to deny the applicability of capital's economic rationality to social life. This is why the environmental movement, when it goes beyond a merely cosmetic or ameliora-tive politics, must become anti-capital. The concept of nature that underpins various philosophies of environmentalism is radically at odds with that which capital has to impose in order to reproduce itself. The environmental movement could, in alliance with others, pose a serious threat to the reproduction of capital. But so far envi-ronmental politics has not, for a variety of reasons, moved very far in this direction. It often prefers to ignore entirely the ecology that capital is constructing and nibble at issues that are separable from the core dynamics of what capital is about. Contesting a waste dump here or rescuing an endangered species or a valued habitat there is in no way fatal to capital's reproduction.

We can now better understand two things. First, how important it is that capital seizes the environmentalist mantle for itself as the legitimate foundation for the big businesses environmentalism of the future. In this way it can dominate ecological discourses – define nature in its own (usually monetised, with the help of cost benefit analysis) terms – and seek to manage the capital–nature contradiction in its own broad class interests. Second, the more dominant the economic engine of capital is within the various social formations that constitute world capitalism, the more the rules of capital's metabolic relation to nature must dominate public discourses, politics and policies.

On what grounds, then, might I upgrade this question of capital's changing metabolic relation to nature to a dangerous, if not potentially fatal, contradiction? Capital's successful past negotiation of this difficulty does not guarantee that things will be the same this time around. 'Successful' is here defined, of course, in capital's terms and those are of sustained profitability. This is an important qualification, because the cumulative negative ecological aspects of capital's past adaptations remain with us, including the legacies of damages inflicted in the past. At each historical step the baseline from which capital's ecosystem functions is very different. Much of the tropical rainforest, for example, is already gone and carbon dioxide concentrations in the atmosphere have been rising for some time. Suburbanisation and the suburban lifestyle are expanding (for example, in China of all places). This way of life is deeply embedded in the cultural preferences, the psyches of people and in a physical landscape lubricated by high energy consumption and wasteful use of land, air and water.

What is different this time is that we are now at a key inflexion point in the exponential growth rate of capitalist activity. This is having an exponential impact upon levels of environmental stress and distress within capital's ecology. To begin with it puts intense pressure on commodifying, privatising and incorporating more and more aspects of our lifeworld (even life forms themselves) into the circuits of capital. Even genetic identifications are now claimed as private property. It also leads to an intensification of pressures most notably in areas such as climate change, loss of habitat diversity and the volatile and stuttering capacity to assure food security and adequate protections against new diseases. There are strong indications, I would argue, of an increasingly cancerous spread and degradation in the qualities of capital's ecosystem. Much of this is associated also with rapid urbanisation and the construction of built environments (sometimes referred to as a 'second nature') of a very low quality (this has been very much the case in Asia's rapid recent urbanisation).

The struggle within capital over how to ameliorate its own ecological conditions is ongoing and sharpening. Ecological effects are typically experienced by capitalist firms as cost-shifting or as what economists call 'externalities' – defined as real costs for which capital does not have to pay (for example, the pollution that is unloaded into the environment or on to others free of charge). Even rightwing economists recognise that there is a problem of market failure here and that there is just cause for state interventions, compensatory taxes and regulatory action. But, as always, uncertainties and unintended consequences attach to both action and inaction on such issues. The greatest danger is that necessary action will be delayed by recalcitrant political and corporate powers and that we might go beyond some irreversible tipping point before the problem is identified, let alone resolved. The reproductive cycle of sardine populations off the California coast, for example, was unknown and overfishing blithely continued in the 1930s to the point of zero reproduction before anyone realised there might be a problem. The sardines have never returned.[4] In the case of the Montreal Protocol, to take another example, the time horizon was long because the CFCs in the stratosphere take many years to dissipate. Capital is understandably not good at dealing with time horizons of this sort. This is one of the big problems with combating the long-term repercussions of climate change and the loss of planetary biodiversity.

Under the pressure of continued exponential growth, cancerous degradation will most likely accelerate. I do not preclude apocalyptic-seeming moments in this process. The frequency of severe weather events is increasing, for example. But catastrophic localised events can readily be accommodated by capital since a predatory 'disaster capitalism' is raring to respond. Capital in fact thrives upon and evolves through the volatility of localised environmental disasters. Not only do these create new business opportunities. They also provide a convenient mask to hide capital's own failings: it is that unpredictable, capricious and wilful shrew called 'mother nature' who is to blame for misfortunes that are largely of capital's making. By contrast, it is the slow, cancerous degradations that are the big problem for which capital is so ill-prepared and for the management of which new institutions and powers have yet to be created.

The temporal and geographical scales of capital's ecosystem have been shifting in response to exponential growth. Whereas the problems in the past were typically localised – a polluted river here or a catastrophic smog there – they have now become more regional (acid deposition, low-level ozone concentrations and stratospheric ozone holes) or global (climate change, global urbanisation, habitat destruction, species extinction and loss of biodiversity, degradation of oceanic, forest and land-based ecosystems and the uncontrolled introduction of artificial chemical compounds – fertilisers and pesticides – with unknown side effects and an unknown range of impacts on land and life across the whole planet). In many instances local environmental conditions have improved, while it is the regional and above all the global problems that have deteriorated. As a result, the capital–nature contradiction now exceeds traditional tools of management and of action. It relied in the past on some combination of market forces and state powers to deal with problems, like the catastrophic London smog of 1952, which produced remedial action in the shape of Battersea Power Station, which dispersed the sulphurous pollutants of coal burning into the upper atmosphere (thus later producing the regional problem of acid deposition in Scandinavia which required complicated regional cross-national agreements to manage). Pollution problems do not only get moved around. They are also resolved by shifting and dispersing them to a different scale. This was what Larry Summers proposed when chief economist at the World Bank. Africa, he said, was 'under-polluted' and it would make sense to use it to dispose of the advanced countries' wastes.

To the degree that so many of the contradictions have already 'gone global' over the last decades, so there are fewer and fewer empty spaces (except for outer-space dumping). This may become a serious problem as compound growth picks up.

Who now speaks and takes effective action for complex interactive problems on a global scale? Periodic international meetings to discuss environmental problems typically go almost nowhere. Occasionally, as in the cases of acid deposition and CFCs, transnational agreements are reached so action is not impossible. But these are drops in the bucket of major problems gradually emerging within capital's global ecosystem. If capital does not successfully manage these contradictions it will not be because of barriers in nature, but because of its own economic, political, institutional and ideological failings. In the case of climate change, for example, the problem is not that we do not know what is happening or that we do not know in very broad terms (complicated though it may be) what to do. The problem is the hubris and the vested interests of certain factions of capital (and of certain capitalist state governments and apparatuses) that have the power to dispute, disrupt and prevent actions that threaten their profitability, competitive position and economic power.

Capital's ecosystem has, of course, been global all along. International trade in commodities entails either a real or a virtual transfer of inputs (water, energy, minerals, biomass and nutrients, as well as the effects of human labour) from one part of the world to another. This trade is the glue that holds capital's ecosystem together and it is the expansion of this trade that expands and intensifies activities within that ecosystem. The category of virtual ecological transfer is important. It refers to the way in which, say, energy used in aluminium smelting in Canada ends up in the USA in the commodity form of aluminium, as opposed to the direct transfer of energy from Canada to the USA through the power grid or an oil pipeline. Capital's ecosystem is riddled with inequalities and uneven geographical developments precisely because of the uneven pattern of these transfers. Benefits pile up in one part of the world at the expense of another. Transfers of ecological benefits from one part of the world to another underpin geopolitical tensions. This also helps explain why the Bolivian approach to the use of 'their' nature is so radically different from that in the USA. The Bolivians want to keep their oil in the ground. Why permit its extraction for use in, say, the United States for a mere pittance of royalties? Why should my resources subsidise your lifestyle?

The valuation put on nature or, as ecological economists prefer to conceptualise it, the monetary value put on the flow of services that nature provides to capital is arbitrary. It leads on occasion to indiscriminate exploitation of available use values to the point of ecological collapse. Capital has often exhausted and even permanently destroyed the resources latent in nature in certain locations. This has been particularly true when capital is geographically mobile. When the cotton growers in the American South or the coffee growers of Brazil exhausted their soils they simply moved on to other more fertile lands where the profitable pickings were even easier. Colonies were mined for their resources without regard to the local (often indigenous) population's well-being. The mining of minerals and the exploitation of energy and forestry resources often follow a similar logic. But the ecological effects are localised, leaving behind an uneven geographical landscape of abandoned mining towns, exhausted soils, toxic waste dumps and devalued asset values. The ecological benefits are located somewhere else.

These extractive and exploitative practices become doubly rapacious and violent under systems of imperial and colonial rule. Soil mining, soil erosion and unregulated resource extractions have left a huge mark upon the world's landscapes, in some instances leading to irreversible destructions of those use values needed for human survival. A more benign capitalist logic can be constructed in certain places and times that combines principles of sound environmental management with sustained profitability. The Dust Bowl of the 1930s in the USA, for example, was followed by the spread of conservationist land practices (sponsored by the state) and the design of a more sustainable agriculture, though based on the capital-intensive, high energy, chemical and pesticide inputs characteristic of profitable contemporary agribusiness.

The existence of destructive ecosystemic practices in one place does not necessarily betoken similar practices elsewhere and vice versa. Doomsayers highlight rapacious and destructive practices here and the cornucopians point to well-balanced ecosystemic practices there. Both coexist within the dynamics of capital's ecosystem. Unfortunately, we lack the knowledge and the instruments to arrive at a full accounting of planetary benefits and losses in use value or even in monetary terms (though satellite imagery will help with some aspects of the former). It is also extremely difficult to account for the real and the virtual ecological transfers occurring through the trading in commodities over space. The steel mills of Sheffield and Pittsburgh close down and air quality miraculously improves in the midst of unemployment, while the steel mills of China open up and contribute massively to the air pollution which reduces life expectancies there. Once again, pollution problems do not get solved but moved around. The uneven benefits and losses nearly always redound, however, to the benefit of the rich and powerful while leaving the vulnerable and the poor far worse off than before. This, after all, is what an extractive imperialism has always been about.

In the absence of any secure knowledge of how capital's ecosystem is actually functioning as a whole, it is difficult to make any clear judgement on how fatal environmental degradations may be for the further continuous expansion of capital. This situation in itself signals, perhaps, a pivotal danger: not only do we lack the necessary instrumental arrangements to manage capital's ecosystem well, but we also face considerable uncertainty as to the full range of socio-ecological issues that must be addressed. We do know that both the spatial and temporal scales at which environmental issues are now being posed have shifted radically and that the institutional framework to handle management at these scales is clearly lagging. We also know the measures necessary to ensure against catastrophic changes may not be designed and implemented in time, even presuming the political willingness on the part of contentious parties to take precautionary action.

The general stance that it seems sensible to take in the face of these reservations is this: there is nothing natural about so-called natural disasters and humanity knows just about enough to ameliorate or manage the threat of most (though never all) environmental catastrophes. But it is unlikely that capital will take the necessary action without a struggle, both between its warring factions and with others who are affected by the cost-shifting that so conveniently goes on. The reasons problems persist are political, institutional and ideological and are not attributable to natural limits.

If there are serious problems in the capital–nature relation, then this is an internal contradiction within and not external to capital. We cannot maintain that capital has the power to destroy its own ecosystem while arbitrarily denying that it has a like potential power to cleanse itself and resolve or at least properly balance its internal contradictions. Usually prodded or mandated by state powers (that are often thoroughly incoherent with regard to environmental policies when taken in aggregate) or influenced by pressures emanating from capitalist society more generally, capital has in many instances successfully responded to these contradictions. The rivers and atmospheres of northern Europe and North America are far cleaner now than they were a generation ago and life expectancies are generally rising and not falling as in northern China. The Montreal Protocol restricting the use of CFCs curbed (though by no means perfectly) a serious environmental threat through international agreement. The harmful effects of DDT have likewise been restricted, to cite one more example out of many. In the case of the Montreal Protocol on CFCs, it was the conversion of the conservative and otherwise free-market cheerleader Margaret Thatcher to the role of an active supporter (in part because she was trained as a chemist and understood the technical issues involved) of the intergovernmental agreement that made all the difference. With climate change, there are simply too many 'deniers' in positions of power to permit ameliorative actions and so far no Margaret Thatcher figure has ridden to the rescue. It has been left to some of the poorer and imme-diately threatened countries, like Bolivia and the Maldives, to plead the cause of climate justice. We are therefore not in a position to find out if capital could accomplish the massive adaptations required to deal with this problem effectively.

The bulk of the evidence now available does not support the thesis of an impending collapse of capitalism in the face of the environ-mental dangers. We will not run out of energy in spite of 'peak oil'; there is land and water enough to feed an expanding population for many years to come even in the face of exponential growth. If there are specific impending scarcities of this or that resource, we are smart enough to find substitutes. Resources are technological, economic and cultural evaluations of use values in nature. If there seem to be natural shortages then we can simply change our technology, our economy and our cultural beliefs. Even problems of global warming, waning biodiversity and new disease configurations – which today have to be accorded the status of the premier threats to human life – could be handled adequately if we could overcome our own short-sightedness and political shortcomings. This is, of course, a tall order for our political institutions to respond to. There will therefore doubtless be resource wars, famines in some places and environmen-tal refugees by the millions elsewhere, and frequent disruptions to commerce. But none of this is dictated by limits in nature. We have no one to blame but ourselves if much of humanity is reduced to penury and starvation. If that happens, it will be more a measure of human stupidity and venality than anything else. There is, alas, abundant evidence that there is plenty of that to go around and that capital itself thrives upon and even foments it. But this has not put an end to capital.

This brings us to the nub of what might be so threatening to the future of capital within the contradictory metabolic unity of capital and nature. The two answers are somewhat surprising. The first concerns the rising power of the rentier class to appropriate all wealth and income without paying any mind to production. The ownership and commodification of land and its 'natural' scarcity allow an unproductive landlord class to extract monopoly rents at the expense of productive capital, ultimately reducing the profit rate (and hence the incentive to reinvest) to zero. This fits, as we have seen, with a broader concept of the rentier, which combines the traditional landlord with all forms of property ownership which are in themselves unproductive but which facilitate the appropriation of wealth and income. The appropriation of natural forces and the occupation of key points in capital's ecosystem may threaten the strangulation of productive capital.

The second reason this contradiction could become fatal lies in a different dimension entirely. It rests on the alienated human response to the kind of ecological system that capital constructs. This ecosystem is functionalist, engineered and technocractic. It is privatised, commercialised and monetised, and oriented towards maximising the production of exchange values (rents in particular) through the appropriation and production of use values. Like all other aspects of capital, it is increasingly automated. It is capital- and energy-intensive with often very little labour input. In agriculture, it tends to be monocultural, extractive and, of course, perpetually expanding under the pressures of exponential growth. In urbanisation, the suburbs are just as monocultural, with a lifestyle that maximises the excessive consumption of material goods in an astonishingly wasteful manner and with isolating and individualising social effect. Capital dominates the practices whereby we collectively and even individually relate to nature. It disregards anything other than functionalist aesthetic values. In its ruinous approach to the sheer beauty and infinite diversity of a natural world (of which we are all a part) it exhibits its own utterly barren qualities. If nature is fecund, given over to the perpetual creation of novelty, then capital cuts that novelty into pieces and reassembles the bits into pure technology. Capital carries within itself a desiccating definition not only of the teeming diversity of the natural world but of the tremendous potentiality of human nature to evolve freely its on capacities and powers. Capital's relation to nature and human nature is alienating in the extreme.

Capital cannot help but privatise, commodify, monetise and commercialise all those aspects of nature that it possibly can. Only in this way can it increasingly absorb nature into itself to become a form of capital – an accumulation strategy – all the way down into our DNA. This metabolic relation necessarily expands and deepens in response to capital's exponential growth. It is forced on to terrains that are more and more problematic. Life forms, genetic materials, biological processes, knowledge of nature and intelligence in how to use its qualities and capacities and powers (whether of the artificial or distinctively human variety matters not a whit) are all subsumed within the logic of commercialisation. The colonisation of our lifeworld by capital accelerates. The endless and increasingly mindless exponential accumulation of capital is accompanied by an endless and increasingly mindless extension of capital's ecology into our lifeworld.

This provokes reactions, revulsions and resistances. The joy of a sunset, the smell of fresh rain or the wonder of a spectacular storm, even the brutality of a tornado, cannot be reduced to some crude monetary measure. Polanyi's complaint that the imposition of the commodity form upon the natural world is not only 'weird' but inherently destructive goes much deeper than the sense that natural forces and powers get disrupted and destroyed to the point where they become unusable for capital. What gets destroyed is the capacity to be human in any other way than that which capital requires and dictates. This is seen by many as an offence against 'true' nature and, by extension, against the possibility of another and better human nature.

This idea that capital mandates the destruction of a decent and sensitive human nature has long been understood. It early on produced an aesthetic revolt, led by the romantic movement, against a purely scientific approach to capitalist modernity. In deep ecology it produced a non-anthropocentric vision of how we should construe ourselves in relation to the world around us. In social and political ecology it produced severely critical forms of anti-capitalist analysis. In the critical work of the Frankfurt School it pioneered the emergence of a more ecologically sensitive Marxism in which the dialectics and the 'revolt' of nature brooked large.[5] What is called 'the revolt of nature' is not that of an irate and out-of-sorts mother nature (as some indigenous thinking would now have it and as every presenter on the weather channels of the world likes to portray it). It is in truth a revolt of our own nature about who we have to become to survive within the ecosystem that capital necessarily constructs. This revolt is across the political spectrum – rural conservatives are every bit as outraged as urban liberals and anarchists at the commodification, monetisation and commercialisation of all aspects of nature.

The seeds are sown for a humanist revolt against the inhumanity presupposed in the reduction of nature and human nature to the pure commodity form. Alienation from nature is alienation from our own species' potential. This releases a spirit of revolt in which words like dignity, respect, compassion, caring and loving become revolutionary slogans, while values of truth and beauty replace the cold calculus of social labour.

## Contradiction 17
# The Revolt of Human Nature: Universal Alienation

It is not entirely beyond the realms of possibility that capital could survive all the contradictions hitherto examined at a certain cost. It could do so, for example, by a capitalist oligarchic elite supervising the mass genocidal elimination of much of the world's surplus and disposable population while enslaving the rest and building vast artificial gated environments to protect against the ravages of an external nature run toxic, barren and ruinously wild. Dystopian tales abound depicting a grand variety of such worlds and it would be wrong to rule them out as impossible blueprints for the future of a less-than-human humanity. Indeed, there is something frighteningly close about some dystopian tales, such as the social order depicted in the teenage hit trilogy *The Hunger Games* by Suzanne Collins or the futuristic anti-humanist sequences of David Mitchell's *Cloud Atlas*. Clearly, any such social order could only exist on the basis of fascistic mind control and the continuous exercise of daily police surveillance and violence accompanied by periodic militarised repressions. Anyone who does not see elements of such a dystopian world already in place around us is deceiving herself or himself most cruelly.

The issue is not, therefore, that capital cannot survive its contradictions but that the cost of it so doing becomes unacceptable to the mass of the population. The hope is that long before dystopian trends turn from a trickle of drone strikes here and occasional uses of poison gas against their own people by crazed rulers there, of murderous and incoherent policies towards all forms of opposition in one place to environmental collapses and mass starvation elsewhere, into a veritable flood of catastrophic unequally armed struggles everywhere that pit the rich against the poor and the privileged capitalists and their craven acolytes against the rest ... the hope is that social and political movements will arise and shout, '*Ja! Basta!*' or 'Enough is enough', and change the way we live and love, survive and reproduce. That this means replacing the economic engine and its associated irrational economic rationalities should by now be obvious. But how this should be done is by no means clear and what kind of economic engine can replace that of capital is an even murkier proposition given the current state of thought and the lamentable paucity of imaginative public debate devoted to the question. In the analysis of this, an understanding of capital's contradictions is more than a little helpful, for, as the German playwright Bertolt Brecht once put it, 'hope is latent in contradictions'.

In excavating this zone of latent hope, there are some basic propositions that must first be accepted. In *The Enigma of Capital*, I concluded: 'Capitalism will never fall on its own. It will have to be pushed. The accumulation of capital will never cease. It will have to be stopped. The capitalist class will never willingly surrender its power. It will have to be dispossessed.'[1] I still hold to this view and think it vital that others do too. It will obviously need a strong political movement and a lot of individual commitment to undertake such a task. Such a movement cannot function without a broad and compelling vision of an alternative around which a collective political subjectivity can coalesce. What sort of vision can animate such a political movement?

We can seek to change the world gradually and piecemeal by favouring one side of a contradiction (such as use value) rather than the other (such as exchange value) or by working to undermine and eventually dissolve particular contradictions (such as that which allows the use of money for the private appropriation of social wealth). We can seek to change the trajectories defined by the moving contradictions (towards non-militaristic technologies and towards greater equality in a world of democratic freedoms). Understanding capital's contradictions helps, as I have tried to indicate throughout this book, in developing a long-term vision of the overall *direction* in which we should be moving. In much the same way that the rise of neoliberal capitalism from the 1970s onwards changed the direction of capital's development towards increasing privatisation and commercialisation, the more emphatic dominance of exchange value and an all-consuming fetishistic passion for money power, so an anti-neoliberal movement can point us in an entirely different strategic direction for the coming decades. There are signs in the literature as well as in the social movements of at least a willingness to try to redesign a capitalism based in more ecologically sensitive relations and far higher levels of social justice and democratic governance.[2]

There are virtues in this piecemeal approach. It proposes a peaceful and non-violent move towards social change of the sort initially witnessed in the early stages of Tahrir, Syntagma and Taksim Squares, although in all these instances the state and police authorities soon responded with astonishing brutality and violence, presumably because these movements had the timerity to go beyond the boundaries of repressive tolerance. It seeks to bring people together strategically around common but limited themes. It can have, also, wide-ranging impacts if and when contagious effects cascade from one kind of contradiction to another. Imagine what the world would be like if the domination of exchange value and the alienated behaviours that attach to the pursuit of money power as Keynes described them were simultaneously reduced and the powers of private persons to profit from social wealth were radically curbed. Imagine, further, if the alienations of the contemporary work experience, of a compensatory consumption that can never satisfy, of untold levels of economic inequality and discordance in the relation to nature, were all diminished by a rising wave of popular discontent with capital's current excesses. We would then be living in a more humane world with much-reduced levels of social inequality and conflict and much-diminished political corruption and oppression.

This does not tell us how highly fragmented though numerous oppositional movements might converge and coalesce into a more unified solidarious movement against capital's dominance. The piecemeal approach fails to register and confront how all the contradictions of capital relate to and through each other to form an organic whole. There is a crying need for some more catalytic conception to ground and animate political action. A collective political subjectivity has to coalesce around some foundational concepts as to how to constitute an alternative economic engine if the powers of capital are to be confronted and overcome. Without that, capital can neither be dispossessed nor displaced. The concept I here find most appropriate is that of *alienation*.

The verb to alienate has a variety of meanings. As a legal term it means to transfer a property right to the ownership of another. I alienate a piece of land when I sell it to another. As a social relation it refers to how affections, loyalties and trust can be alienated (transferred, stolen away) from one person, institution or political cause to another. The alienation (loss) of trust (in persons or in institutions such as the law, the banks, the political system) can be exceedingly damaging to the social fabric. As a passive psychological term alienation means to become isolated and estranged from some valued connectivity. It is experienced and internalised as a feeling of sorrow and grief at some undefinable loss that cannot be recuperated. As an active psychological state it means to be angry and hostile at being or feeling oppressed, deprived or dispossessed and to act out that anger and hostility, lashing out sometimes without any clear definitive reason or rational target, against the world in general. Alienated behaviours can arise, for example, because people feel frustrated at the lack of life chances or because their quest for freedom ended up in domination.

The diversity of meanings is useful. The worker legally alienates the use of his or her labour power for a stated period of time to the capitalist in return for a wage. During this time the capitalist demands the loyalty and attention of the worker and the worker is asked to trust that capitalism is the best system to generate wealth and well-being for all. Yet the worker is estranged from his or her product as well as from other workers, from nature and all other aspects of social life during the time of the labour contract and usually beyond (given the exhausting nature of the work). The deprivation and dispossession are experienced and internalised as a sense of loss and sorrow at the frustration of the worker's own creative instincts. Ultimately the worker stops being melancholic and morose and gets angry at the immediate sources of his or her alienation: either at his boss for working him too hard or at her partner for wanting dinner and sex and not sympathising with her exhausted state. In this totally alienated state, the worker either throws sand in the machine at work or the teacups at her partner at home.

The theme of alienation is present in many of the contradictions already examined. The tactile contact with the commodity – its use value – is lost and the sensual relation to nature is occluded by the domination of exchange value. The social value and meaning of labouring get obscured in the representational form of money. The capacity to arrive democratically at collective decisions gets lost in the perpetual battle between the conflicting rationalities of isolated private interests and of state powers. Social wealth disappears into the pockets of private persons (producing a world of private wealth and public squalor). The direct producers of value are alienated from the value they produce. An ineradicable gulf is created between people through class formation. A proliferating division of labour makes it more and more difficult to see the whole in relation to the increasingly fragmented parts. All prospects for social equality or social justice are lost even as the universality of equality before the law is trumpeted as the supreme bourgeois virtue. Accumulated resentments at accumulation by dispossession in the field of the realisation of capital (through housing displacements and foreclosures, for example) boil over. Freedom becomes domination, slavery is freedom.

The catalytic political problem that derives from all this is to identify, confront and overcome the many forms of alienation produced by the economic engine of capital and to channel the pent-up energy, the anger and the frustration they produce into a coherent anti-capitalist opposition. Dare we hope for an unalienated (or at least less alienated and more humanly acceptable) relation to nature, to each other, to the work we do and to the way we live and love? For this to be so requires that we understand the source of our alienations. And this is exactly what the study of capital's contradictions does so much to illuminate.

The traditional Marxist approach to the revolutionary transformation to socialism/communism has been to focus on the contradiction between productive forces (technology) and social (class) relations. In the lore of traditional communist parties, the transition was seen as a scientific and technical rather than a subjective, psychological and political question. Alienation was excluded from consideration since it was a non-scientific concept that smacked of the humanism and utopian desire articulated in the young Marx of *The Economic and Philosophic Manuscripts of 1844* rather than through the objective science of *Capital*. This scientistic stance failed to capture the political imagination of viable alternatives in spite of the passionate beliefs of adherents to the communist cause. Nor did it provide any spiritually compelling and subjective (rather than scientifically necessary and objective) reason to mobilise arms in a sea of anti-capitalist struggle. It could not even confront the madness of the prevailing economic and political reason (in part because scientific communism embraced much of this economic reason and its fetish attachment to production for production's sake). It failed in fact to fully unmask the fetishisms and fictions peddled in the name of the ruling classes to protect themselves from harm. The traditional communist movement was, therefore, in perpetual danger of unwittingly replicating these fictions and fetishisms. It fell victim in addition to the static and dogmatic views of the leaders of an all-powerful vanguard party. The democratic centralism that often worked well in opposition and at dire moments of violent repression proved a disastrous burden the closer the movement came to exercising legitimate power. Its search for freedom produced domination.

But there is more than a mere kernel of truth in the idea of a central contradiction between revolutions in the productive forces and their conflictual and contradictory social relations. There is, as we saw in the case of Contradiction 8, a deep connection between the technical evolution of capital and the radical transformation of work and of social value. But there are further implications when we address this and other contradictions (such as those arising out of divisions of labour) from the standpoint of alienation. André Gorz has pioneered the way in illuminating these, so I shall simply follow him here.

'The economic rationalisation of work' that occurs with the capitalist development of technological powers, writes Gorz, produces 'individuals who, being alienated in their work, will, necessarily be alienated in their consumption as well, and eventually, in their needs'. The more money individuals can command (and money has the potential, as we have seen, to increase without limit even within individual bank accounts), the more individual needs must increase if those individuals are to perform their economic role as 'rational consumers' ('rational', that is, from the standpoint of capital). A dialectical relation, a spiral of interactions, is established between the desire for money and an economy of needs promoted within the social order. The idea of a stable good life and of good living according to modest requirements is displaced by an insatiable desire for gaining more and yet more money power in order to command more and yet more consumer goods. The effect is to 'sweep away the ancient idea of freedom and existential autonomy' and to surrender true freedom for the limited freedoms of endless striving to participate in and beat the market.[3]

Let us unpack the details of this argument. 'The essential question,' Gorz writes, 'is the extent to which the skills and faculties a job employs constitute an occupational culture and the extent to which there is a unity between occupational culture and the culture of everyday life – between work and life. The extent, in other words, to which involvement in one's work implies the enrichment or sacrificing of one's individual being.' The technology of work is on the surface totally indifferent to this question, but, as we have seen, much of the dynamic of technological change has been orchestrated to disempower and diminish the worker. Such a trajectory for innovation is deeply incompatible with the enrichment of the worker's life. Technology does not and cannot give rise to a distinctive culture over and beyond what it itself commands. The violence of technology resides in the way it cuts the link between the person and sensory interaction with the world. It is, says Gorz, 'a form of repression that denies our own sensitivity'. Tenderness and compassion are not allowed. Nature, as we have seen, is treated 'in an instrumental way' and this does 'violence' to 'Nature and to our own and other people's bodies. The culture of everyday life is – with all the disturbing ambiguity this antinomic creation contains – a culture of violence, or, in its most extreme form, a systematic, thought-out, sublimated, aggravated *culture of barbarism*.'[4] This is most obvious, of course, when we think of drone strikes and gas chambers. But Gorz's point is that it is this that also deeply penetrates to the very core of daily life by way of the instruments we daily use to live that life, including all those we handle in our work.

There is, evidently, a deep longing in popular culture to somehow humanise the impacts of this barren culture of technology. We see that in the way that the replicants in *Blade Runner* acquire feelings, how Sonmi-451 learns an expressive language in *Cloud Atlas*, how the robots in *Wall-E* learn to care and shed a tear while human beings, bloated with compensatory consumer goods, passively float alone, each on their separate magic carpet, above the ruinous world the robots are seeking to order below; and even, more negatively, how HAL the computer in *2001: A Space Odyssey* goes rogue. The sheer impossibility of this dream of humanising technology does nothing to deter its repeated articulation. So where, then, do we go to find a more human way to reconstruct our world?

'Working,' Gorz insists, 'is not just the creation of economic wealth; it is also always a means of self-creation. Therefore we must also ask *a propos* the contents of our work whether the work produces the kind of men and women we wish humanity to be made of.' We know that many if not most of those at work are not happy with what they do. A recent comprehensive Gallup survey in the USA showed, for example, that about 70 per cent of full-time workers either hated going to work or had mentally checked out and become, in effect, saboteurs spreading discontent everywhere and thereby costing their employer a great deal in the form of lost efficiency. The 30 per cent who were engaged were mainly what Gorz called 'reprofessionalised' workers (the designers, engineers and managers of highly complex technological systems). Are these sorts of workers, asks Gorz, 'closer to a possible ideal of humanity than the more traditional types of workers? Can the complex tasks they are allotted fill their life and give it meaning, without simultaneously distorting it? How, in a word, is this work lived?' Can the violence of technical culture be transcended?

Gorz's answer is discouraging. Technology can certainly be used 'to increase the efficiency of labour, and reduce the toil involved and the number of working hours'. But this has a price. 'It divorces work from life, and occupational culture from the culture of everyday life; it demands a despotic domination of oneself in exchange for an increased domination of Nature; it reduces the field of lived experience and existential autonomy; it separates the producer from the product to the point where she or he no longer knows the purpose of what she or he is doing.' If this is not total alienation within the labour process then what is?

'The price we have to pay for technicisation is only acceptable,' Gorz continues, 'if the latter saves work and time. This is its declared aim and it can have no other. It is to allow us to produce more and better in less time and with less effort.' There is no ambition here 'for work to fill the life of each individual and be the principal source of meaning'. This defines the heart of the contradiction within the labour process. In saving time and effort at work technology destroys all meaning for the worker. 'A job whose effect and aim are to save work cannot, at the same time, glorify work as the essential source of personal identity and fulfilment. The meaning of the current technological revolution cannot be to rehabilitate the work ethic and identification with one's work.' It could only have meaning if it released the labourer from drudgery at work for 'non-work activities in which we can all, the new type of worker included, develop that dimension of our humanity which finds no outlet in technicised work'.[5] 'Whether it takes the form of unemployment, marginalisation and lack of job security, or a general reduction of working hours, the crisis of the work-based society (that is, based on work in the economic sense of the word) forces individuals to look outside work for sources of identity and social belonging. It is only outside of work that the worker has the possibility to achieve personal fulfilment, to acquire self-esteem and, hence, 'the esteem of others'.[6]

Society at large has been forced to make an existential choice. Either the economic sphere of capital accumulation had to be curbed to allow for the free development of human capacities and powers outside the tyranny of the market and of work, 'or else economic rationality would have to make the needs of consumers grow at least as quickly as the production of commodities and commodified services'. This is exactly the problem that Martin Ford identifies, except that he eschews all talk of any alternative to capitalist economic rationality. But in this latter eventuality – the path that was actually chosen – says Gorz, 'consumption would have to be [organised] in the service of production. Production would no longer have the function of satisfying existing needs in the most efficient way possible; on the contrary, it was needs which would increasingly have the function of enabling production to keep growing'. The result has been paradoxical:

> unlimited maximum efficiency in the [realisation] of capital thus demanded unlimited maximum inefficiency in meeting needs, and unlimited maximum wastage in consumption. The frontiers between needs, wishes and desires needed to be broken down; the desire for dearer products of an equal or inferior use value to those previously employed had to be created; wishes had to be given the impervious urgency of need. In short, a demand had to be created, consumers had to be created for the goods that were the most profitable to produce and, to this end, new forms of scarcity had unceasingly to be reproduced in the heart of opulence, through accelerated innovation and obsolescence, through the reproduction of inequalities on an increasingly higher level ...[7]

Need creation took precedence over need satisfaction for the mass of the people.

'Economic rationality needed continually to raise the level of consumption without raising the rate of satisfaction; to push back the frontier of the sufficient, to maintain the impression that there could not be enough for everyone.' The stratification of consumption, in which the consumerism of an affluent and parasitic leisure class called the shots and led the way, became crucial to ensuring the realisation of value. This is what Thorstein Veblen's *Theory of the Leisure Class*, published back in 1899, so brilliantly exposed. But what we now know is that if such a class did not already exist it would have to be invented.[8] An alienating consumerism is needed to solve the dilemma of a sagging effective demand produced by wage repressions and technologically induced unemployment for the mass of the workers. The latter, submerged and surrounded at every turn in a sea of increasingly conspicuous consumption, find themselves frantically seeking to maximise their incomes at all costs, working longer and longer hours in order to meet their artificially escalating needs as well as to keep up with the needs of the Joneses.

Instead of working fewer hours, as the new technologies would allow, the mass of the people found themselves working more. But this also served a social end. Allowing free time for more and more individuals to pursue their own objectives of self-realisation is terrifying for the prospects for capital's continuous and secure control over labour, both in the workplace and in the market. Capitalist 'economic rationality has no room for authentically free time which neither produces or consumes commercial wealth,' writes Gorz. 'It demands the full-time employment of those who are employed by virtue not of an objective necessity but of its originating logic; wages must be fixed in such as way as to induce the workers to maximum effort.' Wage demands initiated by the trade unions 'are, in fact, the only demands which do not undermine the rationality of the economic system'. Rational consumption – rational, that is, in relation to perpetual capital accumulation – becomes an absolute necessity for the survival of capital. 'Demands bearing on working hours, the intensity of work, its organisation and nature, are, on the other hand, pregnant with subversive radicalism; they cannot be satisfied by money, they strike at economic rationality in its substance, and through it at the power of capital. The "market-based order" is fundamentally challenged when people find out that not all values are quantifiable, that money cannot buy everything and that what it cannot buy is something essential, or is even the essential thing.[9] As the Priceless ads have it: 'There are some things money can't buy. For everything else, there is MasterCard.'

'Persuading individuals that the consumer goods and services they are offered adequately compensate for the sacrifice they must make in order to obtain them and that such consumption consti-tutes a haven of individual happiness which sets them apart from the crowd is something which typically belongs to the sphere of commercial advertising.' Here the 'mad men' of advertising (who now account for a large portion of economic activity in the USA) take centre stage to wreak their havoc upon the social order. Their focus is private enterprises and private individuals. Their mission is to persuade people to consume goods that are 'neither necessary nor even merely useful'. Commodities 'are always presented as contain-ing an element of luxury, of superfluity, of fantasy, which by designat-ing the purchaser as a "happy and privileged person" protects him or her from the pressures of a rationalised universe and the obligation to conduct themselves in a functional manner.' Gorz defines these goods as 'compensatory goods' which are 'desired as much – if not more – for their uselessness as for their use value; for it is this element of uselessness (in superfluous gadgets and ornaments, for example) which symbolises the buyer's escape from the collective universe in a haven of private sovereignty'.[10] It is precisely this consumerism of excess, this uselessness, that the mad men of advertising have proved so adept at selling. Such consumerism of excess is deeply alien to the satisfaction of human wants, needs and desires. This is a view to which even the current Pope subscribes. 'The limitless possibilities for consumption and distraction offered by contemporary society,' he complains in his recent Apostolic Exhortation, lead 'to a kind of alienation at every level, for a society becomes alienated when its forms of social organisation, production and consumption make it more difficult to offer the gift of self and to establish solidarity between people.'[11]

But, as Gorz notes, 'functional workers, who accept alienation in their work because the possibilities of consumption it offers are adequate compensation for them, can only come into being if they simultaneously become a socialised consumer. But only a market economy sector and commercial advertising that goes with it can produce these socialised consumers.'[12] This is exactly where the revolutionary movement of 1968, with all its vaunted rhetoric of individual liberty and freedom and social justice, ended up – lost in the world of alien consumerism, drowning in a wealth of compensatory goods, the ownership of which was taken as a sign of freedom of choice in the marketplace of human desires.

The progress of alien or compensatory consumerism has its own internally destructive dynamics. It requires what Schumpeter called 'creative destruction' to be let loose upon the land. Daily life in the city, settled ways of living, relating and socialising, are again and again disrupted to make way for the latest fad or fancy. Demolitions and displacements to make way for gentrification or Disneyfication break open already achieved fabrics of urban living to make way for the gaudy and the gargantuan, the ephemeral and fleeting. Dispossession and destruction, displacement and construction become vehicles for vigorous and speculative capital accumulation as the figures of the financier and the rentier, the developer, the landed proprietor and the entrepreneurial mayor step from the shadows into the forefront of capital's logic of accumulation. The economic engine that is capital circulation and accumulation gobbles up whole cities only to spit out new urban forms in spite of the resistance of people who feel alienated entirely from the processes that not only reshape the environments in which they live but also redefine the kind of person they must become in order to survive. Processes of social reproduction get re-engineered by capital from without. Everyday life is perverted to the circulation of capital. The coalition of the unwilling in relation to this forced redefinition of human nature constitutes a pool of alienated individuals that periodically erupts in riots and potentially revolutionary movements from Cairo to Istanbul, from Buenos Aires to São Paulo, and from Stockholm to El Alto.

All this rests, however, upon the possession of sufficient money, the crushing need for which persuades 'previously unpaid strata of society to seek waged work', which further increases 'the need for compensatory consumption'. As a result 'getting paid becomes the primary objective of the activity to the extent that any activity which does not have a financial compensation ceases to be acceptable. Money supplants other values and becomes their only measure.' Along with this goes 'an incentive to withdraw into the private sphere and give it priority, to the pursuit of "personal" advantages'. This then 'contributes to the disintegration of networks of solidarity and mutual assistance, social and family cohesion and our sense of belonging. Individuals socialised by (alien) consumerism are no longer socially integrated individuals but individuals who are encouraged to "be themselves" by distinguishing themselves from others and who only resemble these others in their refusal (socially channelled into consumption) to assume responsibility for the common condition by taking common action.'[13] Affections and loyalties to particular places and cultural forms are viewed as anachronisms. Is this not what the spread of the neoliberal ethic proposed and eventually accomplished?

But the more time has been released from production, the more imperative it has become to absorb that time in consumption and consumerism, given that, as was earlier argued, capitalist 'economic rationality has no room for authentically free time which neither produces nor consumes commercial wealth'. The ever-present danger is that freely associating and self-creating individuals, liberated from the chores of production and blessed with a whole range of labour-saving and time-saving technologies to aid their consumption (microwaves, washing and drying machines, vacuum cleaners, to say nothing of electronic banking, credit cards and cars), might start to build an alternative non-capitalistic world. They might become inclined to reject the dominant capitalist economic rationality, for example, and start evading its overwhelming but often cruel rules of time discipline. To avoid such eventualities, capital must not only find ways to absorb more and more goods and services through realisation but also somehow occupy the free time that the new technologies release. In this, it has been more than a little successful. Many people find themselves with less and less time for free creative activity in the midst of widespread time-saving technologies in both production and consumption.

How does this paradox come about? It takes a lot of time, of course, to manage, run and service all the time-saving household paraphernalia with which we are surrounded and the more paraphernalia we have the more time it takes. The sheer complexity of the support apparatus embroils us in endless telephone calls or emails to service centres, credit card and telephone companies, insurance companies and the like. There is also no question that the cultural habits with which we have surrounded the fetish worship of technological gizmos capture the playful side of our imaginations and has us uselessly watching sitcoms, trawling the internet or playing computer games for hours on end. We are surrounded with 'weapons of mass distraction' at very turn.

But none of this explains why time flies away from us in the way it does. The deeper reason lies, I think, in the structured manner in which capital has approached the issue of consumption time as a potential barrier to accumulation. Producing and marketing goods that do not last or easily become outdated or unfashionable, along with the production of events and spectacles that are instantaneously consumed, culminates, as was earlier argued, in an astonishing categorical inversion as consumers produce their own spectacle on Facebook. While the rents that accrue to capital from these forms of social media are vital, these forms of consumption also absorb an incredible amount of time. Communicative technologies are a double-edged sword. They can be wielded by an educated and alienated youth for political and even revolutionary purposes. Or they can so absorb time (while steadily producing value for others like Google and Facebook shareholders) through idle chatter, gossip and distractive interpersonal banter.

Capitalist economic rationality is difficult if not impossible to refute when people's lives, mental processes and political orientations are taken up and totally absorbed either in the pseudo busy-work of much of contemporary production or in the pursuit of alien consumerism. Getting lost in our emails and on Facebook is not political activism. Gorz has it right: 'If savings in worktime do not serve to liberate time, and if this liberated time is not used for "the free self-realisation of individuals", then these savings in working time are totally devoid of meaning.'[14] Society may be moving towards 'the programmed, staged reduction of working hours, without loss of real income, in conjunction with a set of accompanying policies which will allow this liberated time to become time for free self-realisation for everyone'. But such an emancipatory development is threatening in the extreme for capitalist class power and the resistances and barriers created are strong. 'The development of the productive forces may of itself reduce the amount of labour that is necessary; it cannot of itself create the conditions which will make this liberation of time a liberation for all. History may place the opportunity for greater freedom within our grasp, but it cannot release us from the need to seize this opportunity for ourselves and derive benefit from it. Our liberation will not come about as the result of material determinism, behind our backs, as it were. The potential for liberation which a process contains can only be realised if human beings seize it and use it to make themselves free.' Confronting collectively the multiple alienations that capital produces is a compelling way to mobilise against the stuttering economic engine that so recklessly powers capitalism from one kind of crisis to another with potentially disastrous consequences for our relation to nature and for our relations to each other. Universal alienation calls for a full-blooded political response. So what might that response be?

There is, I repeat, no such thing as a non-contradictory response to a contradiction. An examination of the range of contemporary political responses to universal alienation on the ground produces a profoundly disturbing picture. The rise of fascist parties in Europe (particularly virulent and prominent in Greece, Hungary and France) and the organisation of the Tea Party faction of the Republican Party with its singular aim to defund and shut down government in the United States are manifestations of deeply alienated factions of the population seeking political solutions. They do not shrink from violence and are convinced that the only way to preserve their threatened freedoms is to pursue a politics of total domination. This political current is supported and to some degree meshes with increasingly violent militarised responses to any and all movements that threaten to break through the walls of that repressive tolerance so crucial to the perpetuation of liberal governmentality. Consider as examples the unduly violent police repression of the Occupy movement in the United States; the even more violent response to ongoing peaceful protests in Turkey that began in Taksim Square; police actions in Syntagma Square in Athens that smack of the fascist tactics of Golden Dawn; the continuous police brutality visited on student protesters in Chile; the government-organised attack upon protesters against the unsafe labour conditions in Bangladesh; the militarisation of the response to the Arab Spring movement in Egypt; the murder of union leaders in Colombia and many more. All of this is occurring in the midst of a rapidly widening net of surveillance, monitoring and punitive legislative activism on the part of state apparatuses intent on waging a war on terror and liable to view any active and organised anti-capitalist dissent as akin to an act of terror.

There is widespread agreement on both the far left and the far right of the political spectrum in the United States that the state system as currently constituted is overreaching in its power and that this has to be fought against. This signals a widespread alienation from a state system that has historically taken on the task of trying to manufacture consent and social cohesion (usually out of an appeal to a constructed fiction about national identity and unity) across factional, even class lines. Foucault's analysis of governmentality is helpful here. The autocratic, absolutist and centralised state bequeathed to the world in Europe after a phase of fiscal militarism in the sixteenth and seventeenth centuries had to be adapted to bourgeois principles and practices, which meant adhesion to the utopian politics of an impossible laissez-faire. This transition was successfully accomplished in the English case by using freedom as a means to create governmentality (much as Amartya Sen later advocated for the developing world). This meant that the capitalist state had to internalise limitations upon its autocratic powers and devolve the production of consensus to freely functioning individuals who internalised notions of social cohesion around the nation state. Above all, they had to consent to the regulation of activity through the procedures of the market. Clear limits were placed upon centralised power. The politics of the Tea Party as well as those of the autonomistas and the anarchists in the United States converge in seeking to limit or even to destroy the state, though in the name of pure individualism on the right and some sort of individualistically anchored associationism on the left. What is particularly interesting is how the existing mode of production and its current political articulations define both the spaces and the forms of it own primary forms of opposition. The hegemonic practices of neoliberalism in both the economic and the political arenas have given rise to decentralised and networked oppositional forms.

The specifically right-wing response to universal alienation is both understandable and terrifying in its implications. It is not as if, after all, right-wing responses to these kinds of problem have not had massive historical consequences in the past. Can we not learn from that history and shape anti-capitalist responses more appropriate to a progressive answer to the contradictions of our times?

# Conclusion

# Prospects for a Happy but Contested Future: The Promise of Revolutionary Humanism

From time immemorial there have been human beings who have believed that they could construct, individually or collectively, a better world for themselves than that which they had inherited. Quite a lot of them also came to believe that in the course of so doing it might be possible to remake themselves as different if not better people. I count myself among those who believe in both these propositions. In *Rebel Cities*, for example, I argued that 'the question of what kind of city we want cannot be divorced from the question of what kind of people we want to be, what kinds of social relations we seek, what relations to nature we cherish, what style of life we desire, what aesthetic values we hold'. The right to the city, I wrote, is 'far more than a right of individual or group access to the resources that the city embodies: it is a right to change and re-invent the city more after our heart's desire … The freedom to make and remake ourselves and our cities is … one of the most precious yet most neglected of our human rights.'[1] Perhaps for this intuitive reason, the city has been the focus throughout its history of an immense outpouring of utopian desires for happier futures and less alienating times.

The belief that we can through conscious thought and action change both the world we live in and ourselves for the better defines a humanist tradition. The secular version of this tradition overlaps with and has often been inspired by religious teachings on dignity, tolerance, compassion, love and respect for others. Humanism, both religious and secular, is a world view that measures its achievements in terms of the liberation of human potentialities, capacities and powers. It subscribes to the Aristotelian vision of the uninhibited flourishing of individuals and the construction of 'the good life'. Or, as one contemporary Renaissance man, Peter Buffett defines it, a world which guarantees to individuals 'the true flourishing of his or her nature or the opportunity to live a joyful and fulfilled life'.[2]

This tradition of thought and action has waxed and waned from time to time and from place to place but never seems to die. It has had to compete, of course, with more orthodox doctrines that variously assign our fates and fortunes to the gods, to a specific creator and deity, to the blind forces of nature, to social evolutionary laws enforced through genetic legacies and mutations, by iron laws of economics that dictate the course of technological evolution, or to some hidden teleology dictated by the world spirit. Humanism also has its excesses and its dark side. The somewhat libertine character of Renaissance humanism led one of its leading exponents, Erasmus, to worry that the Judaeo-Christian tradition was being traded in for those of Epicurus. Humanism has sometimes lapsed into a Promethean and anthropocentric view of human capacities and powers in relationship to everything that exists – including nature – even to the point where some deluded beings believe that we, being next to God, are *Übermenschen* having dominion over the universe. This form of humanism becomes even more pernicious when identifiable groups in a population are not considered worthy of being considered human. This was the fate of many indigenous populations in the Americas as they faced colonial settlers. Designated as 'savages', they were considered a part of nature and not a part of humanity. Such tendencies are alive and well in certain circles, leading the radical feminist Catherine MacKinnon to write a book on the question, *Are Women Human?*[3] That such exclusions have in many people's eyes a systematic and generic character in modern society is indicated by the popularity of Giorgio Agamben's formulation of 'the state of exception' in which so many people now exist in the world (with the inhabitants of Guantanamo Bay being a prime example).[4]

There are plenty of contemporary signs that the enlightened humanist tradition is alive and well, perhaps even staging a comeback. This is the spirit that clearly animates the hordes of people employed around the world in NGOs and other charitable institutions whose mission is to improve the life chances and prospects of the less fortunate. There are even vain attempts to dress up capital itself in the humanist garb of what some corporate leaders like to call Conscious Capitalism, a species of entrepreneurial ethics that looks suspiciously like conscience laundering along with sensible proposals to improve worker efficiency by seeming to be nice to them.[5] All the nasty things that happen are absorbed as unintentional collateral damage in an economic system motivated by the best of ethical intentions. Humanism is, however, the spirit that inspires countless individuals to give of themselves unstintingly and often without material reward to contribute selflessly to the well-being of others. Christian, Jewish, Islamic and Buddhist humanisms have spawned widespread religious and charitable organisations, as well as iconic figures like Mahatma Gandhi, Martin Luther King, Mother Teresa and Bishop Tutu. Within the secular tradition there are many varieties of humanist thought and practice, including explicit currents of cosmopolitan, liberal, socialist and Marxist humanism. And, of course, moral and political philosophers have over the centuries devised a variety of conflicting ethical systems of thought based in a variety of ideals of justice, cosmopolitan reason and emancipatory liberty that have from time to time supplied revolutionary slogans. Liberty, equality, fraternity were the watchwords of the French Revolution. The earlier US Declaration of Independence, followed by the US Constitution and, perhaps even more significantly, that stirring document called the Bill of Rights have all played a role in animating subsequent political movements and constitutional forms. The remarkable constitutions recently adopted in Bolivia and Ecuador show that the art of writing progressive constitutions as the basis for regulating human life is by no means dead. And the immense literature that this tradition has spawned has not been lost on those who have sought a more meaningful life. Just think of the past influence of Tom Paine's *Rights of Man* or Mary Wollstonecraft's *A Vindication of the Rights of Woman* within the English-speaking world to see what I mean (almost every tradition in the world has analogous writings to celebrate).

There are two well-known undersides to all of this, both of which we have already encountered. The first is that however noble the universal sentiments expressed at the outset, it has time and again proved hard to stop the universality of humanist claims being perverted for the benefit of particular interests, factions and classes. This is what produces the philanthropic colonialism of which Peter Buffett so eloquently complains. This is what twists Kant's noble cosmopolitanism and quest for perpetual peace into a tool of imperialist and colonial cultural domination, currently represented by the Hilton Hotel cosmopolitanism of CNN and the frequent business-class flier. This is the problem that has bedevilled the doctrines of human rights enshrined in a UN declaration that privileges the individual rights and private property of liberal theory at the expense of collective relations and cultural claims. This is what turns the ideals and practices of freedom into a tool of governmentality for the reproduction and perpetuation of capitalist class affluence and power. The second problem is that the enforcement of any particular system of beliefs and rights always involves some disciplinary power, usually exercised by the state or some other institutionalised authority backed by force. The difficulty here is obvious. The UN declaration implies state enforcement of individual human rights when the state so often is first in line violating those rights.

The difficulty with the humanist tradition in short is that it does not internalise a good understanding of its own inescapable internal contradictions, most clearly captured in the contradiction between freedom and domination. The result is that humanist leanings and sentiments often get presented these days in a somewhat offhand and embarrassed way, except when their position is safely backed by religious doctrine and authority. There is, as a result, no full-blooded contemporary defence of the propositions of or prospects for a secular humanism even though there are innumerable individual works that loosely subscribe to the tradition or even polemicise as to its obvious virtues (as happens in the NGO world). Its dangerous traps and foundational contradictions, particularly questions of coercion, violence and domination, are shied away from because they are too awkward to confront. The result is what Frantz Fanon characterised as 'insipid humanitarianism'. There is plenty of evidence of that manifest in its recent revival. The bourgeois and liberal tradition of secular humanism forms a mushy ethical base for largely ineffective moralising about the sad state of the world and the mounting of equally ineffective campaigns against the plights of chronic poverty and environmental degradation. It is probably for this reason that the French philosopher Louis Althusser launched his fierce and influential campaign back in the 1960s to eject all talk of socialist humanism and alienation from the Marxist tradition. The humanism of the young Marx, as expressed in *The Economic and Philosophic Manuscripts of 1844*, Althusser argued, was separated from the scientific Marx of *Capital* by an 'epistemological rupture' that we ignore at our peril. Marxist humanism, he wrote, is pure ideology, theoretically vacuous and politically misleading, if not dangerous. The devotion of a dedicated Marxist like the long-imprisoned Antonio Gramsci to the 'absolute humanism of human history' was, in Althusser's view, entirely misplaced.[6]

The enormous increase in and nature of the complicitous activities of the humanist NGOs over recent decades would seem to support Althusser's criticisms. The growth of the charitable industrial complex mainly reflects the need to increase 'conscience laundering' for a world's oligarchy that is doubling its wealth and power every few years in the midst of economic stagnation. Their work has done little or nothing in aggregate to deal with human degradation and dispossession or proliferating environmental degradation. This is structurally so because anti-poverty organisations are required to do their work without ever interfering in the further accumulation of the wealth from which they derive their sustenance. If everyone who worked in an anti-poverty organisation converted overnight to an anti-wealth politics we would soon find ourselves living in a very different world. Very few charitable donors, not even Peter Buffett I suspect, would fund that. And the NGOs, which are now at the centre of the problem, would not in any case want that (though there are many individuals within the NGO world who would but simply can't).

So what kind of humanism do we need in order to progressively change the world through anti-capitalist work into another kind of place populated by different kinds of people?

There is, I believe, a crying need to articulate a secular *revolutionary* humanism that can ally with those religious-based humanisms (most clearly articulated in both Protestant and Catholic versions of the theology of liberation as well as in cognate movements within Hindu, Islamic, Jewish and indigenous religious cultures) to counter alienation in its many forms and to radically change the world from its capitalist ways. There is a strong and powerful – albeit problematic – tradition of secular revolutionary humanism both with respect to both theory and political practice. This is a form of humanism that Louis Althusser totally rejected. But, in spite of Althusser's influential intervention, it has a powerful and articulate expression in the Marxist and radical traditions as well as beyond. It is very different from bourgeois liberal humanism. It refuses the idea that there is an unchanging or pre-given 'essence' of what it means to be human and forces us to think hard about how to become a new kind of human. It unifies the Marx of *Capital* with that of *The Economic and Philosophic Manuscripts of 1844* and arrows in to the heart of the contradictions of what any humanist programme must be willing to embrace if it is to change the world. It clearly recognises that the prospects for a happy future for most are invariably marred by the inevitability of dictating the unhappiness of some others. A dispossessed financial oligarchy which cannot any more partake of caviar and champagne lunches on their yachts moored off the Bahamas will doubtless complain at their diminished fates and fortunes in a more egalitarian world. We may, as good liberal humanists, even feel a bit sorry for them. Revolutionary humanists steel themselves against that thought. While we may not approve of this ruthless approach to dealing with such contradictions, we have to acknowledge the basic honesty and self-awareness of the practitioners.

Consider, as one example, the revolutionary humanism of someone like Frantz Fanon. Fanon was a psychiatrist working in hospitals in the midst of a bitter and violent anti-colonial war (rendered so memorable in Pontecorvo's film *The Battle of Algiers* – a film, incidentally, that the US military now uses for anti-insurgency training purposes). Fanon wrote in depth about the struggle for freedom and liberty on the part of colonised peoples against the colonisers. His analysis, though specific to the Algerian case, illustrates the sorts of issues that arise in any liberation struggle, including those between capital and labour. But it does so in stark dramatic and more easily legible terms precisely because it incorporates the additional dimensions of racial, cultural and colonial oppressions and degradations giving rise to an ultra-violent revolutionary situation from which no peaceful exit seems possible. The foundational question for Fanon is how to recover a sense of humanity on the basis of the dehumanising practices and experiences of colonial domination. 'As soon as you and your fellow men are cut down like dogs,' he writes in *The Wretched of the Earth*, 'there is no other solution but to use every means available to re-establish your weight as a human being. You must therefore weigh as heavily as possible on your torturer's body so that his wits, which have wandered off somewhere, can at last be restored to their human dimension.' In this way 'man both demands and claims his infinite humanity'. There are always 'tears to be wiped away, inhuman attitudes to be fought, condescending ways of speech to be ruled out, men to be humanised'. Revolution, for Fanon, was not simply about the transfer of power from one segment of society to another. It entailed the reconstruction of humanity – in Fanon's case a distinctive post-colonial humanity – and a radical shift in the meaning attached to being human. 'Decolonisation is truly the creation of new men. But such a creation cannot be attributed to a supernatural power. The "thing" colonised becomes a man through the very process of liberation.' It was therefore inevitable in a colonial situation, Fanon argued, that the struggle for liberation would have to be constituted in nationalist terms. But 'if nationalism is not explained, enriched, deepened, if it does not very quickly turn into a social and political consciousness, into humanism, then it leads to a dead end'.[7]

Fanon, of course, shocks many liberal humanists with his embrace of a necessary violence and his rejection of compromise. How, he asks, is non-violence possible in a situation structured by the systematic violence exercised by the colonisers? What is the point of starving people going on hunger strike? Why, as Herbert Marcuse asked, should we be persuaded of the virtues of tolerance towards the intolerable? In a divided world, where the colonial power defines the colonised as subhuman and evil by nature, compromise is impossible. 'One does not negotiate with evil,' famously said Vice-President Dick Cheney. To which Fanon had a ready-made reply: 'The work of the colonist is to make even dreams of liberty impossible for the colonised. The work of the colonised is to imagine every possible method for annihilating the colonist ... The theory of the "absolute evil of the colonist" is in response to the theory of the "absolute evil of the native"'. In such a divided world there is no prospect of negotiation or compromise. This is what has kept the USA and Iran so far apart ever since the Iranian Revolution. 'The native sector' of the colonial city, Fanon points out, 'is not complementary to the European sector ... The city as a whole is governed by a purely Aristotelian logic' and follows the 'dictates of mutual exclusion'. Lacking a dialectical relation between the two, the only way to break down the difference is through violence. 'To destroy the colonial world means nothing less than demolishing the colonist's sector, burying it deep within the earth or banishing it from the territory'.[8] There is nothing mushy about such a programme. As Fanon saw clearly:

> For the colonised this violence is invested with positive forma-
> tive features because it constitutes their only work. This violent
> praxis is totalising since each individual represents a violent link
> in a great chain, in the almighty body of violence rearing up in

reaction to the primary violence of the coloniser ... At the individual level, violence is a cleansing force. It rids the colonised of their inferiority complex, of their passive and despairing attitude. It emboldens them and restores their self-confidence. Even if the armed struggle has been symbolic, and even if they have been demobilised by rapid decolonisation, the people have time to realise their liberation was the achievement of each and every one ...[9]

But what is so stunning about *The Wretched of the Earth*, and what indeed brings tears to the eyes on a close reading and makes it so searingly human, is the second half of the book, which is taken up by devastating descriptions of the psychic traumas of those on both sides who found themselves forced by circumstances to participate in the violence of the liberation struggle. We now know much more about the psychic damage suffered by those US and other soldiers who engaged in military action in Vietnam, Afghanistan and Iraq, and the terrible scourge on their lives as a result of post-traumatic stress disorder. This is what Fanon wrote about with such compassion in the midst of the revolutionary struggle against the colonial system in Algeria. After decolonisation there is an immense work that remains to be done, not only to repair the psyches of damaged souls, but also to mitigate what Fanon clearly saw as the dangers of the lingering effects (even replication) of colonial ways of thought and being. 'The colonised subject fights in order to put an end to domination. But he must also ensure that all the untruths planted within him by the oppressor are eliminated. In a colonial regime such as the one in Algeria the ideas taught by colonialism impacted not only the European minority but also the Algerian. Total liberation involves every facet of the personality ... Independence is not a magic ritual but an indispensable condition for men and women to live in true liberation, in other words to master all the material resources necessary for a radical transformation of society.'[10]

I do not raise the question of violence here, any more than did Fanon, because I am or he was in favour of it. He highlighted it because the logic of human situations so often deteriorates to a point where there is no other option. Even Gandhi acknowledged that. But the option has potentially dangerous consequences. Revolutionary humanism has to offer some kind of philosophical answer to this difficulty, some solace in the face of incipient tragedies. While the ultimate humanist task may be, as Aeschylus put it 2,500 years ago, 'to tame the savageness of man and make gentle the life of this world', this cannot be done without confronting and dealing with the immense violence that underpins the colonial and neocolonial order. This is what Mao and Ho Chi Minh had to confront, what Che Guevara sought to achieve, and what a host of political leaders and thinkers in post-colonial struggles, including Amilcar Cabral of Guinea-Bissau, Julius Nyerere of Tanzania, Kwame Nkrumah of Ghana, and Aimé Césaire, Walter Rodney, C. L. R. James and many others, have acted against with such conviction in both words and deeds.

But is the social order of capital any different in essence from its colonial manifestations? That order has certainly sought to distance itself at home from the callous calculus of colonial violence (depicting it as something that must necessarily be visited on uncivilised others 'over there' for their own good). It had to disguise at home the far too blatant inhumanity it demonstrated abroad. 'Over there' things could be put out of sight and hearing. Only now, for example, is the vicious violence of the British suppression of the Mau Mau movement in Kenya in the 1960s being acknowledged in full. When capital drifts close to such inhumanity at home it typically elicits a similar response to that of the colonised. To the degree that it embraced racialised violence at home, as it did in the United States, it produced movements like the Black Panthers and the Nation of Islam along with leaders like Malcolm X and, in his final days, Martin Luther King, who saw the connectivity between race and class and suffered the consequences thereof. But capital learned a lesson. The more race and class get woven seamlessly together, then the faster the fuse for revolution burns. But what Marx makes so clear in *Capital* is the daily violence constituted in the domination of capital over labour in the marketplace and in the act of production as well as on the terrain of daily life. How easy it is to take descriptions of contemporary labour conditions in, for example, the electronics factories of Shenzhen, the clothing factories of Bangladesh or the sweatshops of Los Angeles and insert them into Marx's classic chapter on 'the working day' in *Capital* and not notice the difference. How shockingly easy it is to take the living conditions of the working classes, the marginalised and the unemployed in Lisbon, São Paulo and Jakarta and put them next to Engels's classic 1844 description of *The Condition of the Working Class in England* and find little substantive difference.[11]

Oligarchic capitalist class privilege and power are taking the world in a similar direction almost everywhere. Political power backed by intensifying surveillance, policing and militarised violence is being used to attack the well-being of whole populations deemed expendable and disposable. We are daily witnessing the systematic dehumanisation of disposable people. Ruthless oligarchic power is now being exercised through a totalitarian democracy directed to immediately disrupt, fragment and suppress any coherent anti-wealth political movement (such as Occupy). The arrogance and disdain with which the affluent now view those less fortunate than themselves, even when (particularly when) vying with each other behind closed doors to prove who can be the most charitable of them all, are notable facts of our present condition. The 'empathy gap' between the oligarchy and the rest is immense and increasing. The oligarchs mistake superior income for superior human worth and their economic success as evidence of their superior knowledge of the world (rather than their superior command over accounting tricks and legal niceties). They do not know how to listen to the plight of the world because they cannot and wilfully will not confront their role in the construction of that plight. They do not and cannot see their own contradictions. The billionaire Koch brothers give charitably to a university like MIT even to the point of building a beautiful day-care centre for the deserving faculty there while simultaneously lavishing untold millions in financial support for a political movement (headed by the Tea Party faction) in the US Congress that cuts food stamps and denies welfare, nutritional supplements and day care for millions living in or close to absolute poverty.

It is in a political climate such as this that the violent and unpredictable eruptions that are occurring all around the world on an episodic basis (from Turkey and Egypt to Brazil and Sweden in 2013 alone) look more and more like the prior tremors for a coming earthquake that will make the post-colonial revolutionary struggles of the 1960s look like child's play. If there is an end to capital, then this is surely from where it will come and its immediate consequences are unlikely to prove happy for anyone. This is what Fanon so clearly teaches.

The only hope is that the mass of humanity will see the danger before the rot goes too far and the human and environmental damage becomes too great to repair. In the face of what Pope Francis rightly dubs 'the globalisation of indifference', the global masses must, as Fanon so neatly puts it, 'first decide to wake up, put on their thinking caps and stop playing the irresponsible game of Sleeping Beauty'.[12] If Sleeping Beauty awakes in time, then we might be in for a more fairy-tale-like ending. The 'absolute humanism of human history', wrote Gramsci, 'does not aim at the peaceful resolution of existing contradictions in history and society but rather is the very theory of these contradictions'. Hope is latent in them, said Bertolt Brecht. There are, as we have seen, enough compelling contradictions within capital's domain to foster many grounds for hope.

# Epilogue
# Ideas for Political Praxis

What does this X-ray into the contradictions of capital tell us about anti-capitalist political praxis? It cannot, of course, tell us exactly what to do in the midst of fierce and always complicated struggles on this or that issue on the ground. But it does help frame an overall direction to anti-capitalist struggle even as it makes and strengthens the case for anti-capitalist politics. When pollsters ask their favourite question, 'Do you think the country is headed in the right direction?' that presumes that people have some sense as to what the right direction might be. So what do those of us who believe capital is headed in the wrong direction consider a right direction and how might we evaluate our progress towards realising those goals? And how might we present those goals as modest and sensible proposals – for such they really are, relative to the absurd arguments put forward to deepen the powers of capital as an answer to humanity's crying needs? Here are some mandates – derived from the seventeen contradictions – to frame and hopefully animate political praxis. We should strive for a world in which:

1. The direct provision of adequate use values for all (housing, education, food security etc.) takes precedence over their provision through a profit-maximising market system that concentrates exchange values in a few private hands and allocates goods on the basis of ability to pay.
2. A means of exchange is created that facilitates the circulation of goods and services but limits or excludes the capacity of private individuals to accumulate money as a form of social power.
3. The opposition between private property and state power is

displaced as far as possible by common rights regimes – with particular emphasis upon human knowledge and the land as the most crucial commons we have – the creation, management and protection of which lie in the hands of popular assemblies and associations.

4. The appropriation of social power by private persons is not only inhibited by economic and social barriers but becomes universally frowned upon as a pathological deviancy.

5. The class opposition between capital and labour is dissolved into associated producers freely deciding on what, how and when they will produce in collaboration with other associations regarding the fulfilment of common social needs.

6. Daily life is slowed down – locomotion shall be leisurely and slow – to maximise time for free activities conducted in a stable and well-maintained environment protected from dramatic episodes of creative destruction.

7. Associated populations assess and communicate their mutual social needs to each other to furnish the basis for their production decisions (in the short run, realisation considerations dominate production decisions).

8. New technologies and organisational forms are created that lighten the load of all forms of social labour, dissolve unnecessary distinctions in technical divisions of labour, liberate time for free individual and collective activities, and diminish the ecological footprint of human activities.

9. Technical divisions of labour are reduced through the use of automation, robotisation and artificial intelligence. Those residual technical divisions of labour deemed essential are dissociated from social divisions of labour as far as possible. Administrative, leadership and policing functions should be rotated among individuals within the population at large. We are liberated from the rule of experts.

10. Monopoly and centralised power over the use of the means of production is vested in popular associations through which the decentralised competitive capacities of individuals and social

groups are mobilised to produce differentiations in technical, social, cultural and lifestyle innovations.

11. The greatest possible diversification exists in ways of living and being, of social relations and relations to nature, and of cultural habits and beliefs within territorial associations, communes and collectives. Free and uninhibited but orderly geographical movement of individuals within territories and between communes is guaranteed. Representatives of the associations regularly come together to assess, plan and undertake common tasks and deal with common problems at different scales: bioregional, continental and global.

12. All inequalities in material provision are abolished other than those entailed in the principle of from each according to his, her or their capacities and to each according to his, her, or their needs.

13. The distinction between necessary labour done for distant others and work undertaken in the reproduction of self, household and commune is gradually erased such that social labour becomes embedded in household and communal work and household and communal work becomes the primary form of unalienated and non-monetised social labour.

14. Everyone should have equal entitlements to education, health care, housing, food security, basic goods and open access to transportation to ensure the material basis for freedom from want and for freedom of action and movement.

15. The economy converges on zero growth (though with room for uneven geographical developments) in a world in which the greatest possible development of both individual and collective human capacities and powers and the perpetual search for novelty prevail as social norms to displace the mania for perpetual compound growth.

16. The appropriation and production of natural forces for human needs should proceed apace but with the maximum regard for the protection of ecosystems, maximum attention paid to the recycling of nutrients, energy and physical matter to the

sites from whence they came, and an overwhelming sense of re-enchantment with the beauty of the natural world, of which we are a part and to which we can and do contribute through our works.

17. Unalienated human beings and unalienated creative personas emerge armed with a new and confident sense of self and collective being. Born out of the experience of freely contracted intimate social relations and empathy for different modes of living and producing, a world will emerge where everyone is considered equally worthy of dignity and respect, even as conflict rages over the appropriate definition of the good life. This social world will continuously evolve through permanent and ongoing revolutions in human capacities and powers. The perpetual search for novelty continues.

None of these mandates, it goes without saying, transcends or supersedes the importance of waging war against all other forms of discrimination, oppression and violent repression within capitalism as a whole. By the same token, none of these other struggles should transcend or supersede that against capital and its contradictions. Alliances of interests are clearly needed.

# Notes

**Prologue: The Crisis of Capitalism This Time Around**

1. Karl Marx, *Theories of Surplus Value*, Part 2, London, Lawrence and Wishart, 1969, p. 540.

**Introduction: On Contradiction**

1. Bertell Ollman, *The Dance of the Dialectic: Steps in Marx's Method*, Champagne, IL, University of Illinois Press, 2003.

**Contradiction 1: Use Value and Exchange Value**

1. For a brief overview see David Harvey, *Rebel Cities: From the Right to the City to the Urban Revolution*, London, Verso, 2013.
2. Michael Lewis, *The Big Short: Inside the Doomsday Machine*, New York, Norton, 2010, p. 34.

**Contradiction 2: The Social Value of Labour and Its Representation by Money**

1. This fascinating story is told in Paul Seabright (ed.), *The Vanishing Rouble: Barter Networks and Non-Monetary Transactions in Post-Soviet Societies*, London, Cambridge University Press, 2000.
2. John Maynard Keynes, *Essays in Persuasion*, New York, Classic House Books, 2009, p. 199.
3. Silvio Gesell, (1916); http:www.archive.org/details/ TheNaturalEconomicOrder, p. 121. For some further discussion of Gesell's ideas see John Maynard Keynes, *The General Theory of Employment, Interest, and Money*, New York, Harcourt Brace, 1964,

p. 363, and Charles Eisenstein, *Sacred Economics: Money, Gift and Society in the Age of Transition*, Berkeley, CA, Evolver Editions, 2011.

## Contradiction 3: Private Property and the Capitalist State

1. Silvio Gesell, *The Natural Economic Order* (1916); http:www.archive.org/details/TheNaturalEconomicOrder, p. 81.
2. David Harvey, *The Enigma of Capital*, London, Profile Books, 2010, pp. 55–7.
3. Thomas Greco, *The End of Money and the Future of Civilization*, White River Junction, VT, Chelsea Green Publishing, 2009.
4. Ibid.

## Contradiction 4: Private Appropriation and Common Wealth

1. Karl Marx, *Grundrisse*, Harmondsworth, Penguin, 1973, p. 223.
2. Karl Polanyi, *The Great Transformation: The Political and Economic Origins of Our Time*, Boston, Beacon Press, 1957, p. 72.
3. Ibid., p. 73.
4. Ibid., p. 178.
5. Martin Heidegger, *Discourse on Thinking*, New York, Harper Press, 1966, p. 50.

## Contradiction 5: Capital and Labour

1. Karl Marx, *Capital*, Volume 1, Harmondsworth, Penguin, 1973, p. 344.
2. Andrew Glyn and Robert Sutcliffe, *British Capitalism: Workers and the Profit Squeeze*, Harmondsworth, Penguin, 1972.

## Contradiction 6: Capital as Process or Thing?

1. John Maynard Keynes, *The General Theory of Employment, Interest and Money*, New York, Harcourt Brace, 1964, p. 376.

## Contradiction 7: The Contradictory Unity of Production and Realisation

1. Karl Marx, *Capital*, Volume 2, Harmondsworth, Pelican Books, 1978, p. 391. The parallel passage in Volume 1 is to be found on p. 799 of the Penguin edition.

## Part Two: The Moving Contradictions

1. W. Brian Arthur, *The Nature of Technology: What It Is and How It Evolves*, New York, Free Press, 2009, p. 202.

## Contradiction 8: Technology, Work and Human Disposability

1. W. Brian Arthur, *The Nature of Technology: What It Is and How It Evolves*, New York, Free Press, 2009, pp. 22 et seq.
2. Jane Jacobs, *The Economy of Cities*, New York, Vintage, 1969.
3. Arthur, *The Nature of Technology*, p. 211.
4. Alfred NorthWhitehead, *Process and Reality*, New York, Free Press, 1969, p. 33.
5. Arthur, *The Nature of Technology*, p. 213; Karl Marx, *Grundrisse*, Harmondsworth, Penguin, 1973.
6. Arthur, *The Nature of Technology*, p 191.
7. Joseph Schumpeter, *Capitalism, Socialism and Democracy*, London, Routledge, 1942, pp. 82–3.
8. Arthur, *The Nature of Technology*, p. 186.
9. André Gorz, *Critique of Economic Reason*, London, Verso, 1989, p. 200.
10. Martin Ford, *The Lights in the Tunnel: Automation, Acclerating Technology and the Economy of the Future*, USA, Acculant™ Publishing, 2009, p. 62.
11. Ibid., pp. 96–7.
12. Gorz, *Critique of Economic Reason*, p. 92.
13. Melissa Wright, *Disposable Women and Other Myths of Global Capitalism*, New York, Routledge, 2006.

## Contradiction 9: Divisions of Labour

1. Harry Braverman, *Labor and Monopoly Capital*, New York, Monthly Review Press, 1974.
2. Timothy Mitchell, *The Rule of Experts: Egypt, Techno-Politics, Modernity*, Berkeley, University of California Press, 2002.
3. Robert Reich, *The Work of Nations: Preparing Ourselves for 21st Century Capitalism*, New York, Vintage, 1992.
4. Karl Marx, *Capital*, Volume 1, Harmondsworth, Penguin, 1973, p. 618.

## Contradiction 10: Monopoly and Competition: Centralisation and Decentralisation

1. Joseph Stiglitz, *The Price of Inequality*, New York, Norton, 2013, p. 44.
2. Ibid.
3. Paul Baran and Paul Sweezy, *Monopoly Capitalism*, New York, Monthly Review Press, 1966.
4. Giovanni Arrighi, 'Towards a Theory of Capitalist Crisis', *New Left Review*, September 1978.
5. Elisée Reclus, *Anarchy, Geography, Modernity*, edited by John P. Clark and Camille Martin, Oxford, Lexington Books, 2004, p. 124.
6. David Harvey, 'The Art of Rent', in *Spaces of Capital*, Edinburgh, Edinburgh University Press, 2002.
7. Alfred Chandler, *The Visible Hand: The Managerial Revolution in American Business*, Cambridge, MA, Harvard University Press, 1993.
8. Giovanni Arrighi, *Adam Smith in Beijing*, London, Verso, 2010.
9. Karl Marx, *Capital*, Volume 3, Harmondsworth, Penguin, 1981, p. 490.

## Contradiction 11: Uneven Geographical Developments and the Production of Space

1. Gunnar Myrdal, *Economic Theory and Underdeveloped Regions*, London, Duckworth, 1957.
2. David Harvey, *Spaces of Capital*, Edinburgh, Edinburgh University Press, 2002.
3. Henri Lefebvre, *The Production of Space*, Oxford, Basil Blackwell, 1989.

## Contradiction 12: Disparities of Income and Wealth

1. Michael Norton and Dan Ariely, 'Building a Better America – One Wealth Quintile at a Time', *Perspectives on Psychological Science*, Vol. 6, 2011, p. 9.
2. Oxfam, 'The Cost of Inequality: How Wealth and Income Extremes Hurt Us All', *Oxfam Media Briefing*, 18 January 2013.
3. Branko Milanovic, *Worlds Apart: Measuring International and Global Inequality*, Princeton, Princeton University Press, 2005, p. 149.
4. Craig Calhoun, 'What Threatens Capitalism Now?', in Immanuel Wallerstein, Randall Collins, Michael Mann, Georgi Derluguian and

Craig Calhoun, *Does Capitalism Have a Future?*, Oxford, Oxford University Press, 2013.

## Contradiction 13: Social Reproduction

1. Cited in Samuel Bowles and Herbert Gintis, 'The Problem with Human Capital Theory: A Marxian Critique', *American Economic Review*, Vol. 65, No. 2, 1975, pp. 74–82.
2. Karl Marx, *Capital*, Volume 3, Harmondsworth, Penguin, 1981, pp. 503–5.
3. Gary Becker, *Human Capital: A Theoretical and Empirical Analysis, with Special Reference to Education*, Chicago, University of Chicago Press, 1994.
4. Pierre Bourdieu, 'The Forms of Capital', in J. Richardson (ed.), *Handbook of Theory and Research for the Sociology of Education*, New York, Greenwood, 1986.
5. Robert Reich, *The Work of Nations: Preparing Ourselves for 21st Century Capitalism*, New York, Vintage, 1992.
6. Cindi Katz, 'Vagabond Capitalism and the Necessity of Social Reproduction', *Antipode*, Vol. 33, No. 4, 2001, pp. 709–28.
7. Jürgen Habermas, *The Theory of Communicative Action. Volume 2: Lifeworld and System: A Critique of Functionalist Reason*, Boston, Beacon Press, 1985; Henri Lefebvre, *Critique of Everyday Life*, London, Verso, 1991.
8. Fernand Braudel, *Capitalism and Material Life, 1400–1800*, London, Weidenfeld & Nicolson, 1973.
9. Randy Martin, *Financialization of Daily Life*, Philadelphia, Temple University Press, 2002.
10. Katz, 'Vagabond Capitalism and the Necessity of Social Reproduction', pp. 709–28.
11. Lefebvre, *Critique of Everyday Life*.

## Contradiction 14: Freedom and Domination

1. Christopher Hill, *The World Turned Upside Down: Radical Ideas During the English Revolution*, Harmondsworth, Penguin, 1984.
2. Terry Eagleton, *Why Marx Was Right*, New Haven, Yale University Press, 2011, p. 87.

3. I provide an overview of all of George W. Bush's speeches in David Harvey, *Cosmopolitanism and the Geographies of Freedom*, New York, Columbia University Press, 2009, pp. 1–14.

4. Michel Foucault, *The Birth of Biopolitics: Lectures at the College de France, 1978–1979*, New York, Picador, 2008.

5. Robert Wolff, Barrington Moore and Herbert Marcuse, *A Critique of Pure Tolerance: Beyond Tolerance, Tolerance and the Scientific Outlook, Repressive Tolerance*, Boston, Beacon Press, 1969.

6. Karl Polanyi, *The Great Transformation: The Political and Economic Origins of Our Time*, Boston, Beacon Press, 1957, pp. 256–7.

7. Ibid., p. 257.

8. Ibid., p. 258.

9. Amartya Sen, *Development as Freedom*, New York, Anchor Books, 2000, pp. 297–8.

10. Peter Buffett, 'The Charitable-Industrial Complex', *New York Times*, 26 July 2013.

11. Karl Marx, *Grundrisse*, Harmondsworth, Penguin, 1973, p. 488.

12. Karl Marx, 'On the Jewish Question', in *Karl Marx: Early Texts*, edited by David McLellan, Oxford, Basil Blackwell, 1972.

13. Jean-Jacques Rousseau, *The Social Contract*, Oxford, Oxford University Press, 2008.

14. Eagleton, *Why Marx Was Right*, pp. 75–6.

## Contradiction 15: Endless Compound Growth

1. Michael Hudson, *The Bubble and Beyond*, Dresden, Islet, 2012. This is one of the only economics texts I know that takes the issue of compound growth seriously. I have used some of his materials in what follows. When I raised the question of compound growth in 2011 with two senior economics editors of a major global newspaper, one of them shrugged off the question as trivial if not laughable, while the other said there were still plenty of new technological frontiers to explore so why worry.

2. Robert Gordon, 'Is U.S. Economic Growth Over? Faltering Innovation Confronts the Six Headwinds', *Working Paper 18315*, Cambridge, MA, National Bureau of Economic Research, 2012. The public reaction to

Gordon's arguments are covered in Thomas Edsall, 'No More Industrial Revolutions', *New York Times*, 15 October 2012. The general public reaction was that Gordon probably had a point but that he was too pessimistic on the future impact of innovations. Martin Wolf, an influential economist with the *Financial Times*, however, accepted much of what Gordon had to say and concluded that economic elites in the high-income world would welcome the future that Gordon described but everyone else would like it 'vastly less. Get used to this. It will not change.' Other contributions would be Tyler Cowen, *The Great Stagnation: How America Ate all the Low-Hanging Fruit of Modern History, Got Sick and Will (Eventually) Feel Better*, E-special from Dutton, 2011. All these arguments are, however, US-focused.

3. The Thelluson case is described in Hudson, *The Bubble and Beyond*.

4. Cited in Karl Marx, *Capital*, Volume 3, Harmondsworth, Penguin, p. 519.

5. Angus Maddison, *Phases of Capitalist Development*, Oxford, Oxford University Press, 1982; *Contours of the World Economy, 1–2030 AD*, Oxford, Oxford University Press, 2007.

6. Bradford DeLong, 'Estimating World GDP, One Million B.C.–Present'. Estimates given in Wikipedia entry on Gross World Product.

7. Thomas Malthus, *An Essay on the Principle of Population*, Cambridge, Cambridge University Press, 1992.

8. McKinsey Global Institute, 'The World at Work: Jobs, Pay and Skills for 3.5 Billion People', *Report of the McKinsey Global Institute*, 2012.

9. Guy Debord, *The Society of the Spectacle*, Kalamazoo, Black & Red, 2000.

10. Alvin Toffler, *The Third Wave: The Classic Study of Tomorrow*, New York, Bantam, 1980.

11. Michael Hardt and Antonio Negri, *Commonwealth*, Cambridge, MA, Harvard University Press, 2009.

12. Antonio Gramsci, *The Prison Notebooks*, London, NLR Books, 1971.

13. Gordon, 'Is U.S. Economic Growth Over? Faltering Innovation Confronts the Six Headwinds'.

14. Marx, *Capital*, Volume 3, p. 573.

15. I provided a synoptic account of this in David Harvey, *A Brief History of Neoliberalism*, Oxford, Oxford University Press, 2005.

## Contradiction 16: Capital's Relation to Nature

1. Paul Sabin, *The Bet: Paul Ehrlich, Julian Simon, and Our Gamble over Earth's Future*, New Haven, Yale University Press, 2013.
2. I argue this case in detail in David Harvey, *Justice, Nature and the Geography of Difference*, Oxford, Basil Blackwell, 1996.
3. Neil Smith, 'Nature as Accumulation Strategy', *Socialist Register*, 2007, pp. 19–41.
4. Arthur McEvoy, *The Fisherman's Problem: Ecology and Law in the California Fisheries, 1850–1980*, Cambridge, Cambridge University Press, 1990.
5. Arne Naess, *Ecology, Community and Lifestyle*, Cambridge, Cambridge University Press, 1989; William Leiss, *The Domination of Nature*, Boston, MA, Beacon Press, 1974; Martin Jay, *The Dialectical Imagination: A History of the Frankfurt School and the Institute of Social Research, 1923–50*, Boston, MA, Beacon Press, 1973; Murray Bookchin, *The Philosophy of Social Ecology: Essays on Dialectical Naturalism*, Montreal, Black Rose Books, 1990; Richard Peet, Paul Robbins and Michael Watts, *Global Political Ecology*, New York, Routledge, 2011; John Bellamy Foster, *Marx's Ecology: Materialism and Nature*, New York, Monthly Review Press, 2000.

## Contradiction 17: The Revolt of Human Nature: Universal Alienation

1. David Harvey, *The Enigma of Capital*, London, Profile Books, 2010, p. 260.
2. See the debate in Immanuel Wallerstein, Randall Collins, Michael Mann, Georgi Derluguian and Craig Calhoun, *Does Capitalism Have a Future?*, Oxford, Oxford University Press, 2013.
3. André Gorz, *Critique of Economic Reason*, London, Verso, 1989, p. 22.
4. Ibid., p. 86.
5. Ibid., pp. 87–8.
6. Ibid., p. 100.

7. Ibid., p. 114.
8. Thorstein Veblen, *The Theory of the Leisure Class*, New York, Oxford University Press, 2009 edition.
9. Gorz, *Critique of Economic Reason*, p. 116.
10. Ibid., pp. 45–6.
11. Pope Francis, 'Apostolic Exhortation Evangelii Gaudium of the Holy Father Francis to the Bishops, Clergy, Consecrated Persons and the Lay Faithful on the Proclamation of the Gospel in Today's World', *National Catholic Register*, 15 December 2013, paragraph 192.
12. Gorz, *Critique of Economic Reason*, p. 46.
13. Ibid., pp. 46–7.
14. Ibid., p. 184.

## Conclusion: Prospects for a Happy but Contested Future: The Promise of Revolutionary Humanism

1. David Harvey, *Rebel Cities: From the Right to the City to the Urban Revolution*, London, Verso, 2013, p. 4.
2. Peter Buffett, 'The Charitable-Industrial Complex', *New York Times*, 26 July 2013.
3. Catherine MacKinnon, *Are Women Human?: And Other International Dialogues*, Cambridge, MA, Harvard University Press, 2007.
4. Giorgio Agamben, *State of Exception*, Chicago, Chicago University Press, 2005.
5. John Mackey, Rajendra Sisodia and Bill George, *Conscious Capitalism: Liberating the Heroic Spirit of Business*, Cambridge, MA, Harvard Business Review Press, 2013.
6. Louis Althusser, *The Humanist Controversy and Other Writings*, London, Verso, 2003; Peter Thomas, *The Gramscian Moment: Philosophy, Hegemony and Marxism*, Chicago, Haymarket Books, 2010.
7. Frantz Fanon, *The Wretched of the Earth*, New York, Grove Press, 2005, p. 144.
8. Ibid., p. 6.
9. Ibid., p. 51.
10. Ibid., p. 144.

11. Frederick Engels, *The Condition of the Working Class in England*, London, Cambridge University Press, 1962.
12. Fanon, *The Wretched of the Earth*, p. 62.

# Bibliography and Further Reading

Agamben, G., *State of Exception*, Chicago, Chicago University Press, 2005

Althusser, L., 'Contradiction and Overdetermination' (1964); althusser_overdetermination_nlr41.pdf

—, *The Humanist Controversy and Other Writings*, London, Verso, 2003

Arendt, H., *Between Past and Future: Eight Exercises in Political Thought*, London, Penguin, 2009

Armstrong, P., Glynn, A., and Harrison, J., *Capitalism Since World War II: The Making and Breaking of the Long Boom*, Oxford, Basil Blackwell, 1991

Arrighi, G., 'Towards a Theory of Capitalist Crisis', *New Left Review*, September 1978

—, *The Long Twentieth Century*, London, Verso, 1994

Arthur, W. B., *The Nature of Technology: What It Is and How It Evolves*, New York, Free Press, 2009

Atkinson, T., and Piketty, T., *Top Incomes: A Global Perspective*, Oxford, Oxford University Press, 2010

Baran, P., and Sweezy, P., *Monopoly Capital*, New York, Monthly Review Press, 1966

Becker, G., *Human Capital: A Theoretical and Empirical Analysis, with Special Reference to Education*, Chicago, University of Chicago Press, 1994

Bookchin, M., *The Philosophy of Social Ecology: Essays on Dialectical Naturalism*, Montreal, Black Rose Books, 1990

Bourdieu, P., 'The Forms of Capital', in J. Richardson (ed.), *Handbook of Theory and Research for the Sociology of Education*, New York, Greenwood, 1986

Bowles, S., and Gintis, H., 'The Problem with Human Capital Theory: A Marxian Critique', *American Economic Review*, Vol. 65, No. 2, 1975, pp. 74–82

Braudel, F., *Capitalism and Material Life, 1400–1800*, London, Weidenfeld & Nicolson, 1973

Braverman, H., *Labor and Monopoly Capital*, New York, Monthly Review Press, 1974

Buffett, P., 'The Charitable-Industrial Complex', *New York Times*, 26 July 2013

Chandler, A., *The Visible Hand: The Managerial Revolution in American Business*, Cambridge, MA, Harvard University Press, 1993

Clarke, S. (ed.), *The State Debate*, London, Macmillan, 1991

Cleaver, H., *Reading Capital Politically*, Austin, University of Texas Press, 1979

Debord, G., *The Society of the Spectacle*, Kalamazoo, Black & Red, 2000

Eagleton, T., *Why Marx Was Right*, New Haven, Yale University Press, 2011

Eisenstein, C., *Sacred Economics: Money, Gift and Society in the Age of Transition*, Berkeley, Ca, Evolver Editions, 2011

Engels, F., *The Condition of the Working Class in England*, London, Cambridge University Press, 1962

Fanon, F., *The Wretched of the Earth*, New York, Grove Press, 2005

Ford, M., *The Lights in the Tunnel: Automation, Accelerating Technology and the Economy of the Future*, USA, Acculant™ Publishing, 2009

Foster, J. B., *Marx's Ecology; Materialism and Nature*, New York, Monthly Review Press, 2000

Foucault, M., *The Birth of Biopolitics: Lectures at the College de France, 1978–1979*, New York, Picador, 2008

Gesell, S., *The Natural Economic Order* (1916); http:www.archive.org/details/TheNaturalEconomicOrder

Glyn, A., and Sutcliffe, R., *British Capitalism: Workers and the Profit Squeeze*, Harmondsworth, Penguin, 1972

Gordon, R., 'Is U.S. Economic Growth Over? Faltering Innovation Confronts the Six Headwinds', Cambridge, MA, National Bureau of Economic Research, 2012

Gorz, A., *Critique of Economic Reason*, London, Verso, 1989

—, *The Immaterial*, New York and Chicago, Seagull, 2010

Gramsci, A., *The Prison Notebooks*, London, NLR Books, 1971

Greco, T., *The End of Money and the Future of Civilization*, White River Junction, VT, Chelsea Green Publishing, 2009

Greider, W., *Secrets of the Temple: How the Federal Reserve Runs the Country*, New York, Simon and Schuster, 1989

Habermas, J., *The Theory of Communicative Action. Volume 2: Lifeworld and System: A Critique of Functionalist Reason*, Boston, Beacon Press, 1985

Hardt, M., and Negri, A., *Commonwealth*, Cambridge, MA, Harvard University Press, 2009

Hart, K., 'Notes Towards an Anthropology of Money', *Kritikos*, Vol. 2, 2005

Harvey, D., *Justice, Nature and the Geography of Difference*, Oxford, Basil Blackwell, 1996

—, *Spaces of Capital*, Edinburgh, Edinburgh University Press, 2002

—, *A Brief History of Neoliberalism*, Oxford, Oxford University Press, 2005

—, *Cosmopolitanism and the Geographies of Freedom*, New York, Columbia University Press, 2009

—, *The Enigma of Capital*, London, Profile Books, 2010

—, *Rebel Cities: From the Right to the City to the Urban Revolution*, London, Verso, 2012

—, *A Companion to Marx's Capital*, Volume Two, London, Verso, 2013

Heidegger, M., *Discourse on Thinking*, New York, Harper Press, 1966

Hill, C., *The World Turned Upside Down: Radical Ideas During the English Revolution*, Harmondsworth, Penguin, 1984

Hudson, M., *The Bubble and Beyond*, Dresden, Islet, 2012

Jacobs, J., *The Economy of Cities*, New York, Vintage, 1969

Jay, M., *The Dialectical Imagination: A History of the Frankfurt School and the Institute of Social Research, 1923–50*, Boston, MA, Beacon Press, 1973

Katz, C., 'Vagabond Capitalism and the Necessity of Social Reproduction', *Antipode*, Vol. 33, No. 4, 2001, pp. 709–28

Keynes, J.M., *The General Theory of Employment, Interest, and Money*, New York, Harcourt Brace, 1964

—, *Essays in Persuasion*, New York, Classic House Books, 2009

Klein, N., *The Shock Doctrine: The Rise of Disaster Capitalism*, New York, Metropolitan Books, 2009

Lefebvre, H., *The Production of Space*, Oxford, Basil Blackwell, 1989

—, *Critique of Everyday Life*, London, Verso, 1991

Leiss, W., *The Domination of Nature*, Boston, MA, Beacon Press, 1974

Lewis, M., *The Big Short: Inside the Doomsday Machine*, New York, Norton, 2010

McEvoy, A., *The Fisherman's Problem: Ecology and Law in the California Fisheries, 1850–1980*, Cambridge, Cambridge University Press, 1990

Mackey, J., Sisodia, R., and George, B., *Conscious Capitalism: Liberating the Heroic Spirit of Business*, Cambridge, MA, Harvard Business Review Press, 2013

MacKinnon, C., *Are Women Human?: And Other International Dialogues*, Cambridge, MA, Harvard University Press, 2007

McKinsey Global Institute, 'The World at Work: Jobs, Pay and Skills for 3.5 Billion People', *Report of the McKinsey Global Institute*, 2012

Maddison, A., *Phases of Capitalist Development*, Oxford, Oxford University Press, 1982

—, *Contours of the World Economy, 1–2030 AD*, Oxford, Oxford University Press, 2007

Malthus, T., *An Essay on the Principle of Population*, Cambridge, Cambridge University Press, 1992

Mao Zedong, *Collected Works of Chairman Mao. Volume 3: On Policy, Practice and Contradiction*, El Paso, TX, El Paso Norte Press, 2009

Martin, R., *Financialization of Daily Life*, Philadelphia, Temple University Press, 2002

Marx, K., *The Economic and Philosophic Manuscripts of 1844*, New York, International Publishers, 1964

—, *Theories of Surplus Value*, Part 2, London, Lawrence and Wishart, 1969

—, *Karl Marx: Early Texts*, edited by David McLellan, Oxford, Basil Blackwell, 1972

—, *Grundrisse*, Harmondsworth, Penguin, 1973

—, *Capital*, Volume 1, Harmondsworth, Penguin, 1976

—, *Capital*, Volume 2, Harmondsworth, Pelican, 1978

—, *Capital*, Volume 3, Harmondsworth, Penguin, 1981

Meszaros, I., *Marx's Theory of Alienation*, London, Merlin Press, 1970

Milanovic, B., *Worlds Apart: Measuring International and Global Inequality*, Princeton, Princeton University Press, 2005

Mitchell, T., *The Rule of Experts: Egypt, Techno-Politics, Modernity*, Berkeley, University of California Press, 2002

Myrdal, G., *Economic Theory and Underdeveloped Regions*, London, Duckworth, 1957

Naess, A., *Ecology, Community and Lifestyle*, Cambridge, Cambridge University Press, 1989

Nelson, A., and Timmerman, F. (eds), *Life without Money: Building Fair and Sustainable Economies*, London, Pluto, 2011

Norton, N., and Ariely, D., 'Building a Better America – One Wealth Quintile at a Time', *Perspectives on Psychological Science*, Vol. 6, 2011, p. 9

Ollman, B., *The Dance of the Dialectic: Steps in Marx's Method*, Champagne, IL, University of Illinois Press, 2003

Oxfam, 'The Cost of Inequality: How Wealth and Income Extremes Hurt Us All', Oxfam Media Briefing, 18 January 2013

Peet, R., Robbins P., and Watts, M., *Global Political Ecology*, New York, Routledge, 2011

Piketty, T., and Saez, E., 'Top Incomes and the Great Recession', *IMF Economic Review*, Vol. 61, 2013, pp. 456–78

Polanyi, K., *The Great Transformation: The Political and Economic Origins of Our Time*, Boston, Beacon Press, 1957

Ratcliffe, R., *Revolutionary Humanism and the Anti-Capitalist Struggle*, distributed by the author, Beech Hill House, Morchard Bishop, EX17 6RF, 2003

Reclus, E., *Anarchy, Geography, Modernity*, edited by John P. Clark and Camille Martin, Oxford, Lexington Books, 2004

Reich, R., *The Work of Nations: Preparing Ourselves for 21st Century Capitalism*, New York, Vintage, 1992

Rousseau, J.-J., *The Social Contract*, Oxford, Oxford University Press, 2008

Sabin, P., *The Bet: Paul Ehrlich, Julian Simon, and Our Gamble over Earth's Future*, New Haven, Yale University Press, 2013

Sassower, R., *Postcapitalism: Moving Beyond Ideology in America's Economic Crises*, Boulder, CO, Paradigm Publishers, 2009

Schumpeter, J., *Capitalism, Socialism and Democracy*, London, Routledge, 1942, pp. 82–3

Seabright P., (ed.), *The Vanishing Rouble: Barter Networks and Non-Monetary Transactions in Post-Soviet Societies*, London, Cambridge University Press, 2000

Sen, A., *Development as Freedom*, New York, Anchor Books, 2000

Smith, N., *Uneven Development: Nature, Capital and the Production of Space*, Oxford, Basil Blackwell, 1984

—, 'Nature as Accumulation Strategy', *Socialist Register*, 2007, pp. 19–41

Stiglitz, J., *The Price of Inequality*, New York, Norton, 2013

Storrs, C. (ed.), *The Fiscal Military State in Eighteenth Century Europe*, Aldershot, Ashgate, 2009

Thomas, P., *The Gramscian Moment: Philosophy, Hegemony and Marxism*, Chicago, Haymarket Books, 2010

Toffler, A., *The Third Wave: The Classic Study of Tomorrow*, New York, Bantam, 1980

Veblen, T., *The Theory of the Leisure Class*, New York, Oxford University Press, 2009 edition

Wallerstein, I., Collins, R., Mann, M., Derluguian, G., and Calhoun, C., *Does Capitalism Have a Future?*, Oxford, Oxford University Press, 2013

Whitehead, A. N., *Process and Reality*, New York, Free Press, 1969

Wolff, R., Moore, B., and Marcuse, H., *A Critique of Pure Tolerance: Beyond Tolerance, Tolerance and the Scientific Outlook, Repressive Tolerance*, Boston, Beacon Press, 1969

Wright, M., *Disposable Women and Other Myths of Global Capitalism*, New York, Routledge, 2006

# Index

Numbers in *italics* indicate Figures.

East Asia
  crisis of 1997–98 154; *dirigiste*
  governmentality 48; education
  184; rise of 170
Eastern Europe 115, 230
ecological offsets 250
economic rationality 211, 250, 252,
  273, 274, 275, 277, 278, 279
economies 48
  advanced capitalist 228,
  236; agglomeration 149; of
  dispossession 162; domination
  of industrial cartels and finance
  capital 135; household 192;
  informal 175; knowledge-based
  188; mature 227–8; regional
  149; reoriented to demand-side
  management 85; of scale 75;
  solidarity 66, 180; stagnant xii
ecosystems 207, 247, 248, 251–6, 258,
  261, 263, 296
Ecuador 46, 152, 284
education 23, 58, 60, 67–8, 84, 110,
  127–8, 129, 134, 150, 156, 168, 183,
  184, 185, 187, 188, 189, 223, 235, 296
efficiency 71, 92, 93, 98, 103, 117, 118,
  119, 122, 126, 272, 273, 284
efficient market hypothesis 118
Egypt 107, 280, 293
Ehrlich, Paul 246
electronics 120, 121, 129, 236, 292
emerging markets 170–71, 242
employment 37
  capital in command of job creation
  172, 174; conditions of 128; full-time
  274; opportunities for xii, 108, 168;
  regional crises of 151; of women
  108, 114, 115, 127; *see also* labour
enclosure movement 58
Engels, Friedrich 70
  *The Condition of the English
  Working Class in England* 292

English Civil War (1642–9) 199
Enlightenment 247
Enron 133, 241
environmental damage 49, 61, 110,
  111, 113, 232, 249–50, 255, 257, 258,
  259, 265, 286, 293
environmental movement 249, 252
environmentalism 249, 252–3
Epicurus 283
equal rights 64
Erasmus, Desiderius 283
ethnic hatreds and discriminations
  8, 165
ethnic minorities 168
ethnicisation 62
ethnicity 7, 68, 116
euro, the 15, 37, 46
Europe
  deindustrialisation in 234;
  economic development in 10;
  fascist parties 280; low population
  growth rate 230; social democratic
  era 18; unemployment 108; women
  in labour force 230
European Central Bank 37, 46, 51
European Commission 51
European Union (EU) 95, 159
exchange values
  commodities 15, 25, 64; dominance
  of 266; and housing 14–23, 43; and
  money 28, 35, 38; uniform and
  qualitatively identical 15; and use
  values 15, 35, 42, 44, 50, 60, 65, 88
exclusionary permanent ownership
  rights 39
experts 122
exploitation 49, 54, 57, 62, 68, 75, 83,
  107, 108, 124, 126, 128, 129, 150, 156,
  159, 166, 175, 176, 182, 185, 193, 195,
  208, 246, 257
exponential growth 224, 240, 254
  capacity for 230; of capital 246; of